D1096245

Visufe
vs.
ordinary
comm

HISTORY OF BROADCASTING: RADIO TO TELEVISION

HISTORY OF BROADCASTING: Radio to Television

The Psychology of Radio

HADLEY CANTRIL AND GORDON W. ALLPORT

ARNO PRESS and THE NEW YORK TIMES

New York • 1971

Reprint Edition 1971 by Arno Press Inc.

© 1935 by Harper & Brothers
Reprinted by arrangement with Harper & Row, Publishers, Inc.
All rights reserved

Reprinted from a copy in The Newark Public Library

LC# 72-161159
ISBN 0-405-03574-8

HISTORY OF BROADCASTING: RADIO TO TELEVISION
ISBN for complete set: 0-405-03555-1
See last pages of this volume for titles.

Manufactured in the United States of America

THE PSYCHOLOGY OF
～～～～～RADIO～～～～～

The Psychology of
RADIO

BY

HADLEY CANTRIL, Ph.D.

TEACHERS COLLEGE
COLUMBIA UNIVERSITY

AND

GORDON W. ALLPORT, Ph.D.

HARVARD UNIVERSITY

HARPER & BROTHERS PUBLISHERS

NEW YORK AND LONDON

1935

CONTENTS

CONTENTS

PART III
PRACTICAL INTERPRETATIONS

PREFACE

The present volume is the first attempt on the part of psychologists to map out from their own point of view the new mental world created by radio. There have been previous investigations of special psychological problems related to broadcasting and to listening, but these, conducted in separate and disjointed fashion, have not succeeded in giving a view of the subject as a whole. With but a few years of experience behind us and with the certainty of continuous changes ahead, it is not easy to prepare a comprehensive survey of the psychology of radio. Omissions are inevitable; complete prevision is impossible. Nevertheless, to give the subject its first psychological setting, to list some of the principal problems encountered, and to study a few of these with new methods of research, are justifications enough for our volume.

Social psychology can no longer pretend, as it once did, to solve the problems presented to it with some "simple and sovereign" formula, or with a small handful of theories concerning the instincts or folkways of mankind. The science has passed beyond the stage of *a priorism*. Definitely, if tardily, it is now committed to painstaking research, directed toward single and salient issues within its vast subject matter. Its advance can no longer be measured by the number of textbooks annually produced, nor by the mere plausibility of its pronouncements. The progress of social psychology must be determined, rather, by the incisiveness and validity of its analysis of significant social problems.

The radio is a recent innovation that has introduced profound alterations in the outlook and social behavior of men, thereby creating a significant social problem for the psychologist. Radio is an altogether novel medium of communication, preëminent as a means of social control and epochal in its influence upon the mental horizons of men. Already its ramifications are so numerous and confused that the psychologist hesitates to take the risks of error and misinterpretation besetting a subject so intricate and so new. But a beginning must be made some time, and in the interests of scientific knowledge as well as of practical public policy, the sooner the start is made the better.

Part I is an analysis of the general psychological and cultural factors that shape radio programs and determine the responses of the listeners to these broadcasts. Part II reports five separate experimental investigations in which the mental processes of listeners are studied under conditions of scientific control. In this part, brief summaries of the experiments are placed at the beginning of each chapter to aid the reader whose interest does not extend to the detailed procedures and interpretations contained in the full report. Since so many of the findings reported in Part II depend upon important variables and since single statements taken out of their contexts may be easily misapplied, the reader who is interested in using these results is advised to do so only with due regard to the stated qualifications and conditions.

For practical applications of the experimental work, it would be safer to consult Part III which summarizes our findings for the layman and for the professional broadcaster. Part III also undertakes to apply the experimental results, so far as they are pertinent, to the solution of several perplexing problems that face educators, advertisers, listeners, and psychologists.

In the past decade many writers and many listeners have formed opinions concerning the proper use and control of radio. Some of these opinions reflect a mature and studied analysis while others are mere prejudices. How radio may best be utilized is a question which legislators are bound to face in an era of changing social values. The problem is one of enormous complexity, involving political and economic issues as well as matters of technique and organization. Since the psychology of radio is the psychology of the listener and since the listener is also a citizen, an understanding of his tastes and habits and a knowledge of the way radio affects his everyday life are prerequisite to an intelligent determination of how this medium should be controlled. The data here gathered may ultimately aid those public officials whose duty it is to see that radio achieves its greatest social usefulness.

Without the generous assistance of many representatives of the radio industry our studies could not have been carried out. The broadcasting equipment used in the experiments conducted in the Harvard Psychological Laboratory was loaned and installed by the Edison Electric Illuminating Company of Boston (Station WEEI). This station likewise permitted us to conduct certain of our experiments from their studios. The Westinghouse Station (WBZ) in Boston allowed us access to files and furnished us with much valuable information for our analysis of programs. The Columbia Broadcasting System showed us unusual courtesy, and aided throughout the course of our studies with information and advice. It was especially in their New York studios that we had the opportunity to study the arts of broadcasting at close range. Among the officials of the Columbia Broadcasting System to whom we feel especially indebted are J. J. Karol, P. W. Kesten, Courtney Savage, Knowles Entrikin, John Carlile, Donald Ball, Nila Mack, Helen Johnson, Charles Speer, W. J. Fagan, and Howard Barlow. For similar kindness and assistance we have to thank certain members of the National Broadcasting Company, particularly Franklin Dunham and Frances Sprague. Mr. H. A. Bellows,

Chairman of the Legislative Committee of the National Association of Broadcasters, and Mr. E. C. Buchanan, of the Canadian Radio Commission, provided us with important data concerning commercial and governmental policies and practices. Although we have learned much that we have included in this volume from all these experts, and have at times borrowed from their experience and their interpretations, they are not responsible for the statements and conclusions contained in this study.

The experiments reported in Part II required a great deal of assistance and collaboration. Throughout all of the experimental sessions, Dr. C. E. Smith was in charge of the control panel and his constant and skillful aid was strategic to the entire research. Serving as announcers and speakers were more than thirty associates, among whom we would mention especially Dr. H. D. Spoerl, Mr. C. A. Engvall, Dr. D. W. MacKinnon, and Mr. G. E. Brooks with his colleagues and students from the Emerson College of Oratory. Besides the authors, the principal experimenters were Dr. M. E. Carver, George Houghton, M. Sherif, F. T. Brown, and William Baker. For assistance in arranging certain experiments we are indebted to Station WEEI, to Dr. Kathryn Maxfield, of the Perkins Institute for the Blind, to Dr. A. A. Roback, of the Massachusetts University Extension. For assistance in the treatment of our data we are obligated to Miss Charlotte Croon. Dr. Dwight Chapman and Dr. P. J. Rulon aided with advice on problems of statistical procedure. For gathering data, we are indebted to several of our own students who distributed and collated over twelve hundred questionnaires. If we were to mention the listeners who participated in the numerous parts of our study, giving us the benefit of their judgments and services as experimental subjects, we should have to add over two thousand more names.

It was often necessary to seek advice and assistance of those who had acquaintance with some special phase of our subject. Help of this type was generously given by Clifton R. Reed, of the American Civil Liberties Union, by W. H. Mullen, of the Crowell Publishing Company, by J. L. Swayze, by Dr. E. P. Herring, of the Department of Government in Harvard University, by Professor T. H. Pear, a pioneer investigator in the psychology of radio in Great Britain, and by Mrs. Rupert Emerson who aided with translations from Russian. For their assistance as observant and critical listeners or as readers of the manuscript, we are indebted to C. E. MacGill, A. L. Gould, M. K. Lyman, Robert Bradlee, and G. Radlo.

The studies were executed and prepared for publication with the financial aid of the Committee on Research in the Social Sciences at Harvard. One of the studies included in this volume, *Judging Per-*

sonality from Voice, had previously been published and permission to reprint it with changes and enlargement was kindly given by Dr. C. C. Murchison, editor of the *Journal of Social Psychology*. While our work was under way we received assistance from the reports and publications issued by the Bureau of Educational Research, Radio Division, at Ohio State University. The Yearbook of this Bureau, *Education on the Air*, supplies investigators with information concerning research in progress at various centers. Through the untimely death of Dr. F. H. Lumley, an active member of the Radio Division and author of many studies, the psychological investigation of radio has lost an ardent advocate and contributor.

July, 1935

H. C.
G. A.

PART I

THE MENTAL SETTING OF RADIO

CHAPTER I

RADIO: A PSYCHOLOGICAL NOVELTY

RADIO is the child-prodigy of human inventions. Born less than a generation ago of intellectual and commercial genius, it has already grown from the insignificance of an embryonic idea in the minds of technicians to the stature of a Goliath in industry and public affairs. Vigorously endowed and shrewdly directed, it has developed sturdily, and with lightning speed has fashioned for itself a place in our national life as important and secure as that of two other spectacular but older inventions, the automobile and the moving picture.

Broadcasting companies, conscious of their sudden acquisition of power, have issued embossed brochures which portray with charts, pictograms, and figures of many ciphers the impressive story of radio's growth. They tell us that in this country 100,000 persons are now employed in the radio industry, that 78,000,000 of our citizens are more or less habitual listeners, that more than 20,000,000 of them often listen simultaneously to a single broadcast, and that 21,455,799 homes are equipped with receiving sets. Most of us have already heard the sound of a bell striking the hour in Westminster, and a voice issuing out of the fastness of the antarctic. We realize that the day cannot be far off when men in every country of the globe will be able to listen at one time to the persuasions or commands of some wizard seated in a central palace of broadcasting, possessed of a power more fantastic than that of Aladdin.

Romantic souls thrilled by these marvels wonder, as they turn the dials, what the world is coming to. More practical souls invest their savings in one of the few still expanding industries of the day, and if they are manufacturers or merchants, they hasten to purchase for advertising purposes a time-space segment of the ether from those who now control it. Reflective souls, on the other hand, survey the rapid growth of radio with a feeling of helplessness and dismay. This gigantic industry, they realize, represents a technological advance and a commercial achievement of the first magnitude. They know, too, that it is an agency of incalculable power for controlling the actions of men, that it marks a revolution in communication, and that it is a gigantic tribute to human enterprise.

What they do not know, however, and what they would like very much to know, is the reason for the tenacious grip that radio has so swiftly secured on the mental life of men. If radio had not somehow satisfied human wants, it would never have attained its present popularity. For it is only the interests, the desires, and the attitudes of the listeners that can vitalize the vast inhuman network of the air. The technical and managerial aspects of the radio are much discussed and generally well understood, but the human factors upon which every radio policy is based, and upon which radio as a social institution rests, are for the most part the subject merely of guesswork.

The really important problems of the radio now are psychological problems. Why do people like to listen for hours on end to the impersonal blare of their loud-speakers, or is the blare for them not so impersonal after all? What do they like best to hear, and how much do they understand of what they hear? What is the most effective way to address the listeners, to persuade them, to lead them? How long will they listen, and what will they remember? Are the prevailing programs adapted to the mentality of the listeners? Are the minds of the listeners influenced more by what they hear on the radio, by what they see on the screen, or by what they read? Does the broadcasting of concerts and church services keep people away from concert halls and places of worship? Floods of such questions occur to us and we turn expectantly to the social psychologist for answers. But the radio revolution caught the social psychologist unprepared, and has left him far behind. Radio is a novel phenomenon, something new under the psychological sun. It produces audiences of a size hitherto undreamed of, and plays havoc with the traditional theories of crowd formation and of group thinking. It eliminates the importance of the eye in social relations, and exalts the rôle of the human voice and the auditory sense to a new pinnacle of importance.

Without a fresh beginning, adapted to the nature of the phenomenon with which he must deal, the social psychologist cannot find answers to the questions. The field is unfamiliar and the problems are unique. The best he can do at the outset is to observe for himself typical situations which the radio has created and from them frame strategic questions and devise suitable scientific methods for an orderly attack upon the labor which has fallen to his lot. Above all he must approach his problem with a strictly objective and dispassionate attitude, leaving to the reformer and the legislator the duty of weighing the moral and legal questions radio has created.

AN EVANGELIST AND HIS VOICE

A few years ago a well-known evangelist visited Boston. The large hall which had been hired for his campaign did not accommodate half the people who were attracted to his meetings. The enterprising managers had installed a microphone on the platform and a clear loud-speaker in a second auditorium, nearly as large as the main hall and situated directly below it. On one particular evening the principal auditorium was filled to capacity half an hour before the scheduled time for the service, and the lower half was filled almost as soon as the upper. The overflow audience seemed to differ in no way from the main audience. In both there were the usual loyal supporters, the well-disposed suburbanites, and the customary admixture of curious on-lookers.

Here was an ideal occasion for the social psychologist to begin his observations on the psychological effects of radio. The situation provided for him a kind of "natural experiment." There were two equivalent audiences: one listening to the evangelist face-to-face; one hearing his words distinctly, although unable to see him. In this respect the situation represented the essential contrast between the traditional type of audience and the modern radio audience.

There were certain differences, to be sure. In this case the radio audience was assembled in one hall, not dispersed in many homes. The broadcast itself was local and private, not widespread and commercial. Another important difference was the fact that the appeal of this broadcast was of a more emotional order than is customary over the radio.

In spite of the differences between the present situation and the ordinary broadcast, the social psychologist hoped that by keeping his senses alert he might learn some elementary things about the psychological phenomena of radio. For convenience of observation he took his stand on the stairway connecting the two halls, and from this vantage ground could make observations of the behavior of the two audiences in close succession.

Now the two halls are filled. It is still ten minutes before the evangelist will arrive. The massed choir begins singing familiar hymns which, thanks to the admirable loud-speaker, are heard quite as distinctly by the overflow audience as by the principal audience. In both halls there is a restlessness which subsides more rapidly in the audience that can see the singers. Some members of the upper group join in the choruses and soon many are singing. The lower hall remains silent and impassive while it listens, in spite of the encouragement issued into the microphone by the song-leader.

Finally the evangelist appears in the upper hall. There is a tumult of applause, clearly heard by those in the radio audience but not provoking them to any visible or audible response. Why should they applaud when the evangelist can neither see nor hear them? There is no possibility of give-and-take between the revivalist and his radio audience. The communication between them is "linear" rather than "circular."

As is customary with skillful leaders of crowds, the evangelist engages at once in preliminary announcements, jesting, exhortations for hearty singing, and flattering remarks to his auditors. And, likewise, as is customary with docile crowds well disposed toward a leader, the upper audience responds with increasing laughter and applause to each successive blandishment. The lower audience is more resistant. By the time the sixth hymn is sung (*upstairs* with abandon) a few individuals *downstairs* are humming, but no one in the lower auditorium sings out the familiar words, even though many have their hymnbooks open before them and all can clearly hear the singing of the upstairs congregation. At one time when the evangelist makes an artful witticism, there is loud laughter in the main group, but only a few chuckles below. Those who chuckle subside quickly, some glancing rather shamefacedly around. At a telling sally against infidels in general and against a well-known agnostic in particular there is prolonged applause above but only a few timid handclaps below.

Time has come for the collection to be taken, one of the two climaxes of any evangelical service. After the preliminary appeals, the evangelist suddenly shouts, "All those who are glad that I am in town, raise your hands." Nearly fifteen hundred hands are raised in the upper hall, and only two in the lower. The evangelist immediately issues a command, "Now while your hands are nice and warm put them in your purses and give a large contribution toward the success of these meetings." The collection basins upstairs overflow with silver well silenced by bank notes; downstairs they rattle loosely with copper and nickel.

Soon comes the call for converts. The evangelist makes his most emotional appeal. A lieutenant appears in the lower auditorium to invite members there to go up the steps and "hit the trail." There is an awkward silence, then a fumbling for coats and hats. The group below begins to disintegrate. Most of its members file out into the street, as stolid as when they arrived. A few are drawn upstairs to see the man and the musicians to whom they have been listening. None, so far as can be determined, joins the forward-moving crowds into the aisles, to seek salvation (or some other satisfaction) in shaking hands with the evangelist. There is a striking contrast in the homeward movement, the "depolarization" of the lower group, at the very time when there is a climax of forward motion and continued polarization of the principal crowd. With his major congregation the evangelist's efforts have been eminently successful, but with his radio congregation they have utterly failed.

THE RADIO ORATOR AND HIS CROWD

This episode might seem at first to lead to a surprising conclusion: that the radio is a complete failure as an agency in forming crowds, and that it is incapable of controlling mass behavior. But such a generalization would be too hasty. For reasons already mentioned this situation was not entirely typical of radio. Nor was the evangelist's program designed for broadcasting. It was directed exclusively to the visible audience. He spoke rapidly, more rapidly than is customary in radio discourse. His speech was impromptu and therefore not well organized, and his manner was abrupt, compulsive, and startling. He worked for immediate rather than long-run results, for emotional fervor rather than for future action. The members of the overflow audience were aware that he was appealing primarily to the listeners who were visible and not to them. Since they felt excluded they were not responsive.

A radio spellbinder would have spoken quite differently. He would have used less bombast and more artistry, less brute force and more cunning. He would have directed his attention to the invisible audience and would have made each listener feel welcome as a member of the circle. He would have aroused the listeners' sense of participation in the occasion. "Friends, this is Huey P. Long speaking. I have some important revelations to make, but before I make them I want you to go to the phone and call up five of your friends and tell them to listen in. I'll just be talking along here for four or five minutes without saying anything special, so you go to the phone and tell your friends that Huey Long is on the air."

Such a clever opening makes each member of the audience a fellow conspirator and does much to guarantee friendly attention for the duration of the speech, especially if the discourse throughout is kept on an equally informal plane. Colloquial language and homely American allusions help. Speaking of matters of government, Senator Long does away with all formality and awe. The people are elevated to a position of equality with high officials, or else the high officials are reduced to the common level. "They are," Senator Long assures us in plebeian tones, "like old Davy Crockett who went to hunt a possum . . ."

When the voice of the radio orator is as persuasive and self-assured as that of Senator Long or of Father Coughlin the listener is likely to believe that the statements he hears are true and that the solutions offered for national ills are both dependable and basic. The diagnosis offered is always simple: too many bankers and bank-controlled industries, too much wealth in the hands of too few people. Slogans point the way to salvation. "Share the wealth," "Every man a king," "Join the National Union for Social Justice." Do as you are told. It all seems simple and obvious. Since the listener has identified himself with the orator for the duration of the broadcast, he thinks as the leader thinks, and the leader is careful to point out that he and the listeners are fighting a common battle. The senator says, "You can reach me at Washington, D. C." and Father Coughlin announces himself as "Your Spokesman."

A sound argument is always less important for the demagogue than are weighted words. Senator Long has allied himself in his discourses with God, King Solomon, Christ, the Pilgrim Fathers, Bacon, Milton, Shakespeare, Plato, Socrates, and Abraham Lincoln. By the trick of verbal juxtaposition the glory that is theirs is made to shine upon him. Father Coughlin's listeners are "brothers in Christ," but bankers are "grinning devils," and Communism has a "red serpent head."

To be effective a radio argument need not be sound nor complete, but it must be well organized. It is generally much easier to list or to outline the steps in a radio argument than in an argument heard at a mass meeting. This is true not only because the radio speaker (owing to the value of time) is better prepared, but because he realizes that he cannot rely altogether upon the excitement of the occasion. Although Father Coughlin treats his listeners to a few interludes of bombast, he is as a rule remarkably explicit. His platform has sixteen points, a few of which each week give anchorage to his discourse. He reiterates his main points, he uses numerous concrete examples, his recommendations are specific. He tells his listeners exactly what legislation to support and exactly what to do.

No crowd can exist, especially no radio crowd, unless the members have a lively "impression of universality." Each individual must believe that others are thinking as he thinks and are sharing his emotions. The radio orator therefore takes pains to point out that the listener is supported by vast numbers of people. In the course of an hour's listening Father Coughlin's audience is several times made aware of its size and power. It is announced that millions are listening, that millions of letters have been received, that millions have joined the National Union for Social Justice. The prestige of multitudes allays our misgivings and supports our vacillating decision. Eight million people can't be wrong, and eight million follow this leader, so, too, with impunity may I.

Were it not for Father Coughlin's feat in creating exclusively on the basis of radio appeal an immensely significant political crowd, one could scarcely believe that the radio had such potentialities for crowd-building. In the case of Huey Long, of Mussolini, of Hitler, the leaders were well known in advance, and the listeners had ready-made attitudes toward these leaders that needed only to be intensified and directed through vocal appeal. But in Father Coughlin's case the attitudes required creation as well as shaping. He was not a well-identified leader before he used the medium of broadcasting. His principles were not known nor were they widely accepted. But even a leader known through newspapers and popular discussion finds the radio the most effective agency for enlarging his circle of supporters. After only four radio appearances it is said that Senator Long received the names of over 5,000,000 citizens for enrollment in his "Share Our Wealth Society." It took only a few months of periodic broadcasting for Father Coughlin to secure his alleged membership of 8,000,000 in the National Union.

Significant though the radio undoubtedly is—when artfully used—in forming opinion and in guiding action, it is in many respects unlike all other media of public control. The massed assembly, the talking picture, and the printed word likewise exert immeasurable influence upon the thoughts and sentiments of the people. The unique psychological characteristics of radio will be seen more clearly if we compare broadcasting with these older and better established methods of leadership and control.

THE RADIO AND THE ROSTRUM

At a public meeting or lecture people usually object to sitting where they do not have a good view of the platform. They are anxious to see what the speaker looks like. If they are observant they notice the way he walks to the platform, his stride, his carriage, the speed and rhythm of his gait. When he is on the platform they examine his dress and make more or less conscious judgments concerning his affluence, his neatness, and his taste. They watch his face, perhaps decide that he is a cheerful or a timid soul, that he is intellectual, hard-boiled, or stupid. From his expression they catch moods and points of emphasis. If he walks about, they follow his movements with interest; if he twists his fingers, winds his watch, rattles his keys, clenches his fists, or runs his hands through his hair, they gain various impressions of nervousness or eccentricity. All the while they are aware of what he is saying and how he says it, and their understanding of his message comes through an inextricable blend of visual and auditory impressions. As members of a congregate audience we are all habitual watchers as well as listeners, often finding it difficult to follow the thought of a speaker whom we cannot see.

If we hear this same speaker over the radio the constellation of visual cues disappears. Suddenly deprived of the sense of vision, we are forced to grasp both obvious and subtle meanings through our ears alone. Except for blind people, this is a curious and unnatural state of affairs. Seldom before have we been dependent exclusively upon audition. The cues for judging the personality of a speaker and for comprehending his meaning have been immensely reduced. The visual-auditory-social situation of the rostrum has been skeletonized until a mere fragment remains.

A great many people supply with their own imagery some kind of visual setting to supplement the bare auditory impression. They may see in their mind's eye the glamour of the stage, with its lights and costumes, as a suitable setting for a radio drama; they may create an imaginary appearance and set of mannerisms for the unknown speaker or announcer. In order to enjoy radio humor they may find it necessary to visualize the costume or blackened face of the comedian. The large demand for tickets to studio-theaters where programs are broadcast is probably due as much to the desire to have a complete visual impression of the performers as to curiosity concerning the technical details of putting a program on the air. It is probable that the radio, through giving practice in visualization, is helping to restore in adults some of the keenness of imagery dulled since childhood.

The situation in listening to music is somewhat different. Its comprehension and enjoyment are not to any great extent dependent upon our sight of the musicians or conductor. Long training with the phonograph and with other mechanical renditions of music has accustomed listeners to its impersonality. It seems natural enough to hear music over the radio, and musical programs, it will be noted, eclipse in popularity all other types of broadcasting.

The radio has completely freed the listener from the agelong conventions of the rostrum. As long as he is in the physical presence of an actor, musician, or speaker he is bound by a kind of "social contract" to listen attentively and politely, or at least to refrain from overt expressions of disagreement or displeasure. Heckling and hurling are distinctly bad form. In the theater the actor is not to be disturbed excepting by laughter and applause which are encouraged for their friendly effect upon the actor as well as for the relief they bring to the spectator. It is a rule of civilization that the auditor, having contracted to attend a public meeting, will show respect for the performer even at the price of considerable irritation and boredom to himself.

It is otherwise with the radio audience. The listener may respond in any way he pleases with no more constraint than that imposed upon him by the few people who may be listening with him. He feels no compulsion to laugh at stale jokes, to applaud a bad actor, or to cheer the platitudes of a politician. He is less directly under the sway of the crowd situation, and so is able to form a more objective estimate of the speaker's points. He can flatly and impolitely disagree, and comment as much as he likes without being considered ill-bred. If he chooses, he can sing, dance, curse, or otherwise express emotions relevant or irrelevant.

If he has no emotions to express, he can use the sounds issuing from his loud-speaker merely as a background for some more interesting activity. He does not hesitate to shove the radio performer out to the very periphery of consciousness, or to pay attention to him only when he pleases. He is not conspicuous if he reads or plays cards in front of the radio; he would never do these things before a rostrum or stage. He can even turn off the program abruptly (and often does) when it loses its appeal. But it is not good form to walk out in the middle of a lecture or a play.

This impersonality of the radio creates a marked distance between the listener and the speaker. There is no direct interaction between them. The listener does not as a rule feel that he is supporting the speaker by his presence. A Protestant may listen to a Catholic priest on the air although he might not attend the same speaker's service; a Republican may listen to a Socialist although he would perhaps never be seen at a Socialist meeting. This freedom so congenial to the listener is often a nightmare to the performer who knows neither how many people are listening to him, how attentive they are, nor how well disposed.

There can be no direct give-and-take between the radio performer and his audience. If he is talking too fast, there is no way for the listeners, through subtle attitudes or strained faces, to indicate the fact; if some of his points are not understood, he has no cues which might guide him to repeat or to elaborate his remarks; if his jokes fall flat, he doesn't know it. The facial expressions of auditors are potent aids to brilliant discourse, for the nods of agreement and sympathetic smiles of appreciation encourage a speaker to express himself more naturally and emphatically and to give freer reign to his latent thoughts and feelings. The radio listener at times wishes to ask a question or to express an opinion, but he is unable to do so. Sometimes he wishes to have the speaker explain what he means, but he must forever remain in ignorance unless he takes the trouble to write, and the speaker takes the trouble to reply. There can be no resolution of the difficulties arising in the listeners' minds during an address or an argument. There can be no emergence of new ideas based upon free discussion during or after a talk. This complete absence of "circular relationship" helps account for the fact that speakers often seem to be less challenging

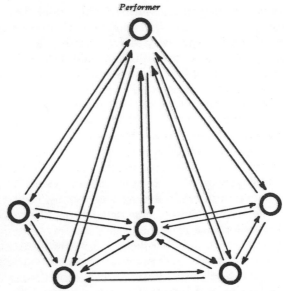

Fig. I.—The social formation of the *congregate assembly*, showing circular relationship between performer and auditors, as well as the influence of one auditor upon another.

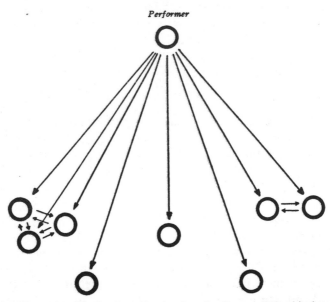

Fig. II.—The social situation in *radio*, showing the linear relationship between the speaker and his auditors, and, excepting where listeners are grouped in their own homes, a complete absence of social facilitation in the audience.

and provocative in their discourse over the air than in a public assembly.

A further difference lies in the fact that members of the radio audience derive little stimulation from one another. There is no touch of a neighbor's arm, no exhilarating influence of unexpected colors, perfumes, attentive postures, whispered comments, applause, and mere animal warmth. Always present in coacting groups such influences create what psychologists call "social facilitation," an augmenting or altering of the natural (solitary) responses of each individual member. As a rule social facilitation results in an enhancement of activity, in conservative and conventional judgment, in a labile attention, in less individualistic and self-centered thought. It tends to make individuals more suggestible, less critical, and more like everyone else. In the congregate assembly our neighbor's laughter enhances our own amusement, and what might have been only a titter becomes a genuine laugh. At a political rally when we see others favorably impressed we tend likewise to approve of the current opinion. The tension of other people in the theater or concert hall reinforces our own tension, and their appreciation magnifies our own.

Radio presentations come to us unaided by social facilitation. We do not feel the compulsion to conform or to express the feelings that others are expressing. We are less emotional and more critical, less crowdish and more individualistic. Broadcasters have tried to supply social facilitation artificially through the use of studio-audiences, whose directed "enthusiasm" and frequently forced laughter are heard in a somewhat ghostly fashion by solitary listeners in their own homes. This device, however, is only partially successful as a substitute for an authentic group influence.

The absence of social facilitation is also important from the performer's point of view. He can no longer depend upon the ready laughter and applause of the jolly fat man in the second row to help him create a more compact and sympathetic audience. There is no self-exciting crowd whose members derive quite as much stimulation and amusement from each other as from him. Deprived both of the circular relationship between his listeners and himself and of social facilitation among the members of his audience, it is no wonder that the most experienced public performer often feels perplexed before the unresponsive microphone. The social situation to which he is accustomed is represented in Figure I, and the social situation of the radio is depicted in Figure II.

By way of summary it may be said that the radio differs from the rostrum and the stage in several important respects:

It places a greater premium upon the use and interpretation of the human voice.

It skeletonizes the personality of the speaker or performer.

It develops the use of imaginative completion of the situation in the minds of the listeners.

It places music in the preferred position among radio programs.

It frees the listener from the necessity of conventional politeness toward public performers.

It interposes a serious psychological barrier between the broadcaster and his audience through the destruction of the normal circular relationship.

It virtually eliminates social facilitation among the auditors with the result that they are less crowdish, more critical and individualistic.

THE RADIO AND THE TALKING PICTURE

With a weekly attendance of approximately 70,000,000, the talking picture rivals the radio as a gigantic vehicle for reaching the masses. But if merely the number of hours which American citizens spend before the radio and the talking pictures are compared, the radio easily wins in the competition. From data available, it may be estimated that our countrymen spend approximately 150,000,000 hours a week before the screen, but nearly 1,000,000,000 hours before the loud-speaker. It is difficult to say whether this rough calculation signifies a greater influence of the radio in forming the opinions, manners, and morals of the public. For various reasons the influence of the talkie may be considered to be more intensive if less extensive than that of the radio.

The talkie employs both sight and sound in all manner of effective combinations and contrasts. It recreates both the song and the lark, the fury and the battle, bringing both closer to the spectator than he has ever experienced them in life. The talking picture needs neither announcers nor captions. The dramatic integration of visual and auditory experience is accomplished, and the impression is realistic and indelible to the highest degree. The only features customarily lacking to make the illusion of the screen complete are color and tridimensionality. Producers have already learned how to add these embellishments, but have at the same time discovered that they are unessential to their audiences.

No one can claim that the radio is able to create an equally realistic illusion. It is evident that human emotions cannot be so fully depicted nor so long sustained in auditory presentation. The spectators before the screen are able to identify themselves with the actors, and to lose themselves for hours in a gripping plot whose conflicts and solution seem profoundly real and personal. By contrast, the radio seems to deal merely with diverting trivia.

For some reason vision is more favorable than audition to the mental process known as "projection." Even when all films were silent the attention of the audience and its addiction to heart-throbs and passion were phenomenal. The addition of sound to moving pictures has scarcely enhanced their emotional appeal. Silent love-making is quite as provocative as audible love-making. Until television is perfected it is probable that the radio will not be able to arouse certain deeper emotional complexes as effectively as does the moving picture.

There are other differences between the radio and the talkie. The latter is designed to give the personality of the actor the fullest display. The star of the talkie is seen and is heard, and in a close-up can almost be tasted. But the radio star is present only to the ear, and his personal qualities and appearance must be left in part to the imagination.

Again, the talkie audience is to a certain extent self-exciting, although, to be sure, social facilitation in a darkened picture palace is much less than in a well-lit hall. Since the audience watching a picture is inevitably a congregate assembly, it is bound by tradition and convention in respect to its conduct. Although neither the radio audience nor the patrons of the talkie are in direct circular relation with the performer, more of the conventional social influences are present in the picture theater. But both are less personal, less human, and more mechanical than the ordinary theater audience and the face-to-face assembly.

The radio has the advantage of being a cheaper source of entertainment. With a receiving set once in the home, it costs little in time, effort, and money to turn the dials. Radio offers an easier escape from unpalatable programs than the theater. It can also command the attention of more people simultaneously, thereby gaining immense prestige in the minds of the listeners.

The radio is designed for the home, whereas the talkie provides an escape from the restraints of the home. For this reason the radio is a more "moral" agency. The radio is a modern substitute for the hearthside, and a family seated before it is obedient to its own conventional habits and taboos. The radio dares not violate those attitudes fundamental in the great American home. It does not dare broadcast programs dealing too frankly with crime, rebellion, or infidelity. Away from the home, before the silver screen, these same home-loving folks may for a time shake off with impunity the very restraints which the radio, as a visitor to the home, is bound to respect. The faithful wife may identify herself for one unholy hour with the glamorous adventuress, and the untalented, obedient son may escape from parental control to see himself as a dashing young hero proceeding from one amorous and professional conquest to another. The talkie caters to those sides of our nature to which the radio—as yet—does not strongly appeal. In the darkened theater, where each spectator is free to drift by himself into the succulent fantasy of the screen, he is unabashed by the presence of others. The same fantasy displayed in the home under the parlor lamps and the critical eyes and ears of the family would cause feelings of guilt and embarrassment.

It seems impossible to decide which is the more influential medium in American social life. Each of the two agencies is immensely important in standardizing public tastes and values. The radio engages the attention of more listeners more hours a week, reaches more listeners at one time, gives more varied programs, and touches more sides of life. The talkie deals almost exclusively with fantasy, but deals with it in such a way as to create an illusion of reality. It is more vivid, more personal, more glamorous. The radio on the whole appeals to the practical interests of men, and the talkie to the repressed desires. Whether people are more influenced by realistic mental intrusions or by absorbing daydreams of adventure, wealth, and delight—who can say?

THE RADIO AND THE PRINTED WORD

In America, where illiteracy is rare, nearly every person reads newspapers, magazines, and books to some extent. Yet it is not uncommon to ask whether the radio may not eventually supplant the printing presses of the country. Publishers already complain that people are listening to the radio so much that they no longer require so many novels for diversion. Educators, both fearing a recession in the meager habits of study and hoping for greater gains through a new mode of appeal, have rushed to the microphone in the interests of public enlightenment. The menace that the radio holds for the printed word cannot be judged until their intrinsic differences are understood.

Most people read what they want to read. They choose their newspapers, their magazines, or their library books more or less unaided. No matter how eccentric his taste, a reader can usually find something to satisfy his interests. Radio, on the other hand, caters to average demands. It is too expensive to broadcast programs for the delectation of individualists. Even the vaunted variety in broadcasting is strictly limited by the common interests of large groups of listeners. If a student is attracted to Byzantine culture, he must read about it or seek out a lecture. If he wishes to know about the life of Goethe, he must turn to books. Should he by chance find a program devoted to Byzantium or Goethe, it would be simplified to suit listeners whose interest in the subject was neither as specialized nor as deep as his.

A man's reading is fitted not only to his interests but to his convenience, while his listening must fit the convenience of the broadcaster. In spite of the efforts to adapt programs to the average habits of average citizens, no broadcaster can place his offering at an hour convenient and inviting to all people. Even though a listener forms the habit of tuning to a certain broadcast at a regular time, he often finds it unpleasurable to adjust his mood to the occasion. The young housewife who is worried chiefly about a dessert for her evening guests is not pleased at recipe hour to learn only about fillet of sole and popovers. She consults her old reliable cookbook. The factory hand, just laid off without warning, is in no mood to listen to a government official telling him how much the status of labor has improved during the administration. Instead, he picks up a pulp magazine for a few hours' escape from his misery. The printed word is a better servant than the radio for the infinite varieties of human moods.

Not only may a man choose what he will read and the time to read it, but he may read it at his own pace. A difficult passage may be read slowly or twice in succession. If the pages ahead look uninteresting they may be skipped. The broadcaster, however, forces the listener to keep the pace thought best for the majority. He does not actually know what this optimum pace may be, but he imposes his judgment in the matter upon his public. Naturally the "right" speed will depend upon the familiarity of the listener with the subject matter, upon his intelligence, his interest, and his attentiveness. The best speed for one auditor is not the best speed for another. Only when reading to ourselves can the proper speed be found and maintained, or varied to suit our mental state.

Radio broadcasting lacks the permanence of the printed page. The listener cannot turn back and make the announcer repeat what he has already said. Nor can he rehear the broadcast at a later date. He must comprehend everything as it comes. If he misses a crucial point in the discourse, he may lose the whole argument, and there is no help for it. The broadcaster tries his best to make every idea clear by means of illustration and repetition, but in so doing he aims only at the average man, thus failing to reach the dullards and risking an insult to those of superior intelligence.

The radio seems to suffer in comparison with the printed word, and yet the case is not one-sided. Most people prefer listening to reading. In the study reported in Chapter V, it turns out that nine out of every ten people prefer to hear a political speech on the radio than to read it in the newspaper. It takes less effort. In reading, one must first decide

what to read; over the radio the decision is more limited and therefore easier. It takes trouble to obtain the particular book or newspaper
one wants; it is simple to turn the dial. The strain and effort involved
in the act of reading are greater than in listening. Therefore, if a
man is not a decided individualist, and is not particular about what he
hears, if he has no guiding interest in seeking out reading matter, he
will sink contentedly before the radio and abandon his reading, perhaps
permanently.

Not only is the radio easy to listen to, it is likewise more personal
than the printed word. A voice belongs to a living person, and living
people arrest our attention and sustain our interest better than do
printed words. The very transiency of the broadcast possesses fascination. Printed words endure; they are polished and perfected, and lack
the spontaneity and human fallibility of the single performance. A
voice broadcasting news possesses an intimacy and eventfulness absent
from the evening newspaper. If the voice is that of a well-known radio
favorite, it seems friendly. We respond to it, and even obey its commands. The voice of Seth Parker requesting a minute of silent prayer
in the course of his Sunday evening program has kept whole families
hushed until his voice again broke the spell.

Finally, the listener has an imaginative sense of participation in a
common activity. He knows that others are listening with him and in
this way feels a community of interest with people outside his home.
He feels less lonely, especially if he is an invalid or if he lives in a
remote spot. Only in a vague sense is the printed word a social stimulus,
whereas the radio fills us with a "consciousness of kind" which at times
grows into an impression of vast social unity. It is for this reason that
radio is potentially more effective than print in bringing about concerted opinion and action.

The social psychologist concludes that the radio is by its very nature
markedly different from the rostrum, the screen, and the printed word.
It is a *novel* means of communication, provoking *novel* effects in the
mental and social life of its devotees and requiring *novel* methods of
investigation.

CHAPTER II

THE INFLUENCE OF RADIO UPON MENTAL AND SOCIAL LIFE

APART from the invention of spoken and written language, which took place in some dim prehistoric time, there have been five major innovations of method in human communication: printing, telegraphy, the telephone, the cinema, and the radio.[1] Each innovation has been followed by social and psychological changes of a revolutionary character. These changes, so far as the printing press, the telegraph, and the telephone are concerned, are already a matter of record, chronicled and celebrated by historians and sociologists. To a certain extent, although much less adequately, the epochal significance of the cinema has been studied. But the changes wrought by radio are virtually unrecorded, primarily, no doubt, because they are not yet fully understood.

Many of the trends that followed the earlier inventions are being speeded and augmented by the radio. The world has become even smaller. The time elapsing between an event of public importance and the popular response it arouses has become still shorter. The clamor for higher standards of living has been increased through more widely disseminated knowledge of the world's goods. And yet, as the preceding chapter showed, radio is in principle a novel method of communication and has brought many effects peculiar to itself. It reaches a larger population of people at greater distances than the other mediums, and it reaches them both instantaneously and cheaply. Through its own peculiar blend of personal and impersonal characteristics it relates the speaker and the auditor in a novel way. These circumstances give it an original character and produce social effects which in part are different from those obtained by the older methods of communication.

The scientists who first mastered the acoustical properties of ether did not know they were preparing a device that within one short generation would bind the earth in a universal network of sound, that would be the greatest single democratizing agent since the invention of printing. Nor could they have foreseen to what extent they were placing public opinion and private taste at the mercy of entrepreneurs. Even now we do not know the ultimate consequences of radio for civilization. We do know, however, that certain important changes have

[1] Excluded from this list are the agencies of transportation, e.g., the locomotive, the automobile, and the airplane, for these are primarily concerned not with the communication of ideas but with the mobility of people.

already been accomplished and that others are under way. But what will happen after years of adaptation and as a consequence of future inventions is a matter only for speculation. In the present chapter we will record those social-psychological changes for which there seems to be good evidence, although for some there is as yet no demonstrated proof.[2]

THE DEMOCRACY OF RADIO

Any device that carries messages instantaneously and inexpensively to the farthest and most inaccessible regions of the earth, that penetrates all manner of social, political, and economic barriers, is by nature a powerful agent of democracy. Millions of people listen to the same thing at the same time—and they themselves are aware of the fact. Distinctions between rural and urban communities, men and women, age and youth, social classes, creeds, states, and nations are abolished. As if by magic the barriers of social stratification disappear and in their place comes a consciousness of equality and of a community of interest.

This consciousness is enhanced by the fact that the radio voice enters directly into our homes, and has a personal appeal lacking in newspapers and magazines. It is enhanced, too, by the informality of the voice, by its conversational rather than oratorical qualities. Although bright lights and bombast in assembly halls have had their place in democracy, they are artificial and do not create, as the radio voice does, the impression of natural equality among men.

When a million or more people hear the same subject matter, the same arguments and appeals, the same music and humor, when their attention is held in the same way and at the same time to the same stimuli, it is psychologically inevitable that they should acquire in some degree common interests, common tastes, and common attitudes. In short, it seems to be the nature of radio to encourage people to think and feel alike.

It is true, of course, that mental differences between people are not easy to eliminate. Nature itself has a way of preferring individuality to uniformity, and the broadcaster knows that his unseen audience is not, after all, of a single mind. Blandishments that will be meat to some of his listeners will be poison to others. This fact creates a problem for the broadcaster. He knows that he is dealing with a *heterogeneous* audience and that in order to make his message effective for all listeners alike he must discover and exploit the common de-

[2]The symposium *Recent Social Trends* (edit. by W. C. Mitchell, *et al.*, New York: McGraw-Hill, 1933) lists without discussion (Vol. I, 152-157) several social changes for which the radio is in part responsible. The present chapter represents a critical sifting and an elaboration of this earlier work.

nominator of their interests. He cannot afford to be either high-brow or low-brow, he must aim at the average intelligence, avoid subtlety and sophistication, and yet if possible flatter his listeners. If he can please them, they will accept his message. His problem is to please everyone if possible, and if he can't do this, to please the majority. Music is one of the solutions to his problem, since music has universal charm. For the rest, he learns how to use phrases and words as inoffensively as possible. He avoids controversy, subtlety, and spiciness. He steers a middle course and appeals to the middle class. He respects the principle of majority rule. His technique is the technique of democracy.

One of the characteristics of a democracy is the ease with which individuals acquire a "crowd mind." The radio, more than any other medium of communication, is capable of forming a crowd mind among individuals who are physically separated from one another. (To a lesser degree, of course, the newspaper does the same thing. But newspaper readers do not have as marked an "impression of universality.") The daily experience of hearing the announcer say "This program is coming to you over a coast-to-coast network" inevitably increases our sense of membership in the national family. It lays the foundation for homogeneity. In times of potential social disruption the radio voice of someone in authority, speaking to millions of citizens as "my friends," tends to decrease their sense of insecurity. It diminishes the mischievous effects of rumor and allays dread and apprehension of what is unknown. Through the use of the radio on March 4 and 5, 1933, President Roosevelt unquestionably diminished the force of the financial panic.

Heretofore "crowds" meant chiefly congregate clusters of people sharing and giving expression to a common emotion. But now, as never before, crowd mentality may be created and sustained without the contagion of personal contact. Although such "consociate" crowds are less violent and less dangerous than congregate crowds—the radio can create racial hatred but not itself achieve a lynching—still to a degree the fostering of the mob spirit must be counted as one of the byproducts of radio.

It is the federal and national type of democracy to which radio contributes, rather than to the older form exemplified politically in the town meeting and culturally in the church and grange. In underprivileged communities the radio offers superior opportunities not only for following the events of the world, but also for hearing musical and educational programs of greater variety and better quality than the community itself can provide. Every city dweller who has suffered that familiar boredom which comes after a few days in a rural community has only to turn on the radio to realize how much stimulation it brings into the cultural wastelands of America. On the other hand, in cities where theaters, symphonies, libraries, and universities are found, the radio offers—as a rule—inferior spiritual nourishment. If it keeps the city dweller from participating in these activities, it has a tendency to level down his cultural outlook. And so radio reflects another of the peculiarities of democracy: it equalizes the opportunity of enjoying art, education, and entertainment, and at the same time makes their level everywhere the same.

In a yet wider sense radio is an agent of democracy. It promotes the interpenetration of national cultures. Canadians tune to American broadcasts; the French may listen to Italians, Germans, and English as readily as to their own countrymen. One continent hears another with increasing ease. When the opinions, the songs, the dramas of another nation are a matter of daily acquaintance, its culture seems less foreign. Radio is no respecter of boundaries. Inherently it is a foe of Fascism and of cultural nationalism. It presses always toward internationalism, toward universal democracy. Dictators, it is true, and nationalists of every description, may exploit the ether to their own ends, but in so doing they are unquestionably perverting the natural properties of radio.

RADIO AND THE STANDARDIZATION OF LIFE

Now we encounter a paradox. Radio brings greater variety into the lives of men, and yet at the same time tends to standardize and to stereotype mental life. Many topics have been introduced into men's circles of interest; they hear a great variety of opinion. There is entertainment and education for all, and those who benefit most are those whose lives are otherwise narrow. The resources of the theater, the university, and the concert hall are made available to the poor, to those who live in remote places, and even to the illiterate. Yet for all the new horizons that it opens, for all its varied and stimulating diversion, radio, for several reasons, is an agency that makes for standardization.

Not every shade of opinion can be put on the air, nor can every variety of cultural interest be represented, although, as we shall see in the next chapter, the degree of standardization varies in different countries. If I am to enjoy my radio, I must adjust my personal taste to the program that most nearly approximates it. I may choose to listen to a political opinion that is somewhat, though in all probability not exactly, like my own. I may choose music that is more or less agreeable, but not exactly as I would have it. I constantly sacrifice my individuality so that I may fit into one of the common molds that radio offers. If I insist on remaining an individualist, I shall dislike nearly all radio programs. I may, on the other hand, choose my own books, phonograph records, and lectures.

In its attempt to cater to the greatest possible number of individuals, radio generally provides typical or modal programs. Music is played because it is "jazz," "sentimental," or "classical"; opinions are given because they are either "pro" or "con." Everything tends to be categorical. The broadcaster attempts to provide a coarse net with which to capture the favorable attention of many listeners at once. Subtle shades of appeal are forfeited.

Suppose war is the subject chosen for broadcast, the chances are that the speech will be one that is clear-cut in its support of militarism ("preparedness") or of pacifism. Think of the shadings of analysis which the subject invites. There might be a dispassionate study of war in terms of biological, psychological, economic, or historical concepts. It might be discussed as a problem in instinct, conscience, propaganda, or patriotism. All such subtler issues are submerged in favor of clear-cut positions. It is as though people were capable of perceiving only two colors, black and white, and were blind to all the shades of gray. Left to themselves the listeners would evolve a large number of attitudes, but under the guidance of radio the potential variety becomes limited through sharply drawn points of view. One must take sides: prohibition or repeal, Republican or Democrat, prostrike or antistrike, Americanism or Communism, this or that. One would think that the universe were dichotomous. Wherever sharp lines are drawn, the complexities of life become oversimplified.

When both sides of an issue are given equal weight, this stereotyping is serious enough, but in practice the radio often favors the emphasis upon only one opinion (for example, in the case of Communism versus Americanism). On many issues the radio is not expected to be impartial, but to favor one view only. This tendency grows more marked, of course, in proportion as the mentality of Fascism displaces the liberal tradition. The Nazi "evening hour" in Germany is an example of the standardizing pressure of the radio carried to its logical extreme.

The radio is likewise responsible, no one can possibly deny, for further standardization of our habits of living. Experts tell us what to eat, what to read, what to buy, what exercise to take, what to think of the music we hear, and how to treat our colds. When the expert signs off, the advertiser takes up the assault on individuality in taste and conduct. (Over the air the distinction between the expert and the advertiser is often intentionally vague.) Radio further emphasizes our time habits. One of the outstanding characteristics of broadcasting is its punctuality. Like train despatching, it is on time. This doubtless has an effect on the already conspicuous habits of punctuality and efficiency in American life and will encourage such habits wherever radio penetrates.

Radio is perhaps our chief potential bulwark of social solidarity. It stems the tide of disrupting influences, and strengthens the ties that are socially binding. It can organize for action in a few hours the emotions of sympathy and indignation. It assists in the apprehension of criminals, in the raising of funds for relief, and in allaying fear. It is such capacities of radio as these that prompted a broadcasting official to declare it to be "one of the greatest solvents of the social problems of the American people." There can be no doubt that broadcasting, by virtue of its standardizing influence, tends to counteract disintegrative forces.

Take the case of the family, the institution that sociologists have always regarded as the keystone of any society. In recent years its functions have obviously been weakened. In a modest and unwitting way radio has added a psychological cement to the threatened structure. A radio in the home relieves an evening of boredom and is an effective competitor for entertainment outside. Children troop home from their play an hour earlier than they would otherwise, simply because Little Orphan Annie has her copyrighted adventures at a stated hour. Young people receive many homilies from the radio, the like of which have not been heard in most American homes for a generation. The adolescent boy frequently prefers to stay home and listen to his favorite comedian than to take a chance on the local movie. Even when father wants to listen to a speech, mother to a symphony, brother to a comedian, and sister to jazz, the resulting conflict is "all within the family," and constitutes an exercise in family adjustment.

One of the abilities of the radio is its reliable and relatively objective news service. Since rumors can be authoritatively denied or converted into fact by the announcer, they are not so likely to become widespread and distorted. To a considerable extent, of course, newspapers have already standardized our information, but radio seems even more decisive. Whereas newspapers sometimes prolong rumors and heighten the suggestion of conflict in order to increase their sales, the radio has more to gain by crisp and conclusive reports. The announcer has little time to waste on innuendo and the creation of atmosphere. Wood-pulp paper is cheap but time is precious. Just as radio allays rumor it may also discourage gossip. The housewife may find the loud-speaker more entertaining than the back fence as her mind becomes occupied with affairs of the outside world rather than with those of her neighbors.

THE RADIO AND AUDITORY HABITS

The ease of tuning in, together with the lack of obligation to listen, has created a new type of auditory background for life within the home. The housewife performs her household duties to the accompaniment of music, advice and advertising: in the afternoon she may sew, read or play bridge with the same background of sound; in the evening, if she is not exhausted, the radio may provide a setting against which dinner is served and guests are entertained. The same auditory ground may be found in restaurants, barbershops, stores, hospitals, hotels, prisons, and dormitories. Students often prepare their assignments to the muted tune of a jazz orchestra (cf. pp. 104ff.). The question naturally arises whether such persistent use of the radio is having an effect upon our powers of concentration, upon our habits of listening, and upon our nerves.

Take, first, the case of the housewife or the student who is completely preoccupied with work. The loud-speaker emits its stream of sound, but it falls on deaf ears. The distraction is completely inhibited. As long as attention does not shift, the radio's effect, if it has any at all, is entirely subliminal. In such a case the effort required (and unconsciously exerted) to overcome the distraction may actually enhance concentration on the task in hand. The story is told of a French mathematician who in the war selected a ruined house within sound of guns at the front because he found that his attention to his problems became sharper. Inattention to one stimulus always means attention to some other; inhibition of one response requires concentration on another. The stronger the potential distraction the greater is the compensatory attention.

But even when distractions are inhibited they may be nerve-racking in the long run. A selection between competing stimuli can be made only at the cost of effort. Recent studies of noise have shown that although it may be unperceived, as in traffic, factories, and offices, it has nevertheless an appreciable effect upon physiological processes.[9] The incessant use of the radio, inhibited though its sounds may be from consciousness, probably causes similar tension. The conclusion must be, then, that working "against the radio" may enhance the degree of attention given to a chosen task, but only at the cost of strain and fatigue.

However, attention is at best a restless thing, always waxing and waning, and shifting from one focus to another. The sounds of the radio are seldom inhibited for more than a few minutes at a time. The mind wanders from the task in hand to the distracting sound, and

[9] M. S. Viteles, *Industrial Psychology*. New York: Norton, 1932, 506-511.

then returns again. The radio provides a secondary focus of attention. The housewife listens "in snatches," and the student divides his attention between "math" and melody. This agreeable diversion is not harmful in those types of work where the task is something so simple and so habitual that its performance does not require the maximum of concentration. Obviously the sounds are not likely to reduce the efficiency of the housewife as greatly as that of the student. In certain lines of manual work such as are required by household duties and in some types of manufacturing, a background of music such as the radio provides has been demonstrated to be actually beneficial.[4]

There is also the phenomenon of accommodation and fatigue in attention. It is possible to keep the radio plugged in until one scarcely hears it at all. From long continued alternations of attention and protracted distraction, irritation is felt, and when at last the radio is turned off, it is with a sense of great relief. Some people reach the point of radio-fatigue sooner than others. Addicts who seldom sign off find themselves, unreasonably enough, ultimately complaining of the lack of originality in programs.

Radio is probably improving the capacity of the average man to listen intelligently to what he hears. In the experiments reported in Chapter IX it was discovered that the college student, with his long training in listening to lectures, is far better able than the untrained listener to understand and to recall what he hears. His advantage, furthermore, is discovered to be greater for *auditory* than for *visual* material. It appears, therefore, that intelligent listening is *par excellence* the mark of the educated man. Although there is a prevailing tendency to use the radio as a background for other tasks, when the dial is turned to a specific program and when attention is directed fully to its message, an auditory training is provided for millions of people and its long-range effects may be exceedingly important. For increasing the world's population of "good listeners" radio deserves an extra star in its crown.

SPECIAL EFFECTS

Such are some of the *general* influences of the radio upon the mental and social life of men. In addition to these there are many others of a *special* order, pertaining only to some one department of human interest and conduct. In most cases the nature of these special influences is self-evident as soon as it is pointed out, although here again it would be difficult in some instances to obtain scientific proof that the change is

[4] C. M. Diserens, *The Influence of Music on Behavior*. Princeton: Princeton University Press, 1926.

actually taking place or that it is due exclusively to the introduction of radio. Social change is usually the result of multiple influences, but in the events reported in the following schedule the radio is clearly a factor of primary significance.

Education

Radio has provided without expense or inconvenience to the listener heretofore unknown educational opportunities. Almost every subject taught in high schools and colleges finds a place on the air—science, literature, languages, agriculture, dietetics. Even violin and dancing lessons are broadcast. Radio instruction, to be sure, is sketchy and quite elementary, but when educators have perfected their methods of instruction and when more money is available for educational broadcasts, radio will have to be recognized as an educational force of the first magnitude.

Since radio instruction is often provided by college instructors, it fosters a more intimate relationship between the community and the centers for higher education. The citizens catch glimpses of what goes on within academic cloisters, and the professor at last talks to the man in the street.

Radio instruction in time may serve to equalize educational differences between members of the same family, and to lessen the intellectual and social distance between college and noncollege men. Its influence is intensely democratic.

Radio instruction stimulates private ambition, efforts at self-education, and intellectual discussion in groups whose interests might otherwise be limited to bridge, movies, and gossip.

A greater knowledge of strange subjects, of foreign countries, and of unfamiliar points of view discourages provincialism and prejudice. The opportunity to hear talks on diverse subjects increases tolerance. The city dweller, for example, who listens to the Farm and Home Hour has his attention sympathetically directed toward the problems of the agricultural population.

It is conceivable that the broadcasting of the best lectures may decrease the demand for teachers, particularly in university extension courses.

Although some educators have dreamt of a national classroom where all citizens might listen to the finest lectures, there are inherent disadvantages in the radio as compared with the rostrum and the classroom (cf. Chaps. I and VIII) which will probably keep this dream from coming true.

New pedagogical devices are being invented. The absence of the blackboard, the lack of circular social relationship, the heterogeneity and lack of preparation in the audience, all force new techniques in teaching. For example, the dialogue is coming into favor. Yet the dialogue as compared with the freedom and spontaneity of the classroom sounds prearranged and stilted. Students are embarrassed by the presence of a microphone, and the instructor does not feel free to digress.

Music

It is now possible for everyone to hear every type of music, classical and popular, vocal and instrumental, old and new. The increased availability of music has doubtlessly increased its popularity. It has been argued that the surfeit of music would eventually destroy its appeal, but there seems to be no more support for this prophecy than for that made centuries ago that the invention of printing would destroy literature. In the arts it is a safe axiom that *appetite grows with eating*.

Radio provides unparalleled opportunity for musical education. It is safe to say that more people listen to better music than ever before in the world's history. Listening alone helps to shape people's taste; but the instruction and interpretations that accompany some of the broadcasts of symphonies, operas, and chamber music accomplish still more. The musical snob, to be sure, is seldom pleased with these "program notes," but for the masses of people they assist in more intelligent listening.

Since music is a cosmopolitan art, familiarity with it draws favorable attention to the culture of other lands. The listener learns to recognize national idioms in music. The styles of various composers become familiar. And their names become pronounceable.

The radio audience demands novelty and variety. The result is that musical broadcasters are exploring the archives of musical literature as never before. There is also increased incentive for composers, particularly, of course, for writers of popular songs where novelty is soon exhausted.

Radio is responsible for the effective revival of old song favorites, including hearth and home songs belonging originally to the plantation and to the frontier. The nostalgic quality of these songs and the "fond recollections" associated with them are not without their significance.

The demands of the radio have a selective effect upon artists. The contralto and baritone are preferred to the soprano and tenor (cf. p. 101f.). Singers with powerful concert voices are no longer at a premium. The physical appearance of the artist is of no consequence. Musicians who are frightened by a visible audience have an advantage before the microphone, whereas those who depend upon an audience for stimulation are the losers. The operator in the control room becomes a musician in his attempts to make up for deficiencies in the performer's radio technique. However, not all performers are pleased to have their art interfered with by a "mechanic."

Increased use of phonograph records in broadcasts has encouraged better recording and reproducing. But there has been a struggle for supremacy between the phonograph and the radio, with the latter the victor. In order to survive the phonograph has turned its attention to class appeal, catering to those connoisseurs who much prefer to have their albums of standard music available at all hours than to depend upon the sporadic benefactions of the radio. The enhancement of standards in the case of the phonograph as a result of competition with the radio is not unlike that which has occurred on the stage as a result of competition with the talking picture.

Drama

Because it has always been expensive to produce, good drama has usually been reserved for the upper economic classes. Radio now provides a type of drama for the masses. Assured of large audiences, the radio producers go to considerable expense in securing talent and fairly long periods of radio time. The popularity of drama on the air is rapidly increasing and its future is assured. Here is an art form that is altogether original, something new under the sun. Novelties are being continually tried, and those that are successful serve as designs for the future.

Radio drama is opposed to the American tendency toward lavish display in staging. Since it depends almost altogether upon the effectiveness and the beauty of the spoken word, it resembles in one respect at least Shakespearean drama. It is not surprising to learn from British broadcasters that "Shakespeare has lent himself better than any other poet or dramatist to the new medium."

The absence of scenery, costumes, and gestures reduces the actor to a single resource—his voice. Radio drama is the antithesis of the pantomime. Vision is altogether subsidiary, its function being no longer sensory but exclusively imaginal. To be sure, the announcer or the actor gives some clues to aid the listener in visualizing the scene portrayed, but most of the imagery is self-created. When television is added, the situation will be different, but for the moment radio drama is quintessentially a vocal art, and as such is undergoing rapid development.

There has been a marked enhancement of interest in diction. Both the actor and the auditor are acutely aware of pronunciation, of inflection, and of the differences between standard and substandard speech.[5] Ro-

[5] Cf. T. H. Pear, *Voice and Personality* (London: Chapman and Hall, 1931) and *The Psychology of Effective Speaking* (London: Paul, Trench, and Trubner, 1933).

meo may be old and bald, Juliet middle-aged and fat, and still their romance may be convincing to an audience that hears but cannot see. But let their speech vary from the standard or their voices quaver and grow husky and the play is undone.

Religion

Although religious services are seldom listed among the most popular programs, they are easily available to all who care to listen. Radio preachers most certainly have a larger congregation than before. Church attendance has not been appreciably reduced, and some people who would not otherwise go to church tune in.

The opportunity to listen to representative services of all denominations probably encourages religious tolerance and weakens further the denominational barriers between Protestant churches. By merely turning his dial on Sunday morning the listener may compare as never before the services of many denominations.

Radio preachers, in order to widen their appeal, tend to speak upon current social problems and matters of interest in everyday life. Their influence in molding public opinion and public policy is thereby increased.

Not infrequently radio preachers receive letters of confession and requests for guidance in personal problems. The radio has thus become unexpectedly an agent in providing spiritual guidance and solace to perplexed souls.

When a church service is broadcast it is necessarily modified. The preacher must keep the radio as well as the present congregation in mind. There must be no awkward pauses in the service, no gaps that are unintelligible to the unseen listeners. The microphone discourages parading, gesticulation, and bombast. The congregation at the church is impressed by the importance of a service which is put on the air. The words that are spoken seem more weighty, and each member feels that when he sings the hymns he contributes ever so humbly to the impressive occasion.

The broadcasting of services offers a few individuals the excuse to stay home. By listening to a service on the radio a lukewarm churchgoer may be religious enough to appease his conscience and still lazy enough to satisfy his Sunday morning lassitude.

Somewhat rarely, perhaps, the family as a group is attentive to a service, and in these cases the almost extinct function of family worship is revived.

To those who listen to services in their own homes, the exclusive religious atmosphere of the church is absent. Attention is not held to the altar, the pulpit, the vestments, but may be diverted by the antics of the puppy or odors from the kitchen. It is inevitable that under such circumstances worship becomes secularized and devotion rather flabby.

Ministers report thàt a certain number of converts are made, and that some people have regained their lost interest in the church and are again attending services.

Politics and Government

The radio has provided an additional channel for reaching the public on political matters. People have an opportunity to hear arguments on both sides of current issues if they take the trouble to tune in at the proper times. This opportunity for obtaining balance in partisan communications is greater than that afforded by the newspaper or the political rally.

Since candidates often broadcast over wide networks, their appeals are directed more to diversified groups and less to sectional interest or local prejudice. The effect is to center the voters' attention upon questions of wider import and probably to diminish interest in municipal and neighborhood issues.

In principle, the use of the radio should increase public enlightenment, encourage responsible citizenship, and enhance interest, intelligence, and tolerance among voters. This sturdy support for the democratic process depends of course upon an honest policy whereby the rights of the air are open to candidates of all parties, irrespective of their ability to pay or to confer favors upon broadcasting companies.

Politicians often find their spoken promises more binding than their printed platform. This is a strange situation, based perhaps on the greater intimacy involved in speech (cf. p. 156f.). If we hear a promise we are more impressed than if we read the declaration in a newspaper.[6]

The radio listener, in his own home, is not as suggestible as the listener in the congregate audience. Emotional appeals of the barnstorming type have less effect upon him. The politician speaking over the radio is forced to be more direct, more analytic, and more concrete than on the rostrum.

Entering the home, as he does, at odd hours, with listeners less well disposed than the enthusiastic partisans who attend political rallies, the candidate's approach will resemble that of the salesman rather than that of the spellbinder. He will avoid long speeches, be more informal and conversational, be better prepared and more succinct.

Radio provides special advantages to officials already in power. The

[6] "From my own experience in writing and speaking on politics, I know that 99 per cent more persons will react to your speaking than to your writing." H. V. Kaltenborn, Radio and Political Campaigns, *Education on the Air* (edit. by J. H. MacLatchy), Columbus: Ohio State University Press, 1932, 3.

air is made readily accessible to officers of the government: they are often invited to explain their policies. In times of emergency this practice makes for security; it is often educational; sometimes, of course, it is a deliberate display of power.

The radio may be used to gain a swift appraisal of public opinion. A few minutes after his address on the banking crisis, March 5, 1933, President Roosevelt began to receive by telegraph unequivocal evidence of public opinion. Such immediate response cannot fail to have a guiding effect upon public policy.

Radio has influenced certain fundamental practices of political parties. Nominating conventions have been somewhat modified since voters themselves may listen in. There is less control by party leaders and cliques, and more by any speaker who is effective over the radio. Events are focused into the microphone, and barnstorming suppressed. To cover the costs of broadcasting, campaign budgets have been greatly increased.

Radio can be used to spread unwelcome political propaganda across national borders. The ether is democratic, no respecter of political boundaries. Its inherent internationalism makes mischief in a world whose political organization has not kept pace with its mechanical genius.

Finally, radio has made necessary new legislation, new licenses, new federal bureaus. Because of its use in the apprehension of criminals, its significance in international communication, the menace of monopoly, the constitutional problems of freedom of speech, and for many other reasons, governments are vitally concerned with the proper control and direction of this mighty medium of communication.

News

The latest news is available to everyone, more swiftly even than through newspaper presses. If a newspaper happens to scoop the first announcement of an important event, radio news-flashes provide a supplement; if the radio has the scoop, the newspaper quickly follows with elaboration. The two agencies interlock and the public definitely gains. Not so many events escape notice as formerly, and the progress of a war, a strike, a man-hunt, or a football game can be closely followed.

In certain ways radio is a dangerous· competitor of the newspaper. In America they are both concerned with advertising *and* with news. By reaching large audiences quickly, the radio can give the high spots of news and take away the "punch" of the newspaper. Election returns and the results of sporting events become rapidly "cold," and when broadcast over the radio, fewer papers are purchased. The newspaper and the radio are likewise lively competitors for advertising booty.

Since radio has come to stay and since newspapers cannot abolish it, the solution is found in supplementation of function, and to some extent in the modification of the policies of newspapers. Radio provides the high spots of news, and the papers give the story with greater completeness, more comment, and with pictures. In advertising, newspapers publish the "follow-up" ads which keep before the public an interest originally stimulated by the radio, or else invite its readers to tune in at such and such an hour to hear the Sextette sponsored by Sunkist Comfits. Many newspapers are meeting the problem of competition by installing broadcasting stations of their own, or by supplying news to studios in return for free advertising.[7]

Popular news announcers speak crisply and briefly. Long comments and interpretations are discouraged, but the announcer's choice of items and his privilege of phrasing them as he wishes place in his hands a subtle but significant power of influencing public opinion.

Language

The standard of any language is determined not by the written, but by the spoken word. In some countries "standard speech" is that heard in the theater, or among the educated inhabitants of a certain city. But in America no social class or locality has clear-cut prestige in linguistic matters. The standard set by the stage and teachers of speech has been affected by the talking picture and it is now quite likely that standard American English will show most of all the influence of the radio. Announcers are chosen for both the uniformity and the clarity of their speech. They must have no foreign accent, no dialect, and no idiosyncrasy; above all, their voices must be agreeable. While announcing is in progress the listener's attention is fixed exclusively upon speech (which is not true of talking pictures). He hears a pleasing voice and correct diction; he hears it several times a day, and day after day. Consciously or unconsciously he may tend to modify his own speech in conformity. As the influence spreads, it is quite possible that local dialects will be suppressed—a result that will have profound effects in nations that are divided into many speech-communities.

On the other hand, the self-conscious use of dialectical forms and

---

[7] In 1934 a Press-Radio Bureau was established as a result of an agreement between the American Newspaper Publishers' Association, NBC, and Columbia. The purpose of the Bureau was "to forestall unfair competition between newspapers and the radio in the gathering and disseminating of news." Two five-minute news broadcasts were provided by the newspapers to the stations with the understanding that the news would not be sold to advertisers and would not be broadcast until several hours after it had appeared in the papers. Independently owned press associations were rapidly established, selling news to independent stations and through them to advertisers. This forced the A.N.P.A. to modify its restrictions and in effect nullified the Press-Radio agreement. (Cf. E. H. Harris, "Radio and the Press," *Annals Amer. Acad. Pol. and Soc. Sci.*, January 1935, 163-169; Isabelle Keating, "Radio Invades Journalism," *The Nation*, 1935, 140, 677f.)

colloquialisms by radio favorites, and the use of deliberately ungrammatical speech by comedians, keeps substandard speech decidedly alive and active. But such distortions are generally employed for dramatic effects or for comedy and are readily recognized as distortions. Even when they are imitated, it is for amusement and with a clear recognition of their difference from "good" speech.

Radio probably increases the vocabulary of the average listener, and for him brings into spoken discourse many terms that previously he had found only in printed literature.

The increasing use of radio in international communication enhances familiarity with foreign languages, and the broadcast of language lessons adds still more to radio's supremacy in linguistic affairs.

Children

Now that we know to what extent our children are movie-made,[8] we naturally wonder what influence the radio has upon their conduct and thought. The following effects have been reported by A. L. Eisenberg on the basis of his study of the preferences, listening habits, and reactions to radio programs of over 3000 children *ten to thirteen years old* in New York City.[9] Further investigations of different ages and in different populations are needed.

Children, it seems, would rather listen to the radio than read. They also prefer the radio to the phonograph and to puzzles, and even regard listening as more desirable than playing a musical instrument themselves.[10] On the other hand, according to their own report, they prefer the movies and the funnies to radio listening.

About one-third of the children say that they lie awake in bed thinking of things they have heard over the radio. The same number report that they frequently dream of radio plots: three-fourths of these dreams are nightmares.

Most children believe that radio has given them many good things, chiefly new information and skills, desirable traits of character, and better food and health habits.

Parents report that radio has brought the following benefits to their children: greater interest in the home, promotion of family ties, increased critical faculties, entertainment, as well as information and skills, desirable traits of character, and good habits in relation to food and health.

[8] H. J. Forman, *Our Movie Made Children*. New York: Macmillan, 1933.
[9] Azriel L. Eisenberg, *Children and Radio Programs*. New York: Teachers College Bureau of Publications, 1935.
[10] P. Lazarsfeld reports that fewer Austrian children have learned to play musical instruments since the advent of radio. (Cf. *Hörerbefragung der Ravag*. Wien: Ravag, 1932.)

A small minority of the children, only about one-tenth of the population studied, say that radio has taught them bad things: disobedience, stealing, mischievousness, fear.

Other effects noted by Eisenberg include the increase in the children's vocabularies, their learning of new games and stories, and their growing familiarity with popular music. He reports likewise a tendency of children to imitate radio stars, in particular to adopt catch phrases, mispronunciations, and queer, amusing sounds.

Industry and Vocation

There have been a number of incidental but exceedingly important effects of radio upon the industrial and vocational life of the nation. Only a few of these will be mentioned.

Within the past fifteen years it has provided a new occupation for almost 100,000 people.

Employment and profits in certain competing industries (e.g., the phonograph) have been adversely affected.

Since radio listening diverts people from other activities, to a certain extent their consumption of shoes, wearing apparel, automobiles, gasoline, magazines, and other commodities may be decreased.

A new medium for writers has been created.

There is more rapid dissemination of business news and stock market quotations.

Nation-wide organizations may bring together scattered local agents to hear pep-talks and to receive instructions from headquarters.

Aviators and navigators are aided by weather reports, radio beams, two-way communication.

Farmers have profited from agricultural instruction and official reports of market conditions and weather.[11]

The ravages of floods and pestilence can be partially averted by prompt broadcasts from government or state agencies.

In discussing these effects of radio we have not taken into account the various systems of broadcasting used in different countries. And we have assumed that the air is everywhere free. In reality, of course, radio is owned and controlled, and many of the trends listed here vary with the type of control in force. In the next chapter we shall survey briefly the differences existing between various systems of broadcasting and consider more specifically how the social-psychological effects of radio in our own country are ultimately determined by the American plan of broadcasting for private profit.

[11] H. Umberger, "The Influence of Radio Instruction upon Farm Practices," *Education on the Air*, 1932. 274-283.

CHAPTER III

THE AMERICAN WAY

THE average American listener may at times complain that there are too many advertisements, too many crooners, or too many stations on the air, but he seldom questions the socio-economic principles underlying the institution of radio. Nor does he realize that what he hears, and therefore much of what he thinks, would be different in a country where radio is supported differently. Programs are not the same under a dictatorship as in a democracy, nor the same under socialism as under capitalism. The composition, the coloring, the variety, and the duration of radio programs are the expression of complex social conditions. Virtually none of the psychological phenomena of the radio can be fully understood apart from the framework of political and economic philosophy under which the industry has developed. All of the findings contained in this volume must, therefore, be considered in part as reflections of the American system.

OWNERSHIP

In every civilized country the government has ultimate authority over communications. As soon as radio became a practicable medium of communication, each government was forced to make a decision. Should it control the new medium democratically or autocratically? Should it own and operate all broadcasting stations, or lease them under contracts calling for conformity to certain rules? Or should it entrust radio to commercial enterprise, interfering as little as possible? The answer, of course, depended ultimately upon the political philosophy of the nation. The result, as Tables I and II show, has been the adoption in different countries of sharply contrasting policies.

The methods of supporting and controlling broadcasting range from complete government ownership and regulation as in Russia to a partial laissez-faire in most countries of the New World. In general, European nations exert more government control. Russia, Germany, and Italy openly utilize the radio for governmental propaganda. Other countries, such as England, France, and Austria, regard radio as an instrument primarily for the education and entertainment of the people, not for governmental propaganda or commercial profit. Most of the nations in North and South America have allowed the radio to be developed almost exclusively by commercial interests.

TABLE I

TYPE OF RADIO OWNERSHIP AND CONTROL IN VARIOUS COUNTRIES (1932)[1]

Country	No. of stations[2]	No. of sets[2]	Ownership	Advertising	Revenue
Argentina.....	38	400,000	Private	Permitted	Advertising
Australia.....	54	330,000	Government (high-power)	Prohibited	License fees[3]
			Private (low power)	Permitted	Advertising
Austria.......	6	439,322	Government owns majority stock in broadcasting club	Prohibited	License fees
Belgium......	12	133,016	Government	Prohibited	License fees
Brazil........	22	7,000	Private	Permitted	Advertising
Canada.......	66	650,000	5 government controlled stations[4]	Restricted[5]	License fees and advertising
			Private	Permitted	Advertising
Chile.........	24	35,000	Private	Permitted	Advertising
Denmark.....	4	437,244	Government	Prohibited	License fees
France.......	30	500,000	13 government stations	Prohibited	License fees
			17 private stations	Permitted[6]	Advertising[6]
Germany.....	30	3,731,948	Government	Restricted	License fees
Great Britain..	21	5,262,953	Public corporation	Prohibited	License fees
Italy.........	12	126,000	Private monopoly	Restricted	License fees and sales tax
Mexico.......	44	100,000	5 government stations	Prohibited	Public funds
			39 private stations	Permitted	Advertising
Russia........	80	2,000,000	Government	Prohibited	License fees and government appropriation
Spain........	15	550,000	Private	Permitted	Advertising and private subsidies
Sweden.......	33	461,721	Government	Prohibited	License fees
United States..	607	17,000,000	Private	Permitted	Advertising

[1] The data contained in Table I were derived chiefly from the following reports: *Commercial Radio Advertising*, U. S. Senate Document, No. 137, Washington: U. S. Printing Office, 1932; *Broadcast Advertising in Europe*, U. S. Dept. of Commerce, Trade Information Bulletin, No. 787, 1932; *Broadcast Advertising in Latin America*, U. S. Dept. of Commerce, Trade Information Bulletin, No. 771, 1931; *Broadcast Advertising in Asia, Africa, Australia, and Oceania*, U. S. Dept. of Commerce, Trade Information Bulletin, No. 799, 1932.

[2] The number of stations and the number of sets listed in the table are only approximations. In some countries there are many small stations not included in this list. It should also be borne in mind that the *number* of broadcasting stations is not

TABLE II

CLASSIFICATION OF TYPES OF CONTROL IN VARIOUS COUNTRIES

1. *Government owned or controlled; little or no advertising; supported by public funds or license fees.*

    Australia—high-power stations
    Belgium
    Canada—5 stations
    Denmark
    France
    Germany
    Great Britain
    Mexico—5 stations
    Russia
    Sweden

2. *Privately owned; exclusive license; revenue from tax; no advertising.*

    Austria

3. *Privately owned; exclusive concession; license fee; limited advertising.*

    Italy

4. *Privately owned; all revenue from advertising.*

    Argentina
    Australia—low-power stations
    Brazil
    Canada—majority of stations not yet nationalized
    Chile
    Mexico—39 stations
    Spain
    United States

Table I shows that there are many more radios in the United States than in any other country. Of the estimated 37,000,000 sets in the world in 1932, the citizens of the United States owned nearly one-half. The broadcasting stations in this country represent an invested capital of over $60,000,000, and in 1931 the gross expenditure of all stations was over $75,000,000.[7] It is inevitable that the owners should adopt policies that will protect and guarantee a return on investments and expenditures. The social psychologist must keep this fact in mind in

always a true index of the amount of coverage in a given country because of the difference in power of broadcasting stations.

[3] License fees are payments made to the government by owners of receiving sets.

[4] Although only five stations are now controlled by the Canadian government (two of which are owned and three leased), the Radio Act of 1932 contemplates eventual government ownership of all large stations.

[5] The programs broadcast on all *networks* by the Canadian Radio Commission carry no advertising.

[6] The French government has prohibited all radio advertising after January 1, 1935. Broadcasting expenses will be defrayed entirely from license fees.

[7] *Commercial Radio Advertising*, U. S. Senate Document, No. 137, 40-46.

his study of the influence of radio upon the attitudes, opinions, and conduct of the listeners.

HOW PRIVATE OWNERSHIP AFFECTS BROADCASTING

Foreign observers are amazed at the abundance of our programs. We owe this quantity and variety to advertisers and other sponsors who pay the bills. The manufacturer whose product has national appeal finds it efficient to advertise on a nation-wide hookup. To this end he may engage any one of three powerful broadcasting chains which compete for the more lucrative programs. All of them broadcast at the same time, thus providing the listener with at least three dependable and expensive programs. The local merchant who wants to cover a restricted area engages the services of a single station or a small chain of stations to broadcast his program simultaneously with the programs of other local manufacturers and national advertisers. Although no single listener can pay attention to more than one program at a time, the fact that this duplication of programs pays is proved by the existence of 607 stations in the United States, almost all of which engage in commercial traffic. As a consequence, the radio listener in America can probably hear more programs at every hour of the day than any other listener in the world.

Broadcasters have had to devise measuring rods by means of which they can charge their customers for the services rendered. One such measuring rod is the amount of coverage (listening area); another is the amount of time the customer is on the air. The hour, which can be conveniently divided up and sold in parts, was selected as the standard unit.

With programs throughout the country beginning on the hour, the quarter hour, or the half, it is possible for broadcasters to rearrange their networks at certain scheduled times when almost all programs in the country are changing. If an advertiser wants nation-wide coverage, he may engage the facilities of a large network from eight to nine in the evening. At nine o'clock, however, various local stations may cut themselves off the nation-wide hookup and sell their time to local customers. From the point of view of advertisers throughout the nation, this is an excellent system. The national advertiser knows that local stations will not plug themselves out in the middle of his program. The local merchant knows that the nation-wide program will end just before nine and that his program will begin on time. There is no danger that the introduction of his program will offend the listeners by cutting them off the nation-wide hookup before an expensive program has finished. From the point of view of the station owner, the system is also highly satisfactory. It is possible for him to sell his time far in advance with almost complete assurance (except in case of emergency) that the period his client engages will not be interrupted in any way.

This wholesale interest in "selling" radio time has forced all radio music, education, and drama to be submissive to the split second. Only the President of the United States may pardonably end his remarks several minutes before or after scheduled time. And the following expression of the listener's point of view shows that even a President would have been wiser not to overstep the time limit by too wide a margin.

Even Americans will rebel if things go too far. At eight-thirty on a recent evening the populace of the United States, respectful if dubious, tuned in on Mr. Hoover's portentous speech in Iowa. At nine-thirty, accustomed to the prompt intervention of the omnipotent announcer, the listeners confidently awaited the President's concluding words. Confidently and also impatiently; for at nine-thirty on every Tuesday evening Mr. Ed Wynn comes on the air. But Mr. Hoover had only arrived at point number two of his twelve-point program. The populace shifted in its myriad seats; wives looked at husbands; children, allowed to remain up till ten on Tuesdays, looked in alarm at the clock; twenty thousand votes shifted to Franklin Roosevelt. Nine-forty-five: Mr. Hoover had arrived at point four; five million Americans consulted their radio programs and discovered that Ed Wynn's time had not been altered or canceled; two million switched off their instruments and sent their children to bed weeping; votes lost to Mr. Hoover multiplied too fast for computation. Ten o'clock: the candidate solemnly labored point number seven; too late to hope for even a fragment of Ed Wynn. What did the N. B. C. mean by this outrage? Whose hour was it anyhow? Ten million husbands and wives retired to bed in a mood of bitter rebellion; no votes left for Hoover. Did the Republican National Committee pay for the half hour thus usurped by its candidate? If so, we can assure it that $5,000 was never less well spent.[8]

On the occasion to which this editorial refers sixty stations received a total of six thousand telephone calls of protest!

The greatest of all broadcasting sins is mistiming. When listening to an American program, one would think that all of Haydn's quartets were meant to be played in 14 minutes and 45 seconds, that all language lessons are of the same length, and that jazz pieces habitually end by fading out in the middle of a refrain just as the clock is striking. The imposition of a rigid time limit on all programs is obviously an artificial device, designed without regard to the nature of the material to be broadcast. We have become so accustomed to this system in America

[8] *The Nation*, 1932, 135, 341.

that we seldom think of it. Although practically all countries use the hour as an approximate unit, it is most strictly adhered to in the United States where time is for sale over large areas. In Great Britain there is no radio advertising, and although programs are adjusted to the hour, they are not so drastically cut nor so artificially prolonged to fit a 30-second deadline. If a conductor sees that his program will be too long, he does not have to change the tempo accordingly, omit the coda, or fade out.

HOW PRIVATE OWNERSHIP DETERMINES PROGRAMS

Although only about 30 per cent of radio time in the United States is sold for commercial programs, this 30 per cent is usually the most effective time to be found in the radio day. That is why it can be sold. The rest of the day is devoted to "sustaining" programs. The broadcasting station either gives a certain amount of time to an unpaid speaker, entertainer, or orchestra, or itself pays the cost of the program. The expense of these sustaining programs is borne by the companies for several reasons: (1) They increase the popularity and use of radio in general. (2) They keep the station on the air and thus increase the station's prestige and enhance its value for commercial programs. (3) They give the station an opportunity to feature certain programs that might attract an advertising client. (4) They enable the station to qualify under the "public interest" clause contained in its license. (5) They build up goodwill, since the broadcaster often includes in the sustaining time educational, symphonic, or dramatic programs in sufficient number and of sufficient quality to quiet the rebellious voices of those who would otherwise protest at programs designed for lower levels of intelligence. As one radio official has said, "Our facilities are at their [the educators'] disposal, if only they will help us to build up the one thing on which our very existence depends—public interest."[9] However, since for the majority of its sustaining programs the station must supply the talent and pay the cost of broadcasting, it sometimes has to economize by offering the listeners mediocre entertainment.

If a commercial organization decides to go on the air, it must first decide what program to put on. The advertiser usually wants to reach the largest audience possible in his allotted time, and the program he selects will be one which he thinks will appeal to the public, the "public" for him being the largest possible audience that might conceivably purchase his goods. The broadcasting companies engage in surveys to de-

[9] H. A. Bellows, "Commercial Broadcasting and Education," *Radio and Education*, 1931, 58.

termine the whims and fancies of this public so they may intelligently advise the potential client in the selection of his program. The client wants to be sure his program is well liked and widely listened to. Many sponsors feel that it is economically safer to underestimate than to overestimate the intelligence of the listening audience.[10] Quite naturally they are not willing to take any chances on a program which because of subtlety or sophistication might repel the majority of the listeners. Commercial broadcasters are not philanthropists; there is no reason why they should make an effort to educate the radio audience to better music, drama, and health, or to progressive political and economic opinions. If any one station or network insisted upon an improved quality in all of its commercial programs, it would lose many advertising clients since at present the supply of broadcasting time is greater than the demand for it and clients may choose their stations and networks.

However, both sponsors and broadcasters are aware that a considerable portion of the citizens appreciates symphonies, operas, and other programs of distinction. The fact that a growing percentage of listeners enjoy these broadcasts of quality accounts for the increasing number of programs of artistic and intellectual merit. Sponsors find that it is good business to satisfy these potential customers and the major broadcasting companies provide a certain number of high class sustaining programs to win the favor of this group. Nevertheless, these quality programs, as well as the more popular variety, are designed for large sectors of public taste and interest. Programs arranged for definite and relatively selected portions of the population (e.g., lawyers, electrical engineers, surgeons) are very infrequently featured over American stations since such "class" appeals are inconsistent with the profit motive of commercial broadcasters.

Another consequence of the American system is the variety and novelty frequently introduced into commercial programs. In order that his program may appeal to all classes of people and to all members of the family, the sponsor often tries to include within the same period a considerable variety of entertainment. Instead of turning to one program to listen to a comedian, another to hear a drama, a third to hear jazz, or a fourth to enjoy a symphony, we may turn to the Canyon Tobacco Hour and hear a little of everything. Perhaps no member of the family enjoys the whole hour, but the chances are that each will

[10] Whether the level of radio programs designed for the average man is too low is a question often asked. Judging from the psychological portrait of the average man, given by H. L. Hollingworth, it would be difficult to underevaluate his abilities and range of interests. Cf. *The Psychology of the Audience.* New York: American Book Co., 1935, 126-137.

like a certain fraction of it. The variety program is the broadcaster's ingenious creation to appeal to the greatest number of people during one period. But a variety program that appeals to the listener "in spots" is quite likely to repel him in spots.

Since radio time is for sale and since the majority of programs are designed to attract the attention of the same sort of individuals at all hours of the day and night, there can be little consistent arrangement of programs according to the *type* of entertainment they provide. In most instances, the listener does not have the assurance that at one time of day he may hear one type of program (such as old song favorites) and at another time a different type (such as drama). Instead, he is made to feel the privilege of hearing a certain *sponsor's* program at a certain hour. In most cases the hour of 3 P.M. is not reserved for education, let us say, but for toothpaste; the hour of 10 P.M. cannot be counted on for drama, but for cigarettes. There are, of course, exceptions to this generalization, particularly in the case of outstanding sustaining programs and week-end symphonies and operas. But, on the whole, broadcasting periods are devoted not to types of programs but to advertisers, whose programs may or may not be consistent over a given period of time. As one broadcasting company has pointed out to its potential customers, "Radio advertising, by its very nature, *can* exploit—powerfully, intimately, and permanently—the *time habits* of the public."[11] While the sequence of programs in the United States follows the interest of sponsors, in other countries—Austria, England, and Russia, for example—certain hours are set aside for definite types of programs or for special groups of listeners.

In order that the reader may appreciate the importance of economic and political determinism, Table III summarizes the effects of private ownership upon the American method of broadcasting together with the effects of three other systems of ownership and control.[12] The contrasts between these four methods illustrate the need for social psychology to consider the cultural and economic framework within which its data are found. Although human nature may be everywhere *potentially* the same, the ways in which it actually develops are limited by the constraints of each particular social system. The constraints become second nature to the individual. He seldom questions them, or, indeed, even recognizes their existence and he therefore takes for granted the great majority of the influences that surround him in everyday life.

[11] "Columbia Broadcasting System," *The Added Increment.* New York: Columbia Broadcasting System, 1934.

[12] For a more critical and complete comparison of the American Way with other systems of Broadcasting, see H. S. Hettinger, *et al.*, "Radio: The Fifth Estate," *Annals Amer. Acad. Pol. & Soc. Sci.*, January, 1935, 1-90.

TABLE III

THE EFFECT OF FOUR SYSTEMS OF OWNERSHIP AND CONTROL UPON BROADCASTING

Country	Ownership and control	Conformity to time unit employed	To what end programs are designed	Coordination, constancy or variety in programs
United States	Private	The hour is divided into 15-minute fractions. The established time periods are strictly enforced. An interval of only 30 seconds is allowed between programs. This makes changes in hookups possible and assures both local and national advertisers of the full time paid for. The great majority of programs are, therefore, exactly 15, 30, or 60 minutes long.	Broadcasters try to sell as much of their time as possible to advertisers. The advertising sponsor is usually represented by an advertising agency. The agency and the station's program staff design a program to attract the largest number of customers to the product advertised. The goal is, then, to please the public, and common denominators of taste and interest are sought. *Sustaining* programs frequently consist of artists who want to advertise themselves, of educators, or of other unpaid speakers. Other sustaining programs (e.g., children's hours, symphonies, operas) are sometimes paid for or made possible by the efforts of the station itself. This is done to satisfy the "public interest" clause in the station's license and to build up the goodwill of the listening public.	*Commercial* programs usually occupy the best hours of the week and are designed for certain common denominators of taste and interest. Some programs, therefore, contain great variety to satisfy every type of listener for a fraction of the program duration. Other advertisers sponsor programs which have a consistent appeal to certain large portions of the population. *Sustaining* programs, however, are more frequently designed for a certain type of listener who may be sure that he will hear a *whole* program suited to his tastes (e.g., symphony, dance band, drama, educational talk).
Austria	Radio	Length of program is adjusted	The government attempts to	General homogeneity in indi-

leased to private club in which government holds majority of stock

to the type of material to be broadcast—a whole evening may be devoted to Viennese waltzes, 20 minutes to a scientific talk, one hour to a jazz band, etc. Strict conformity to the time limit is not compulsory.

educate the people to better music, health, reading, etc., without depriving them of the usual entertainment.

Radio also used for political propaganda in the interests of the government in power.

vidual programs with few "variety" programs. Regular times of the day or week are devoted to symphonies, weather reports, jazz, health, education, cooking, etc. Special times in the week are devoted to special types of listeners, i.e., "Stunde der Frau" or "Stunde der Arbeiterkammer."

England Public corporation

The hour is generally divided into fractions of 15 minutes. There are many 45-minute programs. Established time periods are not enforced, although there is general conformity. Concerts may extend several minutes beyond the allotted period and the next program is postponed.

Programs are arranged by the British Broadcasting Corporation. They are designed with the conscious purpose of disseminating culture. Although the entertainment value of radio is not ignored, no attempt is made to cater to the common denominator of public taste or intelligence. As a medium of popular entertainment, radio is probably therefore less effective than in the United States. Local or national advisory committees make program suggestions.

Political minorities complain that they are not allowed a fair representation on the air. Educational broadcasts are seldom concerned with economic or national issues. However, before general elections, each party is given the same amount of radio time.

Programs are designed not for the "average" listener but for the many different *types* of people who constitute the listening public. Few programs attempt to satisfy everybody. Most programs are consistent with themselves—a program is *all* symphony, *all* light music, *all* drama, etc. The frequency with which a given type of program is broadcast represents a compromise between its cultural importance and the number of people who want to hear it.

TABLE III—*Continued*

Country	*Ownership and control*	*Conformity to time unit employed*	*To what end programs are designed*	*Coordination, constancy or variety in programs*
Russia	Government ownership and control	The hour is the unit of measure and many programs are approximately an hour long. There is an interval of 30 seconds between the established time periods. The length of a program is, however, adjusted to the type of material broadcast. Programs deemed of cultural importance may extend beyond the time limit.	Broadcasts have a three-fold aim: to provide entertainment, to educate the workers, and to propagandize. *Entertainment* is chiefly music of a classical nature. Operas and modern music are popular. Readings of short stories by great actors are frequent. *Education* on the air is a regular part of each day's program. This is designed for different groups according to their ages, needs, and the political ends in view. The *propaganda* consists chiefly in the dissemination of facts which the government reserves the right to interpret. The aim of propaganda is to increase cultural unity and to inspire loyalty to communistic principles in citizens. Loud-speakers are installed in parks, factories, village squares, fields, etc., to provide listening opportunities to the greatest possible number. The contributions of individuals to a given program are minimized. The only names mentioned	Since the radio is used by the government for entertainment, education, and propaganda, programs are adjusted to the needs and time habits of the citizens. Definite hours are reserved for definite subjects—e.g., there is always a concert for the workers at the noon hour, talks on agriculture, construction, beekeeping, aviation, etc., and speeches in foreign languages are broadcast at regular times for interested groups. Frequently these talks are of a highly technical nature—e.g., on new construction materials or the use of rare elements in the electrical industry. Children's programs come daily at regular hours. Programs are also adjusted to the seasons of the year with lectures pertaining to the special tasks of the season. Many programs of general interest are broadcast on the 60-station network, while provincial stations broadcast local material. Since programs are designed for

are those of composers and, occasionally, professors and conductors.

Programs are designed by committees throughout the country and listeners are encouraged to send in suggestions and criticisms.

the workers, and since those who do not work are disregarded, the majority of stations do not begin to broadcast until late afternoon. At least one station, however, broadcasts in the early morning and continues throughout most of the day. But even this station may be silent from 9-12 A.M.

Programs of the American variety type are practically unknown. News reports contain no mention of murders, kidnappings, sports, etc.; but are concerned almost entirely with events of political or economic interest.

HOW PRIVATE OWNERSHIP FASHIONS THE LISTENER'S ATTITUDES AND OPINIONS

The problem of the rights and responsibilities of broadcasting companies is a delicate one, for it involves the two explosive issues of censorship and propaganda. Our interest is not that of the reformer, the political scientist, or the legislator concerned with the moral and legal aspects of the problem. We are observers interested in understanding the psychological mechanisms involved. Radio *censorship*, for social psychology, may be defined as the process of blocking the expression of opinions, and thereby of arbitrarily selecting the listener's mental content for him; radio *propaganda* is the systematic attempt to develop through the use of suggestion certain of the listener's attitudes and beliefs in such a way that some special interest is favored.

The prevailing moral and economic sentiments of the nation make a certain amount of censorship and propaganda inevitable. Neither obscenity nor blasphemy will be tolerated by the majority; the right of censorship in these directions is seldom questioned. Broadcasters must also censor programs that would make them partners in crime. As for propaganda, in the United States the radio depends upon it for its very existence, for all advertising is, psychologically speaking, propaganda (cf. pp. 60ff.). Neither the Federal Communications Commission nor the majority of citizens question the right of broadcasters to issue this particular type of propaganda. Some selection of material for broadcasting is, then, to be expected. But the line between inevitable and arbitrary selection is exceedingly difficult to draw. When does spiciness leave off and obscenity begin? When does virile language pass the boundary of profanity? When does freethinking become blasphemy? When does the propaganda of advertisers cross that indefinite line that separates polite exaggeration from the criminal offense of obtaining money under false pretenses? How can the station expect to sell its time to advertisers for propaganda purposes if it does not also censor programs that might, if placed directly before or after an advertiser's period, prove subversive to that advertiser's interests? The socio-economic framework within which radio operates always creates a temptation for its managers to exert censorship along some lines and to facilitate propaganda along others.

THE SELECTION OF ATTITUDES: CENSORSHIP

The particular type of censorship exercised on broadcasting will depend, of course, upon who controls radio. In Nazi Germany, Soviet

Russia, and Fascist Italy a rigid censorship is maintained by the governments. In the United States, where all citizens are theoretically free to express their opinions, the government does not openly restrict the freedom of the air. Few broadcasting rules are laid down by the Federal Communications Commission. In conformity to the policy of this Commission and to the American creed, broadcasting officials are anxious to maintain the traditions of liberty. "There is no censorship on the basis of political, religious, or other beliefs. Radio has remained impartial, the means through which the nation may hear all sides to a question," write two of radio's spokesmen.[13] A former vice-president of one of the two large broadcasting companies and a former member of the Federal Radio Commission has said that "The censorship bugaboo is a myth from radio's childhood days, kept alive, like all other superstitions, by prejudice and ignorance."[14]

Although, when all things are considered, freedom of the air in America is probably as great as in most other countries and is certainly greater than in some, the claim that censorship does not exist has been vehemently denied, and quite effectively disproved.[15]

The Radio Act and its interpretation.[16] Because of the limitations of the radio spectrum (550 to 1500 kilocycles) there are available to the 607 stations in the United States only 90 clear channels employing 40 frequencies. It is the duty of the Federal Communications Commission to assign these channels to stations in various parts of the country so there will be the least amount of interference. The legal maximum duration of a station's license is for three years, but licenses are sometimes issued on a six months' basis. The Communications Commission, appointed by the President, has the power to issue and to renew licenses.

The Federal Radio Act of 1927 clearly states that the Radio Commission[17] shall exercise no direct censorship. Section 29 of the act says that

Nothing in this Act shall be understood or construed to give the licensing authority the power of censorship over the radio communications or signals

[13] A. N. Goldsmith and A. C. Lescarboura, *This Thing Called Broadcasting*. New York: Holt, 1930.

[14] H. A. Bellows, *op. cit.* 57.

[15] For example, by Miss Lillian Hurwitz (*Radio Censorship*. New York: American Civil Liberties Union, 1932). Some of her examples are given below. The story told by Miss Hurwitz is retold by James Rorty in *Order on the Air* (New York: John Day, 1934) and in *Our Master's Voice: Advertising* (New York: John Day, 1934, Ch. XVII). A more strictly legal analysis of radio censorship may be found in L. G. Caldwell's "Freedom of Speech and Radio Broadcasting" (*Annals Amer. Acad. Pol. & Sci.*, January, 1935, 179-207).

[16] For a recent study of this topic, see E. P. Herring, "Politics and Radio Regulation," *Harvard Business Review*, 1935, 13, 167-178.

[17] The Federal Radio Commission created in 1927 was absorbed by the Federal Communications Commission appointed in 1934.

transmitted by any radio station, and no regulation or condition shall be promulgated or fixed by the licensing authority which shall interfere with the right of free speech by means of radio communications.

Theoretically, the act also insures freedom of the air to political candidates. If a radio station permits one candidate to speak, it must permit all others to speak. But it may legally refuse the air to *all* candidates. This apparent freedom is really a negative freedom when one considers the tremendous expense of hiring a station's facilities and the usual meager budget of minority groups. Political freedom over the radio becomes, legally, proportional to a candidate's campaign funds or his credit. According to reports filed in 1934, the Democratic National Committee still owes the two large broadcasting companies a total of $155,221 for the 1932 campaign, while the Republican debt is $130,274.[18] One wonders whether the same credit would be extended to radical parties and radical candidates.[19]

The single definite form of censorship which the Radio Commission may exercise is that

No person within the jurisdiction of the United States shall utter any obscene, indecent or profane language (Sect. 29).

Other provisions of the Radio Act, however, grant the Radio Commission certain discretionary powers in issuing or renewing a station's license.

If upon examination of any applicant for a station license or for the renewal or modification of a station license the licensing authority shall determine that the public interest, convenience and necessity would be served by the granting thereof, it shall authorize the issuance, renewal, or modification thereof in accordance with said finding (Sect. 11).

The Communications Commission is, then, denied "the power of censorship" and is forbidden to "interfere with the right of free speech by means of radio communications." At the same time, it may "determine that the public interest, convenience, and necessity" shall be served. Accordingly, the Commission may prohibit broadcasts which it believes will not promote the interests of all. And "public interest" is defined chiefly with reference to popular acceptability, interpreted by members of the Commission.[20] Since a new competitor has the right

[18] *New York Times*, June 18, 1934.

[19] Apparently not, according to Upton Sinclair's statement of his difficulties during his campaign for the governorship of California in the fall of 1934. "Nobody in any of our headquarters gets any pay, but there are rent and telephone bills and postage and printing, and, above all, radio time. Our opponents have hired most of it, but there is still a little left—if we are quick. In order to engage time we have to pay cash in advance—no favors are granted to disturbers of the social order." (*The Nation*, 1934, 139, 351.)

[20] Cf. "The Freedom of Radio Speech," *Harvard Law Review*, 1933, 46, 987-993.

to challenge the "program service" of an existing station and request that station's radio channel for itself, station owners must constantly be prepared to defend their "program service" and are not anxious to accept any customers who might give the Commission any cause for alarm.

The Communications Commission may also exercise broad censorship powers by means of admonition and exhortation. For example, Commissioner H. A. Lafount has remarked that "Under the radio act the commission has the right to take into consideration the kind of programs broadcast when licensees apply for renewals. . . . It is to be hoped that radio stations, using valuable facilities loaned to them temporarily by the government, will not unwittingly be placed in an embarrassing position because of the greed or lack of patriotism on the part of a few unscrupulous advertisers."[21] In another connection the same commissioner said that "It is the patriotic, if not the bounden and legal, duty of all licensees of radio broadcasting to deny their facilities to advertisers who are disposed to defy, ignore, or modify the codes established by the N.R.A."[22] There is obviously a distinct connection between such admonitions and the policies of broadcasters in scrutinizing the ethics of their clients' programs and their status.

Thus, although Section 29 of the Radio Act prohibits federal censorship of programs, it is not surprising that many cases have been recorded where censorship has been indirectly applied by the Radio Commission under the "public interest" clause of Section 11. One station, featuring the zealous and at times loose-tongued Rev. "Bob" Schuler who had denounced certain Catholics, local officials, and judges sitting on current cases, was denied a renewal of its license when the Commission reversed the decision of Chief Examiner Yost.[23] Station WCFL, owned by the Chicago Federation of Labor, obtained permission from the Radio Commission to broadcast during the important evening hours only after two years of proceedings and after a bill had been introduced in Congress providing a clear channel for a labor station.[24] The Socialist station, WEVD, was granted a renewal of its license in 1931 after a reversal of the examiner's report and considerable comment by the liberal press.[25]

[21] New York Times, June 18, 1934.
[22] Ibid.
[23] Federal Radio Commission Order, Docket No. 1043, November 13, 1931, in re application of Trinity Methodist Church South, Los Angeles, California, for renewal of license. J. Radio Law, 1932, 2, 132. Also Federal Radio Commission, Examiner's Report, No. 241, 1931.
[24] United States Daily, September 22, 1931, and May 28, 1932.
[25] Federal Radio Commission, Examiner's Report, No. 176, 1931; in re application of Debs Memorial Fund Inc. of New York City for renewal of license decision and order of the Federal Radio Commission, Docket No. 919, J. Radio Law, 1932, 2, 119.

State regulation. Since there are numerous decisions of the Supreme Court prohibiting states from enacting laws which would interfere with federal regulation of interstate commerce,[26] and since radio waves are not stopped by state boundaries, state censorship is comparatively limited. Some states (e.g., California and Illinois) have extended their laws of criminal libel to cover radio utterances of "false and scandalous matter with intent to injure or defame." In New York a bill was proposed to prohibit the broadcasting of any speech or remarks relating to medicine or using medical terms, or the diagnosing of any disease or the recommending of any cure, unless the broadcasting were done by a duly licensed physician.[27] In other states legislation has been introduced in an attempt to equalize the opportunities of speakers by making their radio appearances less dependent upon their ability to pay high prices for radio time. A bill was proposed in North Dakota to compel broadcasters either to grant time to political candidates at $10 per hour or to face confiscation of their stations. The bill was killed in committee.[28] A proposal before the Massachusetts legislature would provide for the establishment and operation by the commonwealth of a radio station for broadcasting information and data deemed important for the public welfare. This bill, like another in the same state to provide for a station to broadcast educational programs, was killed in the House.[29] Such legislative attempts to increase or to decrease the number of points of view which should be expressed in the "public interest" are systematically opposed by broadcasters who are on the whole well satisfied with present government policies.

Stations as censors. Since the stations themselves, rather than the federal or state governments, choose the programs they are to broadcast, the selection of the points of view is in a great majority of cases made directly by the individual broadcasting stations. A Supreme Court decision in the state of Nebraska has held that the owner of a broadcasting station is responsible for any defamatory remarks made by any person broadcasting over the station.[30] The influence of this decision has of course, not been limited to the boundaries of the state in which it was made.

Besides satisfying federal and state restrictions, the station must continually make an effort not to offend two other important groups— the listeners and the sponsors. Broadcasters have stated their interpretation of "public interest, convenience and necessity" as follows:

[26] P. M. Segal and P. D. P. Spearman, *State and Municipal Regulation of Radio Communication.* Washington: U. S. Government Printing Office, 1929.
[27] *J. Radio Law,* 1931, 1, 142.
[28] *Ibid.,* 142.
[29] *J. Radio Law,* 1932, 2, 403.
[30] Radio Act of 1927, Paragraph 18, *U. S. Code Annotated,* 47, Paragraph 98.

1. No program shall offend public taste and common decency.
2. No program shall be planned as an attack on the United States Government, its officers or otherwise constituted authorities of its fundamental principles.
3. No program shall be conceived or presented for the purpose of deliberately offending the racial, religious or otherwise socially-conscious groups of the community.[31]

This Code of Ethics adopted by the members of the National Association of Broadcasters states further that:

> When the facilities of a broadcaster are used by others than the owner, the broadcaster shall ascertain the financial responsibility and character of such client, that no dishonest, fraudulent, or dangerous person, firm, or organization may gain access to the Radio audience.

In putting this code into execution, those in control of broadcasting stations perforce take it upon themselves to define the "fundamental principles" of the government and what constitutes a "dangerous" person.

The form of censorship which broadcasters perhaps use most frequently, particularly in the case of "dangerous" persons, is to refuse them any time on the air. One of the writers was asked to participate in a series of educational broadcasts but was warned by the local station that he should discuss nothing of a "controversial" nature. A speech which a station feels may be unsatisfactory is routed through the station's continuity department and the broadcaster thus learns in advance the content of a speaker's remarks. If the speech is judged by the station to be "dangerous" or not in the "public interest," it may be rejected. Two examples will illustrate how the listener's attitudes are selected in this way at the stations.

Rev. H. J. Hahn was refused permission to broadcast a sermon entitled "Jesus' Way Out" because the station objected to the "tone" of the sermon and particularly to passages in which Mr. Hahn advocated greater taxation of large incomes and an "increasing purchasing power of the workers." The station's action was reported to the Federal Radio Commission. The Commission sustained the station's decision and replied that "Generally speaking, the licensee must be permitted to decide what programs are or are not acceptable."[32] Dr. A. R. Barcelo, former president of the Porto Rican Senate, was denied the use of a station's facilities when he tried to broadcast an address to Porto Ricans in New York, urging them to further Porto Rican independence. The

[31] National Association of Broadcasters, *Broadcasting in the United States.* Washington: National Press Bldg., 1933, 16.
[32] Hurwitz, *op. cit.,* 44-48.

station explained that it did not broadcast the talk because "The Radio Commission might make it hard" for them.[33]

A more drastic form of censorship occurs when the operator in the control room shuts off the microphone. Although rare, this method is not unknown. For example, in 1932, Dr. W. K. Gregory, of the American Museum of Natural History, was to be interviewed by a journalist on the subject of "Evolution and the Depression." A subordinate of the station requested that Dr. Gregory delete the sentence "We have reckless overproduction of goods and reckless overproduction of people. We are a beehive choked with honey, yet full of starving bees." Dr. Gregory refused to omit the sentence. He was allowed to go on the air and when he arrived at this sentence in the interview, the microphone was cut off, leaving a period of silence. The station later apologized to Dr. Gregory.[34] Rev. J. M. Gillis was cut off the air after he had spoken for twelve minutes over a southern station protesting against injustices to the negro.[35] This form of censorship is sometimes the station's method of attempting to avoid profanity on the air. The broadcast of a university football team dinner was interrupted three times by a station in 1931 because of profanity.[36] In the same year the Radio Commission upheld a station when it shut General Smedley Butler off the air because he used the word "hell."[37]

Network privileges may be denied certain speakers. For example, Father Coughlin was unable to hire the network facilities of Columbia and NBC and had to form a chain of his own for his Sunday broadcasts. The individual stations in this chain, being well paid, allowed their microphones to vibrate with his economic heresies.

In a handbook entitled *Broadcasting in the United States,* prepared for public school debaters by the National Association of Broadcasters, the question is asked:[38] "Is it true that broadcasting chains have on various occasions deliberately exercised and imposed an unwise censorship over remarks which were made over their networks?" The mythical debater representing American broadcasters answers the question by citing three instances of alleged censorship. He shows that one was due to the fact that previous speeches in the program took up so much time that there was none left for the complainant. Another instance cited the case of a United States senator who was cut off the air, not because of censorship, but because of the "universal radio cry of distress—SOS" which happened to be broadcast at the

[33] *Ibid.,* 48-50.
[34] *New York Herald Tribune,* November 12, 1932.
[35] *Christian Century,* December 14, 1932.
[36] *New York Times,* October 26, 1931.
[37] *New York Times,* April 27, 1931.
[38] Page 174.

time of the senator's speech. The third and last example given is that of a speaker for the League for Industrial Democracy. The broadcaster admits that there was deliberate censorship of this talk because of its "critical remarks tending to undermine the faith and confidence of the people in their government." The argument is closed with the statement that "All these instances, exceptional as they are, when bulked together tend to show how smoothly, and we might say providentially, the spirit of common sense and the further sense of public responsibility tends to govern the workings of the American Broadcasting System." It is a part of the association's task to refute charges of censorship, and its mission takes it into the public school forum.

Influence of listeners. Since each station attempts to gain and hold popularity, the objections of a large group of listeners to any attitudes expressed in a program may be further grounds for censorship. For example, the subject of birth control is frowned on for fear of offending Catholic listeners. In 1930 the National Birth Control League sent letters to 115 stations requesting permission to broadcast. Only 27 of the letters were answered. Eight of these replies were favorable, two being definitely affirmative. Of the refusals, eight were because of "policy," two said such talks were unsuitable for broadcasting, five regretted that their schedules were filled for months in advance, and the others stated they were "not interested."[39]

Influence of advertisers. Since the advertiser is the man who pays the radio bills, he is also the man who has the privilege of influencing the selection of programs. Station owners must look to the future as well as the present and it is obviously part of their business to please their customers. Hence they are tempted to guard the portals of the air in deference to those sponsors who pay them thousands of dollars a year.

An employee of a station affiliated with a nation-wide network refused to allow Mr. F. J. Schlink, director of Consumers' Research, and an enemy of advertisers, to broadcast his talk on the failure of the NRA to benefit the consumer. A week later, after the refusal had received considerable publicity, the president of the company allowed Mr. Schlink to broadcast the same speech.[40] Another example of the broadcaster's fear of the advertiser was the refusal of a network to allow one of its clients to urge public support of the Tugwell-Copeland Bill. Radio stations receive a large share of their revenue from food and drug companies and the network stated that "our legal department has ruled that this is a matter of such controversial nature

[39] *New York Times,* March 25, 1930.
[40] *New York Times,* January 11, 1934.

that it is too dangerous to use. As a matter of fact, almost any discussion of the Tugwell Bill at this time is dangerous."[41]

Even the radio humorist may be required to frame jokes so that they do not conflict with the sponsor's interest. The Columbia System received a complaint from a large rabbit company when one of Columbia's comedians, Colonel Stoopnagle, insinuated that he got the meat for his rabbit sandwiches by shooting the cats in the alley. A comedian received a letter from a Pullman official objecting to his description of the "meanest man in the world" as the one who rocked the Pullman car when you were trying to sleep. An automobile manufacturer would not allow the same comedian, whose program it was sponsoring, to discuss roller skates in a humorous way, for roller skates, it was pointed out, are a competitive form of transportation.

Broadcasting monopoly. Since a monopoly, by definition, has exclusive control of a particular line of traffic and since it is not customary for monopolies to be equally tolerant of all points of view, we should at least mention the extent to which radio broadcasting has become a monopoly. In the debater's handbook mentioned above, the National Association of Broadcasters answers a question regarding radio monopoly by pointing out that 72 per cent of all stations were independent on June 30, 1932, while only 28 per cent were associated with networks. "These figures," the phantom debater argues, "definitely show up one one of the most flagrant mis-statements of fact and string of innuendoes which has been placed before the American public." But the debater's opponent might reply that of the 40 frequencies available in this country for clear channel broadcasts, 38 are utilized by stations affiliated with chain broadcasting companies, and only two are available for all the independent stations together.[42] The opponent might mention the fact that the average power of the chain stations on one network is 10,000 watts while the average power of independent stations is only 566 watts,[43] that 71 per cent of all station "units" are affiliated with the two large networks,[44] and that the Radio Corporation

[41] *Release of Joint Committee for Sound and Democratic Consumer Legislation.* New York, 1934.

[42] *Commercial Radio Advertising,* 65. Since a clear channel is assigned by the Federal Communications Commission on the basis of service rendered, large broadcasting companies can now best qualify for these channels. Under the present system of ownership and control it is difficult to see how educational, labor, or independent commercial stations can compete with powerful financial organizations.

[43] P. Hutchinson, "Freedom of the Air," *Christian Century,* March 25, and April 1, 1931.

[44] The unit value of a station is based on its power, time schedule, programs, etc. (Cf. *Federal Radio Commission Rules and Regulations,* rule 109.) The percentage of units affiliated with the two large networks is based upon the report of 1932 (*Commercial Radio Advertising,* 66-70, 141-157).

of America owns and controls 3,800 patents affecting radio transmission.

Censorship in the United States is due, then, not so much to direct political influence as to the peculiarities of public taste and above all to the interests of those who (if we overlook the ultimate consumer) pay radio's bills. Radio officials, like the publishers of newspapers, may in principle favor complete freedom of the air. Yet because they are primarily middlemen between the advertiser and the public they must show "discretion." In his pamphlet *Order on the Air*, James Rorty summarizes as follows the principal points of view which those in control of radio try to prevent listeners from hearing over the air.[45]

1. Any attacks by Communists or other radical minorities upon our form of government or upon the specific acts of the administration in power. (A certain amount of liberal criticism is permitted, as for example on the sustaining programs sponsored by the National Council on Radio in Education.) Some exception should also be made for speeches, on purchased time, by radical candidates for political office. But radical minority parties rarely have adequate funds for such purposes.
2. Any criticism of advertisers, or of the advertising business in general.
3. Any radical criticism of the power and utility interests which directly or indirectly dominate the broadcasting industry.
4. Any direct espousal of the cause of a militant labor group involved in a strike or other struggle for power.
5. Any advocacy, or even any mention of birth control, or especially of the rôle of the Catholic Church in opposing birth control.
6. In general, anything that might be construed as "obscene" or even "tactless" or "controversial" by (those) who guard the portals of the air in behalf of the owners and directors of the major broadcasting stations.

Broadcasters reply that such vigorous charges are exaggerations. And since the impartial observer must learn the other side of the story, he must know how the broadcasters themselves reply to Rorty's accusation. The following statement presenting the broadcasters' point of view was prepared for us by Dr. Henry A. Bellows, chairman of the Legislative Committee of the National Association of Broadcasters.

During the year 1934 two official inquiries were made covering the degree of censorship, if any, which is exercised by radio broadcasters in the United States. These were (a) the hearings in March before the Committee on Merchant Marine, Radio and Fisheries of the United States House of Representatives on the so-called McFadden bill, H.R. 7986 and (b) the hearings before the Broadcast Division of the Federal Communications Commission during October under the provision of Section 307 (c) of the Communications Act.

The McFadden bill was expressly designed to provide opportunity, with-

[45] Page 25.

out censorship, for the free expression by radio of the points of view of minority groups in the fields of politics, charity, education, and religion. Despite the wide publicity given in advance to these hearings, it is significant that not a single representative of any political, charitable, or educational group or organization appeared in support of the bill, and the only testimony in behalf of it from any religious group came from a single propagandist organization which, by its own showing, was making extensive use of radio but had been refused certain network privileges.

Testimony at this hearing made it clear that every broadcaster has to exercise a considerable degree of editorial selection. This is an obvious necessity because of the inevitable time limits of broadcasting, and also because every broadcaster is under a definite obligation, within the terms of the Radio Act of 1927, and the Communications Act of 1934, to serve, and therefore to conserve, public interest. This editorial selection consists (a) in determining what subjects are of sufficient public interest to warrant the allocation of radio time, and (b) what organizations or individuals are qualified to discuss such subjects with authority and effectiveness.

It was clearly brought out in the testimony that the broadcasters have consistently maintained an impartial position with regard to the discussion of all controversial subjects, providing facilities equally for all points of view. This testimony was not controverted by a single witness.

It was further made clear that the broadcasters do not exercise any form of censorship over what is said, with the exception of two points : (a) they are constrained by the Federal law to see that no profane, indecent, or obscene language is used, and (b) they are required, under a decision of the Nebraska Supreme Court, to see that no libelous or slanderous statement is broadcast.

The hearings in October before the Broadcast Division of the Federal Communications Commission brought together by far the greatest volume of information regarding the actual conduct of broadcasting stations and networks ever collected. These statements were filed under oath. They covered, among other things, the question of censorship, and included declarations by some 275 individual broadcasting stations, as well as by the major networks, as to their policy in this respect. They also included specific statements, supported by affidavits and letters, of what has been the actual practice with regard to this matter.

Concerning the general field of education, an enormous volume of evidence was presented, including statements by outstanding university, college and school officials, demonstrating that absolutely no censorship of any kind is, or ever has been practiced in connection with educational programs. Not one particle of evidence in opposition to this statement was presented. Exactly the same thing was true with regard to religion, except that most stations have refused to broadcast attacks on the sincerely held faiths of their listeners. Complete freedom of utterance in all matters relating to charity was universally demonstrated, and never challenged.

As regards political, economic and social problems, it was clearly shown that groups opposed to the existing administrations, whether Federal, State or local, have consistently received ample radio time without cost. It was specifically brought out that stations permit without question educational and medical groups to criticize even the commodities or services commercially advertised by those same stations. It was shown that broadcasters have not only permitted, but in some instances have invited, criticism of public utility and power interests, and that there is absolutely no control, direct or indirect, of these interests over the broadcasting industry.

The record with regard to broadcasting by labor organizations particularly in connection with strikes, was particularly significant. The sworn testimony showed that strike leaders had been invited to use, and had freely used, the facilities of networks and stations without charge, and the record contains many significant letters from labor organizations thanking the broadcasters for their fairness in permitting and encouraging such broadcasts.

The testimony at this hearing brought out clearly the fact that the broadcasters earnestly desire further relief from the limitations now imposed upon them by the Federal law in the matter of freedom of speech. Specifically, they feel that the provision of the law regarding profane, obscene, or indecent language constitutes an unjust discrimination against broadcasting as compared with the public press, because of varying and uncertain definitions of what in fact constitutes profanity or indecency. They further feel that the Nebraska Supreme Court decision, holding a broadcaster jointly liable for libel or slander even when the right of censorship is specifically denied by the law, constitutes a very serious barrier against free speech.

The reports of these two hearings before agencies of the Federal Government, which are matters of public record, constitute an overwhelming demonstration of the fact that radio broadcasting in America maintains to an extraordinary degree the traditions of free speech which have been built up under the constitutional guarantee. It is profoundly significant that in neither of these hearings was a single instance of actual censorship brought forward. The problem of editorial selection, in view of the limitations of broadcasting time, is inevitably difficult, and since every broadcasting station potentially includes in its audience every radio-equipped home within its primary service area, it follows that each broadcaster considers the interest of his audience as a whole before the wishes of minority groups. However, since no such minority group has been able or willing to present evidence of having been excluded from the privileges of broadcasting, and since the sworn testimony shows a large amount of time, absolutely free of censorship, given without charge to such groups, it is impossible to avoid the conclusion that in general the broadcasters have been more than liberal in their support of the American traditions of free speech.

THE FORMATION OF ATTITUDES: PROPAGANDA

The type of propaganda, like the type of censorship, found in any particular country, depends upon who owns and controls the air. In

Russia, radio propaganda is used to build up Communism; the Nazi propagandist minister, Goebbels, uses it ubiquitously to spread the doctrines of Hitler and says that "Some day the radio will be the spiritual daily bread of the whole German nation." In the United States most, but by no means all, propaganda is devoted to the selling of merchandise. Much is of the subtle, indirect, concealed variety issued in behalf of political, economic, or religious interests whose identity generally remains hidden. Commercial propaganda by contrast is usually frank and revealed. The average American listener accepts it as an inevitable daily experience. He realizes that if he gracefully submits he will receive free entertainment and beyond this point he worries not at all.

Propagandists' methods have been elsewhere quite thoroughly analyzed.[46] A restatement of some of the basic principles of propaganda with illustrations derived from American broadcasting will help us understand the formation of attitudes by radio.

1. *The propagandist tries whenever possible to connect his proposition to some preëxisting attitude, need, or symbol rich in meaning.* The successful propagandist knows the attitudes and desires of the masses. He studies public opinion to determine what things people are "for" and what they are "against." For example, he knows that such words as "mother," "home," "justice," "health," "purity," "beauty," or "the Constitution" will arouse in the average American a *favorable* attitude. However, since the attitude aroused by any of these words may be different for each individual, the propagandist is careful not to be specific in his appeal. He merely touches off the attitude and lets it serve as a vaguely favorable background for his message. If the propagandist tried to define "justice" or "economy," or if he told specifically how his proposition was related to them, he would inevitably find that there were differences of opinion, and he would immediately come into conflict with a large share of his listeners.

This first and most important principle of propaganda may be detected in many of the advertising programs that go on the air. A cereal manufacturer connects his product to "Americanism," a yeast manufacturer emphasizes "health" and "science," while a coffeemaker shows how his particular product brings "happiness" and "contentment." A chewing gum manufacturer pays a "beauty expert" to direct "health" and "beauty" exercises for the benefit of listeners with fat necks and double chins. The chief feature of these exercises is chewing gum (while standing erect with hands on hips). The expert suggests that if you chew *two* pieces of gum and replace the gum frequently with *fresh* sticks the exercises will be even more beneficial.

⁴⁶L. W. Doob, *Propaganda: Its Psychology and Technique.* New York: Holt, 1935.

The program ends with the advice "Chew your way to beauty." The political candidate tells his listeners that he stands for "liberty," "justice," or "economy" and with the use of such generalities avoids controversial issues.

The same method may be employed by the propagandist to arouse an *unfavorable* response on the part of the listener. By using such words as "communism," "radical," "murder," or "un-American," the propagandist causes his listeners to reject a way of action inimical to his interests. In political broadcasts the speakers frequently associate their opponents with concepts distasteful to the listener. In the New York City mayoralty campaign of 1933, Mr. McKee associated his rival, Mr. LaGuardia, with "communism," "radicalism," and "Moscow"; himself with "America," "Constitution," and "justice." "I shall be an American mayor and not a Moscow mayor," said Mr. McKee.[47] Father Coughlin has described bankers as "grinning devils" who create money with "purple fountain pens" and whose brains have "the functions of a sterile mule."[48]

2. *If no direct appeal can be made to an existing attitude or belief, then the propagandist builds up a new attitude by using indirect suggestion.* Since the radio advertiser must offer some kind of entertainment to gain an audience, his whole radio program is essentially an attempt to build up a favorable attitude toward his product. Radio advertising, more than any other type, depends on the "good-will" of the listener. America's most famous comedians do not necessarily broadcast for Pepsodent because they use the mouthwash or know about the toothpaste. A great symphony orchestra has no inherent relation to Chesterfield cigarettes. The world's most popular crooner is not hired because he was brought up on Fleischmann's Yeast. These programs are sponsored because they engender in the listener a receptive and favorable attitude toward the sponsor's product. The listener may even have a feeling of "indebtedness" to the manufacturer for such a pleasant hour and may, therefore, be a more likely customer.

Indirect suggestion may be used when it is essential that the propagandist conceal his purpose in order to make his propaganda effective. Sunday evening broadcasts, designed to portray French life and culture, were relayed to the United States from France in a costly propaganda campaign to "sell" France to the United States.[49] In tone, the great majority of news broadcasts uphold the status quo. The striker, for example, is more often portrayed as a disturber of the peace than as an individual with legitimate grievances. Certain "news" broadcasts are often propaganda in disguise; thus fashion reports are

[47] *New York Times*. October 26, 1933.
[48] P. Hutchinson, "Heretics of the Air," *Christian Century*, March 20, 1935.
[49] New York *Herald Tribune*, April 10, 1933.

sometimes masked advertisements for particular stores; occasionally reports of new scientific discoveries are veiled encomiums of a commercial product.

Propaganda is likewise disguised as "explanation." Spokesmen for the administration in power are frequently given free use of broadcasting stations and the recent tendency of such spokesmen has been to gain favor by "explanation." The American listener has been bombarded with NRA speakers of every sort who have told him what the officials are doing. Although there has been some criticism of the NRA on the radio, for the most part the amount has been paltry and the severity restrained.

An important but subtle device of oral propaganda is the use of vocal inflection. A skillful speaker while saying one thing may give the listener the impression that he means another; an announcer can convey a hostile impression along with the news he is supposed to report objectively; an educator's manner of speaking may be ironical although his words are orthodox.

3. *Except in rare instances, the propagandist avoids argument.* Rational thought is the propagandist's most deadly enemy. He follows the advice of Edmund Burke and puts his trust not in the right argument but in the right word. The mental mechanism upon which the propagandist relies is not reason but *suggestion*, which brings about the acceptance of a proposition for belief or action without the normal intervention of critical judgment.

The cigarette manufacturer suggests that his particular brand is "mild," "toasted," or "good for the nerves." For these claims no valid proofs are offered. The use of the superlative, a particularly effective type of suggestion which usually will not stand critical analysis, has long been an accepted part of the advertiser's methods. A product is declared, without demonstration, to be the "most economical," the "safest," or the "best on the market." Political speakers are often masters in the use of suggestion, making themselves vaguely attractive to all types of people without engaging in an analysis of issues that would be certain to arouse critical thought.

4. *The propagandist uses repetition to overcome resistance.* Since a single suggestion is seldom sufficient to cause the desired course of action, and since various groups of propagandists are usually competing for the control of the attitudes and response of the listeners, the successful propagandist keeps his way of action, his product, or his idea continually before the people.

This simple principle scarcely needs illustration. In the ordinary half-hour broadcast the sponsor's name is usually mentioned from ten to twenty-five times.[50] The commercial program is repeated daily or weekly and a successful sponsor may be heard on the air at regular intervals for several years. The exponents as well as the critics of any public policy know that they, too, must keep their points of view before the radio listeners by innumerable broadcasts.

5. *Owing to their lack of experience and of critical ability, children are especially susceptible to propaganda.* This principle is not as widely used in radio propaganda as it is in schools, churches, and children's organizations. Nor is it found in the United States as frequently as in Germany, Russia, or Italy where children are systematically indoctrinated over the air. In this country, however, propagandists have become alert to their opportunities. In 1933, for example, an international program, in which groups of children in various lands sang native songs, was sponsored for children by a pacifist organization. The majority of programs designed for children in this country have more immediate ends in view, for example, to encourage the child (or his parents) to purchase a particular brand of cereal.

Take an incident from the life of a seven-year-old radio fan whom we may call Andrew. A company manufacturing a patented food product (chocolate flavoring to be added to milk) is the sponsor of little Andrew's favorite story hour. The advertising appeal is ingenious and effective. It is directed toward the child's desire for physical superiority (victory at games and "pep"). It comes just before the supper hour when hunger facilitates mental associations pertaining to food. It arouses the powerful motive of sympathy and compassion by asking the child to tell his mother about the product and in this way "do a favor" for the little heroine of the story. Through repetition, tedious to the adult but interesting to the child, the association between the fantasy of the story and the product in question is indelibly established. During the day, as he lives the story in his imagination, he thinks of the product.

In Andrew's case, and no doubt in countless others, the well-designed campaign is effective. He talks about the product, and insists that his mother buy it. Being of a modern and skeptical turn of mind, his mother consults unbiased authorities whose only interest is the consumer's welfare. She learns that products of the type advertised "have no significant advantage over cocoa prepared with milk in the home." Furthermore, "as such mixtures are generally unwarrantedly expensive, none is recommended." The specific product in question is considered to be particularly offensive since it is sold "under the most ingenious and implausible advertising claims." In vain does she suggest that Andrew derive his pep from ordinary cocoa, or at least

[50] O. E. Dunlap, *Radio in Advertising*. New York: Harpers, 1931, 110.

from one of the less expensive preparations. Andrew wins his point by refusing to drink milk at all without the costly addition! Having gained his own way, and imbibed of the magic liquid, he feels his biceps with satisfaction and declares that he now has superlative strength.

Children are dependable and effective consumers. Their desires, their interests, and their whims as well, direct an immense portion of the nation's total purchasing power. Unable to see through the implausible claims of advertisers, they are far more suggestible than adults, and therefore are better targets for commercial propaganda. The child is easily "sold" to a product, and is tenacious in his loyalty to it. He believes in it with all his heart, just as he believes in any fairy tale. His credulity is easily turned into profit by those who care to do so. The child provides the desire and demand, and the parent, willingly or unwillingly, provides the money.

In this discussion, we have presupposed that the radio propagandist has succeeded in attracting the attention of the listener. With so many interested parties on the air, and with so many competitors, one of the chief tasks of the commercial propagandist is to be sure that *his* program is heard. To do this he uses various devices. He schedules his program to be broadcast regularly on certain days and certain hours; he employs a theme song or a catch announcement so listeners may easily identify his program; he prints his broadcasting schedule in newspapers and magazines; he uses powerful stations when he can afford them, and tries to select for his broadcast some station with prestige. He may build up the popularity of his program by using a minimum amount of advertising in the first few programs, increasing the advertising when he feels the program has a large following. Famous artists, novelty and variety programs, popular crooners, and great orchestras are employed by the advertiser to arrest the listener's dial at his particular program.

Still more important for the advertiser is the problem of keeping the listener's attention sustained throughout the entire program so he will hear the advertising plug. The radio propagandist bears in mind the fact that the listener is free to turn his radio off. As a result, devices are frequently employed to make the advertising announcements as innocuous and yet as effective as possible. The more daring sponsors use very little advertising, sometimes merely mentioning their names. Others, realizing that the listener may start a conversation or turn his dial when the "plug" begins, place the ads against musical backgrounds or insert them in unexpected places by connecting them to jokes, descriptions of the radio artist, or by making them an integral part of dramatic skits.

Chapter IV

PROGRAMS

THE modern tourist in Manhattan usually visits Radio City, now one of the island's most famous show places. What impresses him most are the intimate glimpses of the studios in which many of his favorite radio programs originate. One of the dozens of uniformed, heel-clicking ushers, who keep the thousands of daily visitors from getting lost in the walled city, will show him all types and descriptions of studios, some large enough to accommodate a thousand people, and some small and cosy, equipped perhaps with antique furniture where the apprehensive speaker is invited to bring his friends so he will feel at home and keep his broadcast intimate. The tourist will be shown how each studio is air conditioned and completely soundproofed, floating in its own air chamber; he will see the office where NBC has its own teletype machines sending messages to its affiliated stations all over the country; he will peek into the rehearsal of a radio star whom the guide names with reverence; he will see the yet unused studios installed for television; and will be shown an exhibit of microphones used by famous announcers and heroes of the air. There will be a demonstration of some of the sound devices used. The tourist learns that radio rain is really birdseed dropping on a smooth board kept clean with a windshield wiper. Only Grade A birdseed is used since Grade B does not bounce and give the proper effect. The rattletrap car he hears is in reality an old-fashioned sewing machine; ocean waves are made by rubbing a scrubbing brush across a drum; a storm at sea comes from sheet iron and Hallowe'en rattles. These illusions *must* be used because through the microphone they sound more "real" than the performances of nature that they imitate. Exclamations of wonder escape the tourist. He is profoundly impressed by one engineering triumph after another, by the luxury of the studio appointments, and by the diabolical ingenuity entering into ethereal art and commerce.

With special permission the sightseer is allowed to enter the sponsors' princely sanctuaries—elaborate and luxurious honeycombs of small rooms with special balconies overlooking each large studio where the advertiser, his friends, and agents may sit during the performance for which they are paying. The tourist will gradually realize that the whole art of radio is built around, and sustained by, salesmanship. The equipment he has just seen must, then, be regarded as a psychological tool to prod him, the average listener, into doing something or thinking something that will increase the profits or the advantage of the man who foots the radio bills.

The promotion booklets sent out by broadcasting companies to potential advertisers frankly regard radio as "the solution to a sales problem." This solution, they say, comes from "creating valuable good-will; associating this good-will definitely with the product; performing unique missionary work; increasing distribution; widening the market; appealing to a desired and specific consumer group in a selective territory—at a receptive time." Psychologically phrased: by broadcasting attractive programs (often not paid for) the industry creates in millions of individuals not only habits of listening but attitudes of favor toward the entire institution of radio. Listeners who are receptive and well disposed, sometimes even aglow with pleasure from the program, are likely to transfer this friendly attitude to the product advertised. If a specific product is mentioned in association with a particularly attractive program the transfer is more intense and more certain, but any product lucky enough to be mentioned over the air, derives some advantage from the benign psychological attitude ("good-will") of the listeners. Such is the argument.

Statistics prove the argument to be sound. A potential sponsor will be shown that radio advertised goods are used 29.3 per cent more than corresponding non-radio advertised goods.[1] He may read for himself a study which demonstrates that the purchase of radio advertised goods is 35.1 per cent higher in radio homes than in non-radio homes.[2] Impressed by these facts the manufacturer asks how much it will cost him to share in the benefits of radio advertising. He finds that an evening hour over one company's network comprising the northeastern part of the country will cost $5,600, a Pacific Coast hookup for an evening hour will cost $1,350, while for a nation-wide hookup in the evening he must pay $15,775 for an hour, $9,865 for a half-hour, and $6,162 for fifteen minutes. Daytime rates are about half the evening rates. None of these prices includes the cost of entertainment which usually approximates 30 per cent of the total expenses but which may in some cases equal or exceed the cost of the radio time.

THE SPONSOR SELECTS HIS PROGRAM

When a manufacturer decides to advertise his product over the radio, he knows that his chief problem is to find a program his prospective customers will enjoy. A "good" program, like a "good" movie, is, from the point of view of the man who puts it on, one that brings satisfactory financial returns.

[1] R. F. Elder, *Does Radio Sell Goods?* New York: Columbia Broadcasting System, 1931.
[2] R. F. Elder, *Has Radio Sold Goods in 1932?* New York: Columbia Broadcasting System, 1932.

The genesis of a commercial program usually involves the following procedure. First of all, the manufacturer is convinced of the merits of broadcast advertising, perhaps by the sales staff of the broadcasting company, perhaps by the manufacturer's advertising agents, or by both in collaboration. The advertising agency is paid a commission by the broadcasting company, the cost of the program to the sponsor being the same whether he arranges it through an agency or directly with the company. Many of the major advertising agencies have highly developed radio departments. They are capable of taking a commercial program from the "idea stage" through to actual public performance, although they may seek the assistance of the broadcasting company in selecting the program and the hour. The networks maintain commercial program departments for individual clients and for agencies that do not possess comprehensive radio bureaus.

The astute advertising manager will not consent to a program which he believes is inappropriate for his client. It must not be out of harmony with his campaigns of published advertising, nor aimed at a class of listeners who represent only a small section of the possible market. Also, much depends upon the talent available for the programs. So important is this factor that some networks maintain "talent agencies" where desirable performers are kept under contract to work for one and only one broadcasting system.

When the program has been finally arranged it is presented to the sponsors in the form of an "audition." For this event large broadcasting companies maintain elaborately furnished audition rooms, some of which reproduce as faithfully as possible the atmosphere of the living room in the great American home. Sometimes these auditions are "piped" over special telephone circuits to the board room of the manufacturer's plant to save the directors of the company a trip to the studios.

Few programs go on the air in exactly the same form in which they are presented in audition. Following the critical deliberations of the client, the agency, and the studio officials, minor and even major operations are performed. Programs must be carefully checked to make sure that they do not infringe upon musical, dramatic, or literary copyrights. Continuity must contain nothing vulgar or repulsive. The music must be scrutinized: "Marching through Georgia" must be deleted if the program is going south; there must be no jazzing of hymn tunes; and the songs of the crooner and "torch" singer must be inspected lest their innuendoes be too suggestive. Broadcasters say that music entering the home must be purer than music on the stage where different traditions prevail; and furthermore that the songs of unseen singers must be especially restrained since they "leave more to the imagination." Commercial announcements, too, are edited so that no illegal claims or reflections upon a competitor's product are put on the air. When preparations have reached this stage the public is informed through the press and fan magazines that a new program will be broadcast at a particular time next week. Be sure to tune in.

While the public is waiting, the production managers, the artists, and musicians rehearse their performance. After the individual rôles have been learned, the program directors of the station and of the advertising agency and the leader of the orchestra whip the program into its final form. Everything is transmitted from the microphone to critics in the control room who in turn send comments to the studio. As the program nears a satisfactory level of performance, each item is carefully timed so the whole program will fit smoothly within the rigid time limit. The orchestra is told where to cut if the music takes too long; cadenzas are introduced and strains repeated if the time is not properly filled. The announcer knows where he can cut or where he can embellish his remarks if he sees during the final performance that a few seconds must be added or subtracted. A rehearsal may occupy the whole day if the program is of the elaborate variety type.

In some performances, studio audiences are admitted and if we care to attend a typical variety show requiring such an audience, we must get a ticket admitting us to the studio. The advertising agent is usually allotted the majority of the tickets, but the broadcasting company has some at its disposal. The demand for tickets is always much greater than the supply, and broadcasting companies rival one another in accommodating large studio audiences, not infrequently leasing an entire theater for the more popular programs.

With ticket in hand, we go to the studio door which opens about twenty minutes before the program begins. In front of us are various microphones, an organ, two pianos, and chairs for the orchestra, with people bustling about arranging music and getting everything in order. Back of us we see the control room separated from the studio proper by soundproof glass. Over the control room is the sponsor's balcony where people in evening dress have come to witness the program for which one of their number is paying. It, too, is separated from the studio by a glass partition, but is equipped, of course, with a receiving set. The sponsors see with the eyes of the leader but hear with the ears of the led.

The members of the studio audience seem to be as diversified a group of people as those who are about to hear the program in their own

homes. No class, age, or sex seems to predominate. As the people file in
we wonder why they have come. By discreet inquiry we discover various
reasons. Many are habitués who find free entertainment much to their
liking during the depression. Others have come for the first time out of
curiosity to witness a broadcast. Others want to see in person the artists
they have often heard. They feel that their acquaintance is incomplete,
and are impelled to supplement their auditory impressions with visual.
The presence of these spectators is the result of the "incomplete closure"
that radio often leaves in the minds of listeners.

But why is the radio audience invited to come at all? There are two
reasons. In the first place, most actors and singers are stage-trained
and they like to perform in a theatrical setting before a responsive
audience of flesh and blood. One comedian, whose habits were formed
on the stage, prefers to change his costume for each act in his radio
show. Relatively few artists are trained for the microphone alone, and
only when they are do they prefer to give their performance in solitude.
Secondly, the sponsor also likes to see people in the studio. It gives him
local publicity, and he has the comfort of knowing that at least a few
hundred people appreciate his efforts. For him, too, the visible audience
is tangible evidence that his expensive program is at last reaching its
human destination.

Now the artists begin to assemble. Children point with excitement
to Lanny Ross and Mary Lou, a famous "love pair." Parents are glad
to see that Captain Henry really looks like a kindly old southern gen-
tleman. Friends go down to greet the performers and the whole atmosphere is one of bustle and excitement. The orchestra practices a few
strains, the manager makes sure that all directions are understood, the
various sound devices are tested, and the control room operator makes
the final mechanical adjustments. Just before the performance, the
master of ceremonies introduces himself to the audience and welcomes
us to the studio. We are told that we can help to make this program
a success by applauding enthusiastically so the listeners will think the
show is unusually good. The audience titters a bit but joins the con-
spiracy with good humor. The host then informs us that we won't be
able to hear some of the vocal numbers because they will be sung softly
and directly into the microphone. Anyway, we are to take his word for
it that the songs are good and we are to applaud just as loudly as
though we had heard them. Our applause is directed by a sign "Applause" which the master of ceremonies carries in his hand and holds
up at the proper time. We practice our applause and are given the cue
when to stop. Our cooperation, the final link in the long chain of
preparation, is now assured.

Complete silence for a few long seconds. The production manager stands with his eye on the second hand of the clock and one arm stretched above his head. Suddenly he drops his arm and with the strains of the theme song the show goes on the air. We notice one official exchanging signals with the control room operator and transmitting them to the conductor of the orchestra. These signals tell him how the program sounds through the loud-speaker, whether it is too loud or too soft, whether or not the instruments are blending properly. The orchestra stops, the announcer makes his program announcement, the sound device expert splashes some water in a box, drags a chain across the platform in front of his microphone, as the listener is told that he is boarding the Show Boat. Captain Henry and other members of the ensemble talk about the trip and the progress of the local love affair. The toastmaster keeps an eye on the audience and with his studio smile tells us that this is a fine program and we must surely appreciate it. After a humorous remark he puts up his sign and we applaud. Lanny Ross sings a song which we barely hear and again we applaud good-naturedly. Molasses 'n' January at another microphone exchange their wit in negro dialect. Tonight they are not blackened up, although during another program in which they participate they appear in full disguise because the sponsor wants them to. Their jokes are greatly appreciated by the audience, for they are clearly heard and well constructed. Next the advertisement is brought slyly into the program when two southern gentlemen discuss the origin of the sponsor's brand of coffee. The applause sign is raised after the ad. Then some more talk about the progress of the love affair after which the lovers sing a duet. We see that there are two Mary Lous, one who sings and one who talks. At the end of the duet there is spontaneous applause. Two famous radio stars have been seen together in action. Then a nine-year-old boy is introduced by Captain Henry who tells the radio world that there is one kind of love transcending all others—the love of father and son, whereupon the boy reads a very sentimental piece about his mother's death. There is a piano duet. There are more songs, more orchestral numbers, another appearance of the comedians, another ad, and again the theme song is played and the announcer says we shall be back on the air again at the same time next week. The applause sign appears for the last time. The uplifted arm of the production manager is conspicuous. The orchestra leader watches it. It falls and the program is over. Into this single variety program have been squeezed comedy, jazz, semi-classical songs, homely drama, advertising, and sentiment. The program is all things to all people.

Other types of programs do not require studio audiences; only a few privileged spectators are admitted and these must sit quietly in an out-of-the-way corner of the studio. On such an occasion we may see the "March of Time," a dramatization of the week's news. Again there is tense silence as the red hand of the clock approaches the hour. At a signal from the control room, the announcer in a crisp, staccato voice launches the rapidly moving program. One event follows another with breath-taking speed. The cast first reënacts a discussion in the House of Representatives. Most of the listeners, of course, have never seen nor heard the congressmen who are portrayed, but the listener's previous ideas concerning the personalities of the congressmen seem somehow confirmed by the actors' voices. When this scene is over the announcer shifts us rapidly to Jericho where a stentorian actor bemoans the fate of the Jews, while in the background other actors sob and wail. Listeners in their homes are not troubled by this shift of thousands of miles. Many of them no doubt are not certain whether they are listening to Jericho or to New York. Nor do they care. In annihilating auditory distance, the radio has to some extent destroyed for the listener his capacity to distinguish between real and imaginary events. Now the announcer takes us to a hospital where a child is dying from a rare disease. We hear the doctors conferring in serious tones, and we can almost smell the disinfectant. The next minute we are transported to Kansas City for a scene between the mayor and gangsters. The speakers are tense; the studio vibrates with excitement. Rough words fly back and forth. Another artist especially engaged for this program portrays with the proper accent an incident in Peru. On the heels of the Peruvian incident comes an Oklahoma flood. The father of a family wakes his children in the middle of the night and carries them to the roof. Soon the house is torn from its foundations and floats rapidly away. A fat man with a handkerchief to his mouth has been hired to cry like a baby. This is one of his specialties. The family bunches together. They are about to strike a bridge. They know it will be the end. Near another microphone a berry box is broken—the terrible crash of the house against the bridge. This tragic scene ended, the actors bring us to South Germany where the Nazis are trying to enforce the worship of Wotan. The exciting program comes to an end with the sound of two busy typewriters placed in front of a microphone. One clicks noisily while the announcer tells his public that this is an old typewriter. Then we hear the gentle purr of the modern noiseless. This is the advertisement of the company furnishing the program. So much for the "March of Time."

Now we visit a theater that has been converted into a studio. A huge package of cigarettes suspended in mid-air provides a stage background as well as visual propaganda for the studio audience, and a foretaste of what television will bring into the home. The announcer thanks us for coming, presents the fifty-piece orchestra with its sparkling instruments, and tells us that a fine orchestra, like a fine cigarette, must be made of choice ingredients. The orchestra plays a number, individual musicians standing up as their instruments are featured, while any musician playing a solo part must leave his seat and come down to the microphone. A well-trained chorus sings and then a famous operatic tenor makes his appearance. For the benefit of the visible audience he wears evening clothes, but for the benefit of the unseen audience he places himself considerately ten feet from the microphone. His voice, unlike the crooner's, is not suited to a more intimate range. The program is exclusively musical, but since all classes and types of people smoke cigarettes, it has sufficient variety to please them all. At the middle and end of the program a brief advertisement is spoken; in order that his voice may sound as persuasive as possible the announcer stands very close to the mike and uses a low and ingratiating tone. At this moment the visible audience is entirely forgotten; the unseen listeners represent the larger market.

Next we interview a popular radio philosopher about his work. He has been on the air almost every morning for years and has sold nearly half a million copies of his compiled broadcasts. We ask him how he manages to make such a success of his work, and he tells us that the secret is to speak with sincerity and to include a bit of philosophy for every type of person. "If I'm not sincere I'm flooded with letters telling me that 'It didn't sound like you.' " Most people, he says, are in trouble and are worried about one thing or another. They want comfort and inspiration for the day. But the audience is diverse, and therefore the help he offers must be varied. For men he includes a robust joke, for the tender-minded a homely poem contributed by one of his devoted listeners, for older people a homily tried and true, for the sick some religious solace, and at the end a sentimental theme song for everybody. He always closes his talk with the reassuring statement that "All is well." Issuing day after day from a mighty skyscraper in a mighty city, this pronouncement seems almost supernatural and is calculated to bring comfort to a thousand isolated regions where thousands of confused souls vaguely wonder what the world is coming to. As we listen to the philosopher we are profoundly impressed by his voice. Upon its sincerity his whole appeal depends. Psychologists will do well to notice that "sincerity" is an unmistakable attribute of voice. Whether to sound "sincere" must correspond to inner conviction or whether it may be a pose is another question. In the case of the philosopher we confess our surprise at hearing him speak so convincingly over the air just after analyzing for us so cold-bloodedly the structure of his program. Something for everyone plus "sincerity": an almost perfect psychological formula for the type of broadcast that attempts to reach a large population.

THE CONTENT OF PROGRAMS

The American public hears a potpourri of commercial and sustaining programs, but it is difficult for the casual listener to know what the ratio is between them. A group of 75 persons was asked to estimate the percentage of radio time that is commercially sponsored. The estimates averaged 72 per cent, and ranged from 20 per cent to 98 per cent. Actually their mean estimate is approximately 39 per cent too high. When asked the percentage of time devoted to music, the average judgment was 68 per cent (actually about 7 per cent too high); the judgments ranged from 30 per cent to 90 per cent. When asked how much time is consumed by commercial announcements, the average estimate was 17 per cent (12 per cent too high), and the range from 1 per cent to 40 per cent. Such errors show that the listener lacks perspective. Preoccupied with individual programs, his attention and his memory become too confused to permit him to make sound judgments concerning the composition of broadcasters' offerings. An objective rather than a subjective analysis of the auditory bill of fare is needed.

Table IV represents a classification of the programs broadcast during the second week of April, 1934, by several stations affiliated with the Columbia Broadcasting System.[3] The figures indicate the percentage of time devoted to each type of program on each day of the week.

Table IV shows that for the stations concerned:

(1) over 60 per cent of all broadcasts were musical programs;
(2) popular music occupied a much larger share of radio time than any other type of program;
(3) more classical music was broadcast on Sunday than on weekdays, while Monday contained more light and popular music than any other day;
(4) script, including drama and dialogue, was broadcast more than any other nonmusical type of program;
(5) educational broadcasts, in the narrower sense of the word, represented about 5 per cent of the total radio time;
(6) few educational programs were broadcast over the weekend;

[3] The writers wish to thank Mr. John J. Karol of the Columbia Broadcasting System for permission to publish Tables IV and V. Analyses of radio programs will be found in H. S. Hettinger's *A Decade of Radio Advertising* (Chicago: University of Chicago Press, 1933, Chaps. XI and XII). The more detailed classifications used in the tables in the present chapter are more satisfactory for our purposes than Hettinger's coarser classifications, even though the general tendencies reported here agree with his findings.

TABLE IV

PERCENTAGE OF TIME DEVOTED TO VARIOUS TYPES OF PROGRAMS DURING ONE REPRESENTATIVE WEEK

Component	Mon.	Tue.	Wed.	Thu.	Fri.	Sat.	Sun.	Total
Music								
Popular	43.21	36.00	34.09	34.92	40.74	34.40	30.07	36.18
Novelty	1.09	1.77	2.82	2.21	6.20	5.47	....	2.79
Semiclassical	3.81	7.45	8.30	6.77	1.12	5.44	3.05	5.13
Classical	7.71	3.36	7.21	11.88	0.57	8.68	15.93	7.86
Light	12.15	8.66	9.25	8.28	5.05	9.74	6.11	8.42
Religious	....	....	0.10	....	0.04	....	8.55	1.24
Total Music	67.97	57.24	61.77	64.06	53.72	63.73	63.71	61.72
Nonmusical								
Church programs (actual services)	....	....	....	....	....	2.99	5.54	1.21
Educational	5.98	7.99	5.75	4.27	6.14	0.50	1.30	4.64
Special events (flights, receptions, etc.)	3.40	2.97	3.47	2.15	7.31	2.74	1.44	3.36
Announcements of program content (noncommercial)	7.00	5.59	6.30	6.27	5.76	4.91	7.34	6.17
Humorous	....	1.42	0.99	0.77	....	....	1.59	0.69
Church of the air	....	0.05	....	....	....	....	....	0.01
Political	....	5.72	1.41	1.24	1.39	....	....	1.42
Functions (banquets, presidential balls, etc.)	....	1.74	....	0.21	5.76	13.48	....	2.99
Script (dramatic programs, serial dialogue, etc.)	10.30	11.47	14.26	15.93	13.21	10.48	13.76	12.79
Commercial announcements	5.35	5.81	6.05	5.10	6.71	1.17	5.32	5.10
Total	100.00	100.00	100.00	100.00	100.00	100.00	100.00	100.00

(7) commercial announcements represented over 5 per cent of the total time used during the week and on Saturday commercial announcements were scarce;

(8) humorous and political programs appeared irregularly.

Table V classifies the same programs according to the total time devoted each day to commercial and to sustaining broadcasts.

TABLE V

PERCENTAGE OF TIME DEVOTED TO COMMERCIAL AND SUSTAINING PROGRAMS
DURING THE REPRESENTATIVE WEEK

Day of week	Total minutes broadcast	Percentage commercial broadcasts	Percentage sustaining broadcasts
Sunday	990	39.39	60.61
Monday	1020	36.76	63.24
Tuesday	1020	35.49	64.51
Wednesday	1020	42.16	57.84
Thursday	1020	33.82	66.18
Friday	1020	38.23	61.77
Saturday	1020	10.29	89.71
Totals	7110	33.76	66.24

This table shows that the amount of time devoted to sustaining programs is twice that devoted to commercial programs. It shows also that there is much less commercial broadcasting on Saturday than on any other day of the week. This is the day when sponsors feel that the time and place habits of listeners are least dependable. People are quite likely to be away from home or engaged in duties or recreations interfering with their customary habits of listening.

The following tables are based on a detailed analysis of the programs broadcast over a single station for a single month.[4] The broadcasts of the station chosen (WBZ, Boston) were felt by broadcasting officials to be typical of American stations since they consisted of relays of national network programs as well as regional and local broadcasts reaching both urban and rural listeners. The month chosen (October, 1933) was suggested by broadcasting officials as representative.

Table VI gives a detailed analysis of American radio fare as provided by a typical station during a typical month. It shows

(1) that the offerings are remarkably varied;

(2) that almost half of all broadcasts were musical programs;

(3) that dance music and skits hold first and second place respectively;

[4] The National Broadcasting Company and its affiliated station, WBZ, kindly provided the data for the analysis and the permission to publish the tables.

(4) that programs sponsored entirely by educational organizations occupy less than 5 per cent of the total time.

TABLE VI

PERCENTAGE OF TIME DEVOTED TO VARIOUS PROGRAMS
BY THE STATION IN A TYPICAL MONTH

Program	Percentage of broadcasts
Dance orchestras	13.85
Skits	10.07
Semiclassical music	7.28
Vocal artists—popular	6.65
Sports	5.96
Advertisements	4.82
News reports	4.77
Education[5]	4.48
Organ music	4.02
Variety programs—popular	3.98
Drama	3.33
Children's programs	3.24
Phonograph records	3.19
Recipes, household hints	2.89
Religious services	2.70
Mountain and barn music	2.47
Vocal artists—classical	2.20
Conventions and celebrations	2.03
Station announcements, weather, time	1.66
Talks on national policies	1.28
Symphonies	1.13
Old song favorites	1.10
Negro spirituals	1.01
Business, stock reports	.96
Fashion talks and Hollywood	.90
Variety—semiclassical	.74
Detective stories	.72
Band concerts	.63
Safety talks	.60
Short stories and travel	.54
Political speeches	.41
Brain teasers	.39
Total	100.00
Total music	46.27

Table VII demonstrates that less than one-third of this station's time is sold to commercial sponsors; also that

[5] Only programs formally sponsored by educational organizations were included in this classification under "education." This narrow use of the term obviously excludes programs which are educational in the broader sense, e.g., some children's programs, symphony concerts, dramas, and current topics. For a more complete discussion of this problem, see p. 250.

(1) nothing but sustaining programs are provided early in the morning (6-8) and late at night (12-1);

(2) there are striking differences in the sales values of different hours. From the advertiser's point of view, evening hours are most popular, while the hours in the middle of the morning and the middle of the afternoon are next in preference.

TABLE VII

PERCENTAGE OF THE STATION'S TIME SOLD EACH
HOUR OF THE BROADCASTING DAY
DURING THE MONTH

Rank order	Hour	Percentage of time sold
1	9–10 P.M.	72.00
2	7– 8 P.M.	70.00
3	8– 9 P.M.	63.00
4	6– 7 P.M.	58.00
5	10–11 A.M.	52.00
6	5– 6 P.M.	48.00
7	9–10 A.M.	39.00
8	3– 4 P.M.	39.00
9	11–12 P.M.	30.00
10	4– 5 P.M.	29.00
11	12– 1 P.M.	22.00
12	2– 3 P.M.	10.00
13	10–11 P.M.	9.00
14	8– 9 A.M.	5.00
15	1– 2 P.M.	3.00
16	11–12 M.	0.50
17	7– 8 A.M.	0.00
18	6– 7 A.M.	0.00
19	12– 1 A.M.	0.00
Average		28.93

The sales value is proportional to the dependability of the time and place habits of the listeners. The broadcaster can be comparatively sure that between the hours of 6 10 P.M. a large portion of the population will be at home and will not be greatly preoccupied with other tasks. On the other hand, the broadcaster knows that from 6-9 A.M. most people are busy getting the day started and have little time for radio. The midmorning and midafternoon hours provide the housewife entertainment while she goes about her duties.

This table, like Table V, shows that the advertiser finds Saturday and Sunday less effective than other days, for the time and place habits of listeners are less dependable over the week-end.

TABLE VIII

PERCENTAGE OF TIME SOLD ON THE DIFFERENT
DAYS OF THE WEEK

Sundays.................................. 21
Mondays................................. 38
Tuesdays................................. 36
Wednesdays.............................. 34
Thursdays................................ 35
Fridays.................................. 36
Saturdays................................ 15

Table IX gives the percentage of broadcast time which was devoted at each hour of each day of the week to network and to local programs. This table shows that

(1) a slight majority of this station's hours are devoted to network programs;

(2) far more network programs are broadcast on Sundays than on weekdays;

(3) the broadcasts on Fridays and Saturdays contain more network programs than do other weekdays;

(4) the early morning hours (6-8) contain entirely local programs;

(5) three-fourths of the programs broadcast during the best evening hours (7-10) are network relays;

(6) local programs are abundant in the middle of the afternoon (3-4), at the dinner hour (6-7), and late in the evening;

(7) there is comparatively little regularity either by days of the week or by hours of the day.

(8) In conjunction with Tables VII and VIII, it appears that network programs are broadcast during the hours when listeners' habits are most dependable for a large commercial sponsor; and

(9) the days when listening habits are least dependable (over the week-end) are filled with sustaining network broadcasts to keep the station on the air most economically and with better quality programs than it could arrange locally.

Table X contains a description of each type of program according to the days it most usually occurs, the time of day at which it is offered, whether it is sustaining or commercial, local or national. Since in most programs there is considerable variability, the table cannot be considered as a rigid classification. It represents average tendencies rather than inviolable laws. The numbers after "sustaining" and "com-

TABLE IX

PERCENTAGE OF TIME DEVOTED TO NETWORK AND TO LOCAL PROGRAMS

Hours	Mon.		Tue.		Wed.		Thu.		Fri.		Sat.		Sun.		Total	
	N	L	N	L	N	L	N	L	N	L	N	L	N	L	N	L
6– 7 A.M.	0	100	0	100	0	100	0	100	0	100	0	100			0	100
7– 8 A.M.	0	100	0	100	0	100	0	100	0	100	0	100			0	100
8– 9 A.M.	78	22	75	25	76	24	76	24	70	30	70	30	96	4	77	23
9–10 A.M.	50	50	50	50	44	56	50	50	49	51	75	25	100	0	60	40
10–11 A.M.	90	10	95	5	75	25	87	13	81	19	56	44	67	33	79	21
11–12 M.	47	53	68	32	50	50	43	57	100	0	18	82	50	50	54	46
12– 1 P.M.	60	40	58	42	50	50	63	37	38	62	50	50	97	3	59	41
1– 2 P.M.	75	25	60	40	75	25	81	19	75	25	100	0	100	0	81	19
2– 3 P.M.	65	35	98	2	87	13	87	13	87	13	100	0	100	0	89	11
3– 4 P.M.	10	90	25	75	44	56	31	69	38	62	100	0	80	20	47	53
4– 5 P.M.	70	30	40	60	81	19	56	44	63	37	75	25	60	40	67	33
5– 6 P.M.	60	40	60	40	56	44	50	50	50	50	13	87	100	0	64	36
6– 7 P.M.	48	52	30	70	31	69	31	69	31	69	50	50	64	36	35	65
7– 8 P.M.	90	10	100	0	75	25	56	44	87	13	13	87	100	0	80	20
8– 9 P.M.	43	57	100	0	87	13	81	19	81	19	75	25	90	10	71	29
9–10 P.M.	50	50	50	50	100	0	75	25	100	0	37	63	95	5	78	22
10–11 P.M.	45	55	55	45	55	45	12	88	56	44	100	0	50	50	44	56
11–12 P.M.	35	65	50	50	25	75	25	75	44	56	37	63	65	35	49	51
12– 1 A.M.	100	0	95	5	100	0	100	0	100	0	100	0	100	0	99	1
Total	53	47	58	42	58	42	53	47	61	39	60	40	83	17	60	40

TABLE X
DESCRIPTIVE ANALYSIS OF PROGRAMS

Type of program	Time of day	Day	Sustaining-Commercial	National-Local
Advertisements	midmorning midafternoon evenings	less on Saturdays and Sundays	Commercial	Both
Band concerts	midmorning midafternoon	midweek and Sundays	Sustaining	National
Business, stock market reports	12–1 P.M. 5–6 P.M.	daily except Saturdays and Sundays	Sustaining	Local
Children's programs	Sunday mornings.......... Weekdays from 5–6 P.M..........		Sustaining 2 Commercial 1	National Local
Conventions and celebrations	scattered with more in evenings	irregular	Sustaining	
Dance orchestras	early afternoon and late evening	daily with more on Sundays	Sustaining 8 Commercial 1	National
Detective stories	8–9 P.M.	midweek	Commercial	National
Drama	scattered	daily with less on Saturdays and Sundays	Commercial 4 Sustaining 1	Both
Educational	scattered	daily with less on Sundays	Sustaining	Both
Fashion talks and Hollywood gossip	afternoons	irregular	Commercial 4 Sustaining 1	Local
Mountain, hillbilly, barn music	mornings, some from 6–7 P.M.	irregular	Sustaining 4 Commercial 1	Both
Negro spirituals	10–12 A.M.	daily, more on Sundays	Sustaining	National
News reports	11–1 P.M. 5–7 P.M. 10–11 P.M.	daily, less on Saturdays and Sundays	Sustaining 4 Commercial 1	Both
Old song favorites	12–1 P.M. 6–9 P.M.	weekdays Saturdays	Commercial 2 Sustaining 1	Both
Operas		— None Broadcast —		

			Sustaining	National
Organ music	scattered with more in mornings	daily, more on Sundays	Sustaining	National
Phonograph records	7– 8 A.M. / 9–10 A.M.	daily, except Sundays	Sustaining 2 / Commercial 1	Local
Political speeches	scattered with more in afternoons	irregular	Commercial 3 / Sustaining 1	Local
Radio brain teasers	4–5 P.M. / 6–7 P.M.	daily, more on Sundays	Sustaining 3 / Commercial 2	Local
Recipes, cooking, household hints	scattered with more in mornings	daily, except Sundays	Commercial 10 / Sustaining 1	Local
Religious services	mornings 1–2 P.M. } 5–6 P.M. } afternoons	Sundays and weekdays / Sundays	Sustaining	Both
Safety talks	scattered with more in afternoons	irregular	Sustaining	National
Semiclassical music		irregular, more on Sundays	Sustaining 10 / Commercial 1	National
Short stories and travel talks	scattered with more in evenings	irregular	Sustaining 4 / Commercial 3	National
Skits	scattered	daily, less on Sundays	Sustaining 7 / Commercial 4	Both
Sports	1– 5 P.M. / 6–10 P.M.	daily, more on Saturdays	Sustaining 2 / Commercial 1	Both
Station announcements, weather, time	scattered	irregular	Sustaining 2 / Commercial 1	Local
Symphonies	mornings, some 8–12 P.M.	irregular	Sustaining	National
Talks on national policies	evenings	irregular	Sustaining	National
Variety programs—semiclassical	scattered but more in afternoons	irregular	Sustaining	National
Variety programs—popular	11 A.M.– 7 P.M. / 7 P.M.–10 P.M.	irregular	Sustaining 8 / Commercial 5	Both
Vocal artists—classical and semiclassical	afternoons and evenings	irregular	Sustaining 6 / Commercial 1	Both
Vocal artists—popular	scattered	irregular	Sustaining 9 / Commercial 2	Both

mercial" represent the ratio of programs paid for and those broadcast gratis by the station.

The descriptive analysis of Table X should not create the impression that there is striking uniformity in the practices of broadcasters. They seem to have no ironclad habits, perhaps because they wisely conclude that an experimental attitude toward their policies is best, and perhaps because the listeners themselves are so diverse and undependable that it is impossible to know just when and how and where they can be reached with greatest certainty. We must give up all hope of discovering strict orderly sequence in radio programs. The most that we can derive from Table X is a list of certain prevailing tendencies within our typical station.

The programs broadcast chiefly in the *mornings* were

> mountain, barn, and hillbilly music
> negro spirituals
> organ music
> phonograph records
> recipes and cooking
> religious services

Programs broadcast mainly in the *afternoons* were

> business and stock reports
> children's programs
> fashion talks and Hollywood gossip
> political speeches
> safety talks
> semiclassical variety programs
> sports

Programs broadcast primarily in the *evenings* were

> conventions and celebrations
> dance orchestras
> detective stories
> short stories and travel
> talks on national policies
> popular variety programs

The following programs were scattered throughout the radio day:

> advertisements
> band concerts
> drama
> educational talks
> news reports
> old song favorites
> radio brain teasers

semiclassical music
skits
station announcements, weather, time
symphonies
classical and semiclassical vocal artists (afternoons and evenings)
popular singers

On *Saturdays* and *Sundays* there were fewer of the following programs than on other days:

advertisements
business and stock reports
drama
educational talks
news reports
phonograph records
recipes, household hints
skits

On *Sundays* there were more of the following programs than on week days:

dance orchestras
negro spirituals
organ music
radio brain teasers
religious services
semiclassical music

On *Saturdays* there were more broadcasts of sporting events.

The following programs were more often *commercial* than sustaining:

detective stories
drama
fashion talks, Hollywood gossip
old song favorites
political speeches
recipes, cooking, household hints

All other programs are broadcast more often as sustainers than by commercial companies.

The following types of programs were chiefly *network* broadcasts:

band concerts
children's programs
dance orchestras
detective stories
negro spirituals

organ music
religious services
semiclassical music
short stories and travel
symphonies
talks on national policies
semiclassical variety programs

The following programs were mainly *local*:

business and stock reports
fashion talks and Hollywood gossip
phonograph records
political speeches
radio brain teasers
recipes and cooking
safety talks
station announcements, weather, time

Table XI is taken from Hettinger[6] and shows the percentage of pro-grams of different lengths broadcast over networks during the second week of May, 1932.

TABLE XI

Length of program	Commercial	Sustaining
Under 15 min...............	——	2.8
15 min....................	75.6	55.9
16–29 min.................	——	2.5
30 min....................	20.5	33.8
31–44 min.................	——	——
45 min....................	——	1.1
46–59 min.................	——	——
60 min....................	2.1	3.9
Over 60 min...............	1.8	——

According to this analysis, fifteen-minute programs constitute over half of all broadcasts and represent three-quarters of all commercial programs. It can also be seen that virtually all programs are multiples of the quarter-hour unit, particularly in the case of commercial broadcasts.

Such is the situation in respect to programs. They are numerous and varied, on the whole expertly directed and presented with talent, and ever though they are still to a degree experimental, they aim always to be sensitive to public taste and public opinion. Just how successfully they achieve their aim can be determined only through a study of the radio audience itself. The locus of our investigation therefore shifts from the broadcasting studio to the American home.

[6] H. S. Hettinger, *A Decade of Radio Advertising*, 1933, 251. Reprinted by permission of the University of Chicago Press.

CHAPTER V

THE LISTENER'S TASTES AND HABITS

ENTREPRENEURS in radio, no less than social psychologists, are keenly interested in the habits, the tastes, and the opinions of the radio public. The industry itself constantly collects what facts it can. It knows approximately how many people listen to the radio in the United States, how the listeners are distributed by states, what proportions live in cities, in towns, in rural districts, what their incomes are, how much time they devote to listening, and at what hours they tune in. As a means of assuring advertisers that their investments in radio time are not wasted, such facts are, of course, indispensable. Although psychologically considered they are somewhat superficial, these statistics of the industry do reveal certain elementary facts that serve as a necessary background for more detailed research; accordingly they are not without their value for social psychology.

THE LISTENERS

Of the 29,904,663 homes reported in the U. S. Census for 1930, approximately 21,455,799, or 70 per cent, were supplied with radios in January, 1935.[1] Almost 50 per cent of all the receiving sets in the world are found in the United States, and with the exception of Denmark, the per capita ownership of sets in the United States is greater than in any other country. The number of receiving sets is twice as large as the number of telephones in American homes.[2] It has been estimated that the average size of the radio family (excluding infants) is 3.62 persons,[3] bringing the total number of possible home listeners in the United States to approximately 78,000,000. The number of people who actually listen to a radio set at any one time has been estimated by broadcasters as 2.3 in the evening and slightly more than one in the daytime.[4]

The Distribution of Listeners by States. Although a large majority of the citizens of the country have the privileges of radio, the distribution of these privileges is strikingly uneven. Whereas 96 per cent of the homes in the District of Columbia are equipped with receiving sets, only 24 per cent of the homes in Mississippi are supplied. The disparity

[1] Columbia Broadcasting System, *Lost and Found.* New York: Columbia Broadcasting System, 1935.

[2] *Ibid.*

[3] Columbia Broadcasting System, *Vertical Study of Radio Ownership 1930-1933.* New York: Columbia Broadcasting System, 1933, 50.

[4] F. H. Lumley, *Measurement in Radio.* Columbus: Ohio State University Press, 1934, 200.

85

between Massachusetts (86 per cent) and Arkansas (27 per cent) is almost as marked.[5] Grouping the states by regions, the uneven distribution of sets becomes apparent at a glance.

PERCENTAGE OF HOMES SUPPLIED WITH RADIO, JANUARY 1, 1935

Northeast	80.7
Pacific	77.1
Central	73.2
West	64.4
Middle West	62.2
Southwest	50.3
Southeast	48.0

The Distribution of Sets in Rural and Urban Communities. Another noticeable difference in the ownership of receiver sets is found in communities of various sizes. The following figures are for January 1, 1935.[6]

Size of Community	Ownership of sets
Cities over 250,000	93% of all homes
Cities of 25,000–250,000	92% of all homes
Cities of 1,000–25,000	88% of all homes
Towns under 1,000	77% of all homes
Rural	34% of all homes

These data represent averages for the country as a whole. If sectional differences are taken into account, the picture is altered to some extent. Data gathered in 1933 show, for example, that in rural districts *south* of the Mason-Dixon line, only 5 per cent of the farmers owned radios; whereas the corresponding figure for farmers in the *North* and *Far West* was 45 per cent. In the country at large, approximately 45 per cent of the native white families had receiving sets, 44 per cent of foreign-born whites, and only about 7 per cent of colored families.[7]

The Incomes of Radio Listeners. The following tabulation was made by the Columbia Broadcasting System and demonstrates that people who have the most money to spend also as a class own a greater proportion of radios.[8] The figures are for 1935.

Annual family income	Percentage of homes in this income group owning radios
Over $10,000	90
$10,000–$5,000	85
$5,000–$3,000	79
$3,000–$2,000	72
$2,000–$1,000	65
Under $1,000	52

[5] Columbia Broadcasting System, *Lost and Found.*
[6] *Ibid.*
[7] H. S. Hettinger, "What We Know About the Listening Audience," *Radio and Education* (edit. by L. Tyson). Chicago: University of Chicago Press, 1933, 47.
[8] Columbia Broadcasting System, *Lost and Found.*

However, the majority of comparisons made between *owners* and *users* of radio sets show a tendency for the middle class to listen most, the lower financial class next, and people with higher incomes still less.[9] To be sure, the upper levels of income have higher standards of living and therefore *own* more radios. But an *embarras de richesse* prevents the privileged class from using the radio intensively. The wealthy usually support churches though they seldom attend them; in the same spirit they purchase radios but do not so often listen to them. People with fewer privileges make more intensive use of what they have. Whatever statistics may show concerning the concentration of sets in affluent homes, radio flourishes in America because of loyal support from the great middle class, and not because almost every rich family owns a receiving set.

How Much People Listen. A survey of the habits of 4,375 listeners in Minneapolis brought out the following facts:[10]

> 7.5 per cent listen less than 1 hour per day
> 19.7 " " " from 1 to 2 hours " "
> 17.8 " " " " 2 to 3 " " "
> 16.5 " " " " 3 to 4 " " "
> 21.2 " " " more than 4 " " "
> 17.3 " " failed to answer the question

The mean listening time was 19.6 hours a week (2.8 hours a day) in one sample of 507 listeners. For women the average was 21.7 hours a week; for men, 17.8 hours.[11]

Considered in relation to educational background the time devoted to listening shows a noteworthy tendency:[12]

Amount of education	Average listening hours per week
College students......................	10.9
17–20 years of schooling...............	16.9
13–15 " " "	18.6
9–12 " " "	23.7
1– 8 " " "	21.8

[9] Studies which show that radio listening is chiefly a middle class habit are: R. Riegel, *The Buffalo Radio Audience* (Buffalo: Station WBEN, 1932); H. S. Hettinger and R. R. Mead, *The Summer Radio Audience* (Philadelphia: Universal Broadcasting Company, 1931); and C. Kirkpatrick, *Report of a Research into the Attitudes and Habits of Radio Listeners* (St. Paul: Webb, 1933). On the other hand, D. Starch found no significant differences between the listening habits of those in different income groups in his two studies *Revised Study of Radio Broadcasting* (New York: National Broadcasting Company, 1930) and *More Facts on Radio Listening by Income Levels* (New York: Columbia Broadcasting System, 1934).

[10] C. R. Reed, "The Radio," *Report of Superintendent of Schools to the Board of Education.* Minneapolis: Board of Education, 1931.

[11] C. Kirkpatrick, *op. cit.,* 28.

[12] *Ibid.,* 25.

Generally speaking, those who have greater educational advantages devote less time to the radio. Again it appears that the chief supporters come from the middle class, determined by education as well as by income.

When people are asked in such studies as these to estimate the amount of time they spend before the loud-speaker, are their judgments reliable? Recently a mechanical device has been invented to tell accurately the length of time the radio has been turned on. Eventually it may tell also to what stations the dial has been turned. Preliminary work with this contrivance indicates that, on the average, people *under-estimate* the amount of time the receiving set is in operation. Such a behavioristic check upon subjective report undoubtedly has its value. But it may in the long run be quite as misleading. A record of how many hours the set is tuned in does not automatically reveal whether people are *listening*. Perhaps the subjective report is, after all, quite as acceptable as the testimony of this detector.

It is probably true, however, that Kirkpatrick's estimate of an average listening day of 2.8 hours is too small. In summarizing other studies, Lumley concludes that the average time is more likely four to five hours a day.[13] One study indicates that the number of hours the radio is turned on varies directly with the length of time it has been in the home :[14]

No. years of ownership	Hours of listening
1–2	4.2
3	4.4
4	4.4
5	4.5
6–10	4.7

Radio listening is, then, a well-sustained habit, not an activity engaged in only by those who are curious to hear what their new sets will bring them. It is, of course, impossible to determine accurately the division of this time between *attentive* listening and preoccupation with other matters. From one study on the attentiveness of women listeners it was discovered that only about 13 per cent of the housewives pay complete attention to the morning broadcasts, 22 per cent to afternoon programs, and about 55 per cent to evening programs.[15]

Children as well as adults have become radio fans. In one study of children's listening habits it was found that 40 out of every 100 children interviewed listened to the radio at least a half-hour every day.[16]

[13] Lumley, *op. cit.*, 196.

[14] Columbia Broadcasting System, *A Study of Radio Listening*. New York: Columbia Broadcasting System, 1934.

[15] H. S. Hettinger, "What We Know About the Listening Audience," *op. cit.*, 50.

[16] S. M. Gruenberg, "Radio and the Child," *Annals Amer. Acad. Pol. and Soc. Sci.*, January, 1935, 123.

Another investigation reports that children from 10 to 13 years of age in New York City spend an average of 6 hours and 16 minutes before the loud-speaker each week.[17]

When People Listen. Various surveys on the *hours* when people like to listen have been summarized by Lumley:[18]

First	preference	7– 9 P.M.
Second	"	9–10 P.M.
Third	"	6– 7 P.M.
Fourth	"	10–11 P.M.
Fifth	"	12– 1 P.M.
Sixth	"	5– 6 P.M.
Seventh	"	11 P.M.–midnight
Eighth	"	10 A.M–noon
Ninth	"	8–10 A.M.
Tenth	"	3– 5 P.M.

More women listen in the daytime; and in the evening an equal proportion of men and women.[19]

Whether one day of the week is more favored than another seems to depend upon the popularity of individual programs. Lumley concludes that there is probably less listening on Saturday evenings than on other evenings, although reports on this point are conflicting.[20]

The size of the radio audience varies less with the *months* of the year than might be expected. It has been estimated that only 10 per cent of the radio audience is away on a vacation during any two-week period in the summer. Since radios are popular in camps, summer hotels, and automobiles, the great majority of the habitual listeners are reached by radio throughout the summer.[21]

What Programs Listeners Like. The program preferences of listeners have received more attention from investigators than has any other problem. Advertisers would like to know what type of program they should invest in, while broadcasters in all countries are curious to learn the tastes of the public. Lumley has drawn up the following composite rank order of listeners' preferences based on results obtained in eight separate investigations.[22]

Overlooking differences of age and sex and considering the radio audience only as one large undifferentiated group, it is clear that music heads the list of preferences, with other forms of entertainment following in favor. Broadcasts of serious subjects are less popular.

[17] Azriel L. Eisenberg, *Children and Radio Programs.* New York: Teachers College Bureau of Publications, 1935.

[18] Lumley, *op. cit.,* 194.

[19] *Ibid.,* 195.

[20] *Ibid.,* 197.

[21] Columbia Broadcasting System, *A Larger Summer Audience in 1934.* New York: Columbia Broadcasting System, 1934.

[22] Lumley, *op. cit.,* 274–276.

Program	Median rank-order
Music	2.5
Popular	2.0
Classical	4.5
Comedy	2.5
Dramatic programs	3.5
Sport broadcasts	4.0
Talks (general)	6.0
Religious programs	6.5
News and market reports	7.0
Educational programs	7.0
Children's programs	7.5
Special features	8.5
Women's programs	10.0

Finally, as would be expected in a study of *composite* tastes, those programs appealing to special groups take the lowest average position.

To obtain a more discriminating account of listeners' tastes, giving due consideration to differences of age and sex, and employing a more detailed classification of programs, a new investigation was undertaken by the writers. A questionnaire listing forty-two types of programs was distributed to 1,075 people, as representative a sample of listeners as it was possible to obtain, drawn partly from an urban community in Massachusetts and partly from small towns and rural areas in New York State. Both sexes were equally represented. The group included approximately the same number of people over and under thirty years of age. The occupational and cultural level of both men and women represented a typical crosscut of the American population. The questionnaires were personally distributed and collected. No names were put on the questionnaires, but data on sex, age, and occupation were obtained. All individuals were told to be frank and honest in expressing their opinions. They were instructed to *check once* those programs they would like to hear *somewhat more* frequently; to check *twice* those programs they would like to hear *much more* frequently; to place a *cross* beside programs they would like to hear *somewhat less* frequently and *two crosses* beside those they would like to hear *much less* frequently.

The results of this study can be most clearly expressed by the method of rank-orders. The ranks are calculated by weighing a double check as plus two, a single check as plus one, a single cross as minus one, and a double cross as minus two. The algebraic sum of individual judgments on each type of program determines its place in the rank list. A minus sign before a type of program therefore indicates that the listeners, taken as a group, would like to hear it *less* frequently than it is now presented. All other programs are wanted *more* frequently. Ties in the rank-order of preferences are indicated by braces.

TABLE XII

Men's Rank-Order of Preferences

Rank	Men under 30	Men over 30	Total men
1	Sports	⎰Old song favorites	Football
2	Football	⎱Football	Sports
3	Dance orchestras	Humorists	⎰Old song favorites
4	Boxing	News events	⎱Boxing
5	Baseball	Sports	News events
6	Hockey	Boxing	Baseball
7	News events	Baseball	Humorists
8	Old song favorites	National policies	Dance orchestras
9	Tennis	Drama	Hockey
10	Symphonies	⎰Educational talks	Symphonies
11	Humorists	⎱Symphonies	Drama
12	Drama	Health talks	Educational talks
13	Engineering	Short stories	⎰National policies
14	Dance music	Famous people	⎪Psychology
15	Psychology	History	⎨Short stories
16	Famous people	Psychology	⎪Health
17	Short stories	Detective stories	⎱Famous people
18	New jazz songs	⎰Vocal artists	Detective stories
19	Educational talks	⎨Educational methods	History
20	Health talks	⎱Hockey	Engineering
21	Detective stories	Organ music	⎰Vocal artists
22	Physics or chemistry	Dance orchestra	⎨Physics or chemistry
23	History	Literature	⎱Tennis
24	National policies	Operas	Dance music
25	Classical music	Physics or chemistry	Operas
26	⎰Vocal artists	Engineering	Literature
27	⎨Operas	Classical music	Educational methods
28	⎱Literature	⎰Church music	Organ music
29	Phonograph records	⎨Astronomy	Classical music
30	Jazz singers	⎰Tennis	New jazz songs
31	Organ music	⎱Dance music	Astronomy
32	Educational methods	New jazz songs	Jazz singers
33	Astronomy	Political speeches	⎰Church music
34	−Foreign language instruction	Business and stock reports	⎱Phonograph records
35	−Poetry	Sermons	−⎰Poetry
36	−Church music	Poetry	⎱Foreign language instruction
37	−Political speeches	Foreign language instruction	−Political speeches
38	−Business and stock reports	−Jazz singers	−Business and stock reports
39	−Sermons	−Phonograph records	−Sermons
40	−Advertisements	−Recipes and cooking	−Recipes and cooking
41	−Fashion reports	−Advertisements	−Advertisements
42	−Recipes and cooking	−Fashion reports	−Fashion reports

In these tables of preferences, the classification of programs is arbitrary and overlapping. For example, "dance music" and "new jazz songs" might be included within the same category as "dance orchestras." "Classical music" is frequently synonymous with "symphonies" or "vocal artists." Since, however, each individual indicated his preferences for all of the types of programs listed, the overlap resulted merely in a reaffirmation of judgments. Fine distinctions, even though the resulting categories are not mutually exclusive, are on the whole of more interest to the psychologist, and of greater value to the broadcaster than the coarser distinctions reported by Lumley (p. 90). It is easy enough for practical purposes to combine these detailed categories into general types, but it is impossible to obtain a discriminating view of public taste if only coarse categories are employed.

General preferences. Most people want to hear *more* of almost all types of programs. This is the first fact to strike the eye. In the com-

TABLE XIII

WOMEN'S RANK-ORDER OF PREFERENCES

Rank	Women under 30	Women over 30	Total women
1	Dance orchestras	Operas	Symphonies
2	Symphonies	⎰Old song favorites	⎰Old song favorites
3	Drama	⎱Symphonies	⎰Dance orchestras
4	Old song favorites	Humorists	⎱Drama
5	⎰New jazz songs	News events	Operas
6	⎱Operas	Drama	News events
7	News events	Organ music	Short stories
8	Short stories	Educational talks	Humorists
9	⎰Literature	⎰Vocal artists	Literature
10	⎱Psychology	⎰Famous people	⎰Organ music
11	Football	National policies	⎰Educational talks
12	Organ music	Literature	⎱Psychology
13	Humorists	Educational methods	Vocal artists
14	Educational talks	Dance orchestras	Health talks
15	Dance music	Health talks	New jazz songs
16	⎰Health talks	Short stories	Famous people
17	⎱Tennis	Psychology	Educational methods
18	History	Classical music	History
19	Vocal artists	History	National policies
20	Fashion reports	Church music	Dance music
21	Jazz singers	Dance music	Classical music
22	⎰Sports	Poetry	Football
23	⎱Classical music	Recipes and cooking	Fashion reports
24	Hockey	Detective stories	Poetry
25	Famous people	Sermons	Sports
26	Boxing	Fashion reports	Detective stories
27	Educational methods	New jazz songs	Church music
28	National policies	⎰Astronomy	⎰Recipes and cooking
29	Detective stories	⎱Football	⎱Baseball
30	Baseball	Sports	Jazz singers
31	Poetry	Baseball	Tennis
32	⎰Church music	Foreign language instruction	Boxing
33	⎰Astronomy	−Jazz singers	Astronomy
34	⎱Phonograph records	−Physics or chemistry	⎰Sermons
35	Recipes and cooking	−Political speeches	⎱Hockey
36	Foreign language instruction	−Boxing	Foreign language instruction
37	−Sermons	−Phonograph records	−Phonograph records
38	−Physics	−Engineering	−Physics or chemistry
39	−Political speeches	−Tennis	−Political speeches
40	−Engineering	−Business and stock reports	−Engineering
41	−Advertisements	−Hockey	−Business and stock reports
42	−Business and stock reports	−Advertisements	−Advertisements

bined tabulations for all groups, only six types of programs (sermons, recipes, political speeches, business reports, and advertisements)[23] met with majority disapproval.

The most popular programs are the *old song favorites*. This finding will not surprise anyone engaged in arranging radio programs. According to Irving Berlin, "Radio's most valuable asset is old songs. The old songs have a quality of association to the listener; they are like old friends. The aged catalogues are the backbone of radio. The old song is valuable because it is old; it's like old wine that is good."[24]

The *dance orchestra* maintains a high level of popularity. *News reports* in this survey are found to be much more appreciated than Lumley's summary indicated (p. 90). *Symphonies, drama,* and *humorous*

[23] Advertising is not, of course, a type of radio "program." However, since all listeners knew the reference was to advertising as included in regular programs, its use in this connection seemed legitimate.

[24] *New York Times,* May 6, 1934.

TABLE XIV

ORDER OF PREFERENCES BY AGE

(BOTH SEXES TAKEN TOGETHER)

Rank	Total under 30	Total over 30	Grand total
1	Dance orchestras	Old song favorites	Old song favorites
2	Football	Humorists	Dance orchestras
3	Symphonies	News events	News events
4	Sports	Symphonies	Symphonies
5	{ Old song favorites	Drama	Football
6	{ Drama	National policies	Drama
7	News events	Educational talks	Humorists
8	Boxing	{ Vocal artists	Sports
9	New Jazz songs	{ Football	{ Educational talks
10	Hockey	{ Famous people	{ Psychology
11	Baseball	Operas	{ Operas
12	Tennis	Short stories	{ Short stories
13	Humorists	Health	{ Boxing
14	{ Psychology	Organ music	{ Famous people
15	{ Short stories	Educational methods	{ Health
16	{ Operas	Sports	{ Baseball
17	{ Educational talks	History	Literature
18	Literature	{ Dance orchestras	{ National policies
19	Dance music	{ Psychology	{ History
20	Health	Literature	Vocal artists
21	History	Baseball	Organ music
22	Famous people	Boxing	Dance music
23	Vocal artists	Detective stories	New jazz songs
24	Detective stories	Classical music	Educational methods
25	Organ music	Church music	{ Hockey
26	Classical music	Dance music	{ Detective stories
27	National policies	Physics or chemistry	Classical music
28	Jazz singers	{ Poetry	Tennis
29	Educational methods	{ Engineering	Engineering
30	Engineering	Astronomy	Physics or chemistry
31	Physics or chemistry	{ New jazz songs	Church music
32	Phonograph records	{ Hockey	Astronomy
33	Astronomy	Sermons	Poetry
34	Poetry	Recipes and cooking	Jazz singers
35	—Foreign language instruction	{ Foreign language instruction	Phonograph records
36	—Church music	{ Tennis	Foreign language instruction
37	—Fashion reports	Political speeches	—Sermons
38	—Sermons	—Jazz singers	—Recipes and cooking
39	—Recipes and cooking	—Business and stock reports	—Fashion reports
40	—Political speeches	—Phonograph records	—Political speeches
41	—Business and stock reports	—Fashion reports	—Business and stock reports
42	—Advertisements	—Advertisements	—Advertisements

programs are again found among those most preferred. The educator will be heartened to see that *educational programs* are almost as popular as *sports* when listeners of both sexes and of all ages are considered together. *Advertisements* are given last place, three fourths of the people desiring fewer of them.

Apart from these general preferences, there are marked differences of taste depending upon the age and the sex of the listener. Many programs that appeal to men do not please their wives and daughters, and certain subjects that interest youth often do not appeal to middle age. Variety programs, designed by some broadcasters, to delight every listener for *part* of the hour, run the danger of boring or offending some of the listeners for a portion of the time.

Sex differences. For the American male the chief blessing conferred by radio is its provision for a vicarious enjoyment of sports, especially football. For women, sport features are among the less enjoyable programs; women like symphonies best of all. Both sexes like old song favorites; women also enjoy operas and dance orchestras, while men are less appreciative, particularly of operas, which rank twenty-fifth for them and fifth for women. Other programs preferred by *women* are: short stories, literature, organ music, vocal artists, new jazz songs, dance music, classical music, poetry, educational methods, church music, sermons, and, of course, fashion reports and recipes. Programs more popular with *men* are: sports of all kinds, talks on national policies, detective stories, talks on engineering, physics or chemistry, and business news. Men even prefer advertisements to fashion reports.

Age differences. Dance orchestras and sports rank highest with youth, while listeners over thirty list old song favorites, humor, and news as their favorites. Other programs that *young people* enjoy considerably more than old people are: new jazz songs, talks on psychology, dance music, jazz singers, phonograph records, and fashion reports. *Older people* rate the following programs higher than young people: talks on national policies, educational talks in general, vocal artists, talks by famous people, operas, health talks, organ music, talks on educational methods, history, church music, physics or chemistry, poetry, sermons, recipes and cooking, and political speeches. While younger people would like to hear less of eight of the 42 types of programs listed, the majority of older people find only five types particularly objectionable.

Our study has not dealt directly with the *preferences of children.* Lumley studied the preferences of ten- to fourteen-year-old children for the current programs coming to them in school hours.[25] The choices fell in the following order:

1. dramatized stories;
2. dramalogues based on the lives of great explorers and inventors;
3. programs coming from foreign countries;
4. historical events told by eyewitnesses;
5. talks by famous men and women;
6. musical programs with songs for them to sing;
7. accounts of a child's travels around the world.

Preferences of *high school students* in one city were:[26]

1. short plays
2. variety programs

[25] F. H. Lumley, "Suitable Radio Programs for Schools," *Thirteenth Yrbk., Bull. Dept. of Elem. School Principals, Natl. Educ. Assoc.,* Washington, 1934, 13, 412.
[26] K. Tyler, "Radio Studies in the Oakland Schools," *Education on the Air,* 1934, 306.

3. sports (play-by-play)
4. comedy
5. dance music
6. news broadcasts
7. crooners
8. quartets
9. symphony
10. classical music
11. talks

Occupational differences. The preferences of occupational groups were not included in our own survey, but have been studied by other investigators. Kirkpatrick found that professional people rate news and classical music high; students rate popular music highest; housewives rate classical music high and sports low; laboring groups have marked preference for news and popular music and a distaste for classical music and sports.[27] Lazarsfeld's study of listeners in Vienna shows that the more highly educated classes prefer symphonies, chamber music, opera, and educational talks; that women who work outside the home during the day (professional women, peasants, laborers) like these "better" programs more than do those women who work inside the home during the day (housewives, servants).[28] Evidently the woman whose duties confine her to the house looks upon the radio as an instrument of entertainment rather than edification. Hettinger found that simple music and homely drama were more popular in rural districts, and that old-fashioned melodies, news reports, religious services, and women's programs were more popular in small towns than in cities.[29]

THE HABITS AND ATTITUDES OF THE LISTENER

The psychological study of the listener is by no means exhausted by an account of his predilections for certain types of programs. There are other mental characteristics determining his behavior in the presence of the radio, and with fifteen years of alert experience, broadcasters have learned what some of these characteristics are.

Fan mail teaches them many things about listeners. Studies of fan mail indicate that it is heavily weighted by listeners in the lower economic classes and in nonurban areas.[30] Over half of it contains requests of some kind, e.g., for information, photographs, samples, booklets, premiums. A cereal manufacturer, for example, receives an average of

[27] Kirkpatrick, *op. cit.*, 32.
[28] P. Lazarsfeld, *Hörerbefragung der Ravag.* Wien: Ravag, 1932.
[29] Hettinger, *op. cit.*, 57.
[30] Lumley, *Measurement in Radio*, 49-88.

20,000 requests a week for an illustrated booklet. Letters of appreciation or criticism also flood the studios, sponsors, and artists. After one anniversary program, a single station received over 225,000 letters of congratulation, and when Western Union announced that anyone could send a free telegram in response to one of its programs, 360,000 listeners jumped at the chance. Other writers make specific requests for changes in programs. Many letters come from neurotics who tell the broadcasters their troubles. The large mailbags of radio character analysts, mystics, and horoscope experts show that many bewildered souls turn to these oracles of the air for consolation and advice. Others release their prejudices, objecting to broadcasts that disturb their comfortable beliefs, even calling the announcer's attention to faults in pronunciation. It is difficult to broadcast on any subject without receiving some letters of both commendation and criticism.

In spite of its impressive volume, this audience mail is sent by isolated, unorganized listeners composing only a small fraction of the total listening population. The response does not represent crowd behavior in the usual sense. The individual listener writes a letter, not because he thinks others are doing so, but because it is a sure and immediate way for him to resolve some tension the program has created. Fan mail from both children and adults pours into the studios particularly after *sad* broadcasts, not because they are preferred to humorous and happy programs, but because listeners feel a need to express their sympathies. In laughter, emotions are immediately released, but the sympathetic emotions are of greater duration and require some overt action to reduce the tension they create. The large proportion of fan mail coming from the lower economic classes and nonurban areas suggests that the writers are comparatively limited in other means of self-expression. Instead of praising or condemning a program to their friends, arguing about it with other people, or finding some substitute outlet for their emotions, these listeners apparently gain relief and satisfaction only by responding directly to the person or organization that has provoked them. Writing and mailing a letter of praise or of protest achieves a rapid emotional "closure." The strain thus relieved the auditor is emotionally free to resume his listening or to turn to other activities.

Broadcasters know, then, that it is essential to respect the sectional, political, racial, and religious attitudes of their audiences; that it is offensive to jazz hymn tunes, that it is injudicious to play "John Brown's Body" on a program reaching south of the Mason-Dixon line, that people listening to a chain program do not like to be reminded of the time of day in other sections of the country. They know that the safest bet for any program is simple, comprehensible, and somewhat familiar music. They have found that the public despises "affected" voices and on the average program dislikes feminine announcers. They know that the best radio entertainer is the person who can carry showmanship with the utmost possible impression of naturalness. They know that listeners like to hear a program accompanied by the laughter and applause of a studio audience. They know that every artist, every program, every station must be well identified, must have "personality," if it is to be long-lived. Above all, they know that even though advertising over the air annoys and offends a majority of the listeners, it none the less pays lavish returns to both the advertiser and the studio. When it comes to such practical information, the psychologist has little to teach the broadcaster and much to learn from him.

A number of practical-minded investigators have gone out into the field and through their discoveries have supplemented the wisdom of the studios. They have found out, for example, that the average listener is not accustomed to tune in to all available stations. His habits at the dial are likely to be rutted: 5.6 per cent listen regularly to only one station while 76.6 per cent never listen to more than three stations.[31] The majority of listeners do not always pay complete attention to the programs they hear. Some of them tune in a few moments after the program has started and tune out toward the end to avoid advertising plugs.[32]

These practical investigators have discovered also that housewives are strong supporters of radio, and that 67 per cent of them say they receive valuable assistance from the programs. Nearly half of the women learn new recipes, about 20 per cent obtain information concerning the care of children, and the same percentage praise the health talks. About 10 per cent find that the radio enhances their appreciation of music, and the same number claim other educational benefits.[33]

Freeman reports that a short intelligence test given over the air suggests, but does not prove, that the radio listener is somewhat above the average citizen in intelligence.[34] On the other hand, a slight negative correlation was obtained in another study between the intelligence and the amount of listening of high school students.[35] Since the radio audience is so vast, it is probably safest to conclude that its intelligence is *precisely average*, no more and no less. If any intellectual difference exists between this vast sample and the population at large it is probably in terms of *range*: those who are extremely gifted and those who are

[31] Hettinger, *op. cit.*, 52.
[32] *Ibid.*, 50.
[33] *Ibid.*, 59.
[34] F. N. Freeman, "A Radio Intelligence Test," *New York Times*, June 25, 1933.
[35] F. H. Lumley, "Research in Radio Education at Ohio State University," *Education on the Air*, 1933, 358.

very deficient in intelligence undoubtedly spend little time before the radio. Broadcasters can make no mistake if they assume that their audience, by and large, is of dead-average intelligence. Likewise they can make no mistake if they assume that a dead-average audience likes to have its intelligence flattered. An insult to one's intelligence is much more likely to be resented than a challenge to one's intelligence. It is better, says a Canadian radio official, to overestimate the capacities of the radio audience than to underestimate them "for something worth while may result from the former course, whereas only successive vacuities can be the product of the latter."[36]

Those who work with radio know that too much listening makes a person "stale."[37] The habitual listener may find the radio as tiresome as an overmasticated piece of chewing gum. It is not always the program's fault if the listener doesn't like it. For such adaptation there is only one remedy, and that is to tune out. Spaced-listening is the best way to enhance the entertainment value of radio.

In spite of the accumulation of such practical wisdom, there is much still to be learned concerning the habits and the attitudes of listeners. As the following chapters will show the experimental method is best adapted to some of the problems, but the method of the questionnaire can be used to obtain information on many issues that are disputed or obscure.

Table XV contains a summary of the results of a questionnaire study derived from the same population of 1,075 cases used in our investigation of tastes and preferences. The figures in the table represent the percentages of listeners in each group answering the question in the manner specified.

Summary of questionnaire. Although the majority of older people know in advance what program they will turn to, two-thirds of the younger listeners tune in blindly. This age difference is noteworthy. However, considering the population as a whole, it is almost always a previously announced program or else the "favorite station" that determines where the dial shall be set. Almost nine-tenths of the listeners prefer network programs to local broadcasts, and the majority feel that America should have better quality at the sacrifice of the present variety in programs.

Two-thirds of the listeners would rather hear news broadcast than read it in the papers, while nine-tenths prefer to hear a speech over the radio than to read it. Also 90 per cent prefer music to spoken material over the radio. They give as their reasons, first, that spoken material

[36] M. Denison, "The Preparation of Dramatic Continuity," *Education on the Air,* 1932, 126.
[37] O. E. Dunlap, "Ears Become Weary," *New York Times,* January 28, 1934.

TABLE XV

Questionnaire Results

Abbreviated statement of the question asked, with alternative answers provided for checking	Men	Women	Percentage of respondents checking answers Younger people (under 30)	Older people (over 30)	Total
1. Usually turn radio on only to programs previously announced					
Yes	44	43	33	53	44
No	56	57	67	47	56
2. Usually listen to					
First program heard	13	5	12	6	9
Favorite station	47	49	41	53	47
Something looked-up	40	46	47	41	44
3. Radio tuned to same station for considerable time					
Usually	29	31	28	32	29
Sometimes	51	56	58	50	55
Seldom	20	13	14	18	16
4. Prefer					
Local programs	10	15	11	17	12
Network programs	90	85	89	83	88
5. Prefer quality to variety in programs					
Yes	61	61	59	63	61
No	39	39	41	37	39
6. Would like more children's programs					
Yes	51	68	53	62	58
No	49	32	47	38	42
7. Prefer news events					
Over the radio	62	72	64	69	66
In the newspapers	38	28	36	31	34
8. Prefer a speech					
Heard on radio	88	91	91	86	89
Read in newspaper	12	9	9	14	11
9. Prefer to hear on radio					
Music	84	90	91	83	87
Spoken material	16	10	9	17	13
10. Reasons for preferring music over radio					
Miss speaker's personality	23	24	21	24	23
Spoken material uninteresting	50	41	47	44	45
Takes too much effort to listen to a talk	27	35	32	32	32
11. Prefer a joke					
When heard over radio	90	62	91	88	89
When read	10	38	9	12	11

TABLE XV (*Continued*)

12. Prefer hearing a joke

When told in person.....	57	56	53	59	56
When given over radio...	43	44	47	41	44

13. When listening *alone* do you laugh aloud?

Frequently.............	19	24	24	19	22
Sometimes.............	54	57	52	57	54
Seldom................	27	19	24	24	24

14. When listening *with* others do you laugh aloud?

Frequently.............	27	35	32	30	31
Sometimes.............	57	56	54	59	57
Seldom................	16	9	14	11	12

15. Find radio humor is improved by hearing laughter of studio audience

Yes...................	61	62	63	55	61
No....................	39	38	37	45	39

16. Like to hear studio audiences applaud[38]

Yes...................	60	69	—	64	64
No....................	40	31	—	36	36

17. Prefer to listen to a speaker with whom you

Agree.................	54	57	49	60	56
Disagree..............	46	43	51	40	44

18. When views presented by radio speaker do not agree with yours, do you

Tune out..............	26	29	26	30	28
Continue to listen.......	74	71	74	70	72

19. Are you usually doing something else while listening to *music* over the radio?

Yes...................	64	74	76	57	66
No....................	36	26	24	43	34

20. Are you usually doing something else while listening to *talks* over the radio?

Yes...................	32	40	40	31	36
No....................	68	60	60	69	64

21. Do you prefer to attend a concert than to hear it over the radio?

Yes...................	73	75	76	69	74
No....................	27	25	24	31	26

[38] This question was added after the questionnaire had already been distributed to 500 people under 30 and to 225 over 30. It represents, therefore, only the opinion of 350 people over 30 years of age and equally divided according to sex.

TABLE XV (*Continued*)

Abbreviated statement of the question asked, with alternative answers provided for checking	Men	Women	Percentage of respondents checking answers Younger people (under 30)	Older people (over 30)	Total
22. Do you prefer to attend a lecture than to hear it over the radio?					
Yes	54	59	56	56	56
No	46	41	44	44	44
23. Do you spend more time					
Reading	63	55	56	62	59
Listening to radio	37	45	44	38	41
24. Because of having a radio, do you go to *movies*					
More often	5	3	4	3	3
Less often	20	18	15	23	10
The same	75	79	81	74	87
25. Because of having a radio, do you go to *church*					
More often	3	2	3	2	3
Less often	5	5	4	6	5
The same	92	93	93	92	92
26. Because of having a radio, do you go to *concerts*					
More often	4	2	5	2	4
Less often	18	16	17	15	18
The same	78	82	78	83	78
27. Because of having a radio, do you go to *dances*					
More often	7	4	8	3	5
Less often	10	11	10	10	10
The same	83	85	82	87	85
28. Because of having a radio, do you go to *vaudeville*					
More often	6	3	6	3	4
Less often	14	10	11	15	13
The same	80	87	83	82	83
29. If the radio is on does it distract your attention from any work or recreation you are engaged in?					
Usually	20	19	16	27	22
Sometimes	53	56	57	53	50
Never	27	25	27	20	28
30. Which type of *male* voice do you prefer to hear over the radio?					
Tenor	28	33	31	31	31
Baritone	63	60	59	63	62
Bass	9	7	10	6	7

TABLE XV (*Continued*)

Abbreviated statement of the question asked, with alternative answers provided for checking	Men	Women	Percentage of respondents checking answers Younger people (under 30)	Older people (over 30)	Total
Which type of *female* voice do you prefer?					
Soprano...............	28	23	20	29	25
Alto....................	72	77	80	71	75
31. Do you wonder what type of person the radio announcer or artist is?					
Always................	16	27	22	21	23
Usually................	23	28	28	23	25
Sometimes.............	42	38	39	40	40
Never.................	19	7	11	16	12
32. Do you enjoy a radio program more when you are					
Alone..................	33	38	35	36	35
With others............	11	10	10	12	11
Makes no difference.....	56	52	55	52	54
33. If you are alone in the house, do you feel less lonesome with the radio turned on?					
Yes...................	79	87	83	82	83
No....................	21	13	17	18	17
34. Do you think advertising should be given					
More time on radio.....	2	2	2	3	2
Same time on radio.....	41	45	40	46	43
Less time on radio......	47	40	48	42	46
No time at all..........	10	13	10	9	9
35. Do you record the *names* of radio advertised products?					
Frequently.............	5	5	3	7	5
Sometimes.............	28	45	36	37	36
Never.................	67	50	61	56	59
36. Do you record the *phone numbers* or *addresses* of advertising sponsors?					
Frequently.............	6	4	4	6	5
Sometimes.............	25	38	29	33	31
Never.................	69	58	67	61	64
37. Do you buy products because you have heard them advertised over the radio?					
Frequently.............	10	7	7	10	8
Sometimes.............	57	70	64	64	64
Never.................	33	23	29	26	28

TABLE XV (*Concluded*)

Abbreviated statement of the question asked, with alternative answers provided for checking	Men	Women	Percentage of respondents checking answers Younger people (under 30)	Older people (over 30)	Total
38. Does radio advertising annoy you?					
Always...............	9	5	7	7	7
Usually...............	18	14	19	17	16
Sometimes............	55	60	58	56	59
Never................	18	21	16	20	18
39. Would you be willing to pay a small tax (about $2 a year) to have the same programs you now have only without advertising?					
Yes..................	28	20	25	24	24
No...................	72	80	75	76	76

is usually uninteresting; second, that it requires too much effort to listen to spoken material; and third, that the absence of the speaker's personality reduces the appeal of radio talks.

The data on humor show that the great majority prefer to hear jokes over the radio than to read them, but at the same time slightly more than half prefer to hear jokes "in person" than over the air. More people laugh aloud at radio jokes when there are other people listening in the same room; women and listeners over thirty seem somewhat more affected by this social influence. Most people feel that radio humor is improved if they can hear studio audiences laughing at the comedian's joke. The majority also like to hear audiences applaud.

Most people prefer to listen to a speaker with whom they agree; one-fourth of the listeners tune a speaker out if they do not agree with him.

Two-thirds of the people are engaged in some other activity while listening to radio music and this proportion rises to three-fourths for listeners under thirty years of age. When talks are being broadcast, however, the majority give them undivided attention (at least they engage in no other occupation). Three-fourths of the listeners find that radio is a distraction when they attempt other activities while listening to it.

Approximately three-fourths of the listeners would rather attend a concert than hear it over the air and over half prefer the face-to-face lecture to one over the radio. Attendance at churches, movies, concerts, dances, and vaudeville has in no case been diminished by more than 18 per cent on account of the radio. Attendance at concerts seems to be most affected; attendance at church least.

Although only 13 per cent of the listeners state that radio has decreased their attendance at vaudeville shows, this figure undoubtedly obscures an important type of social change. For in recent years the majority of vaudeville houses have closed. Radio entertainment is more like vaudeville than it is like any other established type of amusement. An evening before the loud-speaker provides a typical variety show. Most of our replies came from people who had already ceased to patronize vaudeville and who did not consciously realize that radio, the great middle-class family-style of entertainment, is largely responsible for the demise of vaudeville.

Alto and baritone voices are preferred by the great majority of listeners to soprano and bass. Almost nine-tenths of the listeners wonder, at least occasionally, what sort of person the announcer is, women showing a greater curiosity than men about the personality behind the voice.

Although the majority report that they enjoy radio as much when they are with others as when they are alone, still a large number state that their enjoyment of a radio program is greater when they are alone. This finding is perhaps accounted for by the fact that 83 per cent of the listeners feel less lonesome when the radio is on.

The data on advertising reveal that the majority think advertising should be given less time on the air. Although 82 per cent are annoyed at least some of the time by radio advertising, yet only 24 per cent (28 per cent of the men and 20 per cent of the women) would be willing to pay a small tax and have the same programs without advertising. Most listeners—whether annoyed or not—admit that they sometimes buy goods because of advertising over the air. One-third of the listeners occasionally write down the addresses or phone numbers of dealers who advertise.

RADIO AND THE STUDENT

Those who have walked past college dormitories and heard the rhythmic strains of jazz orchestras or the voices of crooners issuing from numerous loud-speakers may have wondered what effect radio is having on the scholastic habits of the younger generation. A questionnaire was given to 200 students of both sexes to see whether they actually try to combine listening with studying. Seventy-one per cent of these students reported that they had radios in their rooms. How listening and studying mix is shown in Table XVI. The percentages represent the combined reports of the 142 students who owned radios.

This table shows that over two-thirds of the students who have radios in their rooms (or 48 per cent of all the students answering the

TABLE XVI

How College Students Who Have Radios in Their Rooms Combine
Listening with Studying

%

1. Do you study while the radio is on?
   Yes.. 68
   No.. 32
2. How often do you listen to the radio while studying?
   Always.. 2
   Frequently.. 42
   Seldom.. 56
3. Do you listen to selected programs or to any program?
   Selected.. 85
   Any... 15
4. What type of program do you generally listen to while studying?
   Jazz music.. 59
   Classical... 29
   Comedy.. 8
   Drama... 3
   Talks... 1
5. What type of program most hinders your studying?
   Jazz music.. 2
   Classical... 3
   Comedy.. 27
   Drama... 28
   Talks... 40
6. Do the announcements between musical numbers distract you?
   Yes... 65
   No.. 35
7. What volume do you use on your radio while studying?
   Loud.. 2
   Medium.. 45
   Soft.. 53
8. Do you think your studying is more effective with the radio on?
   Yes... 3
   Equally effective... 29
   Less effective.. 68
9. Do you have the radio on even when doing very important work?
   Yes... 8
   No.. 92
10. Does the radio provide merely a background for your studying or is it
    equally strong in consciousness?
    Radio in background.. 86
    Equally strong... 14
11. If the radio is on while you are studying, how much of the program do you
    think you remember?
    Almost all... 14
    About half... 29
    Only a little.. 54
    None... 3

questionnaire) sometimes combine studying with listening. Since an auditory language pattern coming from the loud-speaker interferes seriously with the visual language pattern of the textbook, they generally select a musical program, especially jazz, as a background for the more serious business of studying. Although important assignments keep the loud-speaker muzzled, more casual study is accompanied by melodies soon forgotten. No appreciable correlation was found between a student's academic standing and the amount of radio background to his study. Listening to the muted tones of a jazz orchestra or to the movements of a symphony seems to be a habit which, like chewing gum, smoking, or humming, alleviates for some students the task of acquiring an education, even though they admit that it makes their labors less efficient.

This chapter has drawn together psychological information concerning the tastes, the habits, and the attitudes of the listener, as obtained from the methods of the *census, statistical inquiry, practical experience* in the studio, and the *questionnaire*. The data tell their own instructive story. For the reader whose interest is primarily in the practical application of these findings to broadcasting, the discussion will be resumed in Chapters XI, XII, XIII, and XIV, and for those whose interest lies in psychological theory, in Chapter XV. In the meantime, one important method for exploring the mental processes of the listener remains to be studied: the psychological experiment conducted in the psychological laboratory.

PART II

EXPERIMENTS

~~~~~~~~~~

With the exception of a few of the experiments reported in Chapter VI, all of the investigations described in Part II were conducted in the Harvard Psychological Laboratory where complete broadcasting and receiving equipment had been installed. The apparatus included a microphone, a control panel, several loud-speakers, and a system of signaling devices. The loud-speakers were of the 540 AW cone-shaped type manufactured by Western Electric. A two-button, carbon microphone was used. A qualified technician operated the control panel throughout the experiments. All of the apparatus was generously loaned and installed by the Edison Electric Illuminating Company of Boston (Station WEEI).

CHAPTER VI

VOICE AND PERSONALITY

Summary. Fourteen experiments were conducted in the laboratory and from Station WEEI in Boston. Twenty-four male speakers and over six hundred judges participated. The method consisted chiefly in matching objective information obtained for twelve features of personality (e.g., age, photographs, handwriting dominance, extroversion) with the corresponding voices. In comparing these matchings with chance it was found that the majority were successful, often by large margins, but that no single feature of personality was always matched correctly with voice nor was any individual voice always correctly judged in every respect. It was also found that the uniformity of opinion regarding the personalities of the speakers was somewhat in excess of the accuracy of such opinion, showing the importance of the phenomenon of stereotyped judgment.

In general, better results were obtained from the use of summary sketches of personality than from single qualities, and judgments were more often correct for the organized traits and interests of personality than for physical features. When the speakers read from behind a curtain instead of over the radio, it was found that on the average approximately 7 per cent higher results were obtained. Two experiments showed that free descriptions of personality as judged from voice sent in by listeners were in general successfully recognized by other listeners and by acquaintances of the speakers. Experiments designed to study the ability of the blind to judge personality from voice showed them on the whole to be less accurate than judges with normal sight.

In the last chapter we found that the majority of listeners are interested in the personalities of the announcers and the speakers whom they hear. Voices have a way of provoking curiosity, of arousing a train of imagination that will conjure up a substantial and congruent personality to support and harmonize with the disembodied voice. Often the listener goes no further than deciding half-consciously that he either likes or dislikes the voice, but sometimes he gives more definite judgments, a "character reading" of the speaker, as it were, based upon voice alone.

Some people believe that these judgments are highly dependable. One radio commentator, for example, shows his confidence in the following rather extravagant opinion: "The human voice, when the man is not making conscious use of it by way of impersonation, does, in spite of himself, reflect his mood, temper and personality. It expresses the character of the man. President Roosevelt's voice reveals sincerity, goodwill and kindness, determination, conviction, strength, courage and abounding happiness."[1] A psychologist would be obliged to point out that these traits of President Roosevelt are discussed first of all in newspaper articles, magazines, and biographies, and that it is by no

---

[1] *New York Times,* June 18, 1933.

means certain that the listener's judgment is based upon voice alone rather than upon popular legend and publicity. One wonders whether *unknown* voices reveal as much as this writer believes. Are there not many jokes concerning people who fall in love with radio voices and then learn to their sorrow that the voice seriously misrepresents the character?

The whole question is obviously one for the psychologist to settle with the best methods at his command. Without controlled experimentation he cannot possibly give an opinion. An auspicious beginning has been made by T. H. Pear, working with the British Broadcasting Corporation.[2] Using nine speakers of different ages, sex, and interests, he secured over 4,000 listeners' judgments concerning the vocation, place of residence, age, and birthplace of these speakers. Although Pear's chief interest was in such phonetic problems as accent and dialect, the free descriptions submitted by the auditors enabled him to make some tentative statements concerning the accuracy of judgments of other personal characteristics. Sex was stated quite correctly (except in the case of an eleven-year-old child) ; age, in spite of a strong central tendency in the judgments, was on the whole estimated with fair success. Physical descriptions seemed frequently apt, and vocation was sometimes stated with surprising exactness. Since Pear did not prescribe how the judgments should be made or instruct the listeners concerning all the features of personality which they might judge, his results are difficult to express quantitatively or to compare with chance.

In Vienna, Herzog employed a number of radio speakers and asked the listeners to judge sex, age, vocation, height, weight, whether the speakers were accustomed to giving orders, and whether they had agreeable voices.[3] Answers were received from 2,700 listeners. In general her results show that all of these characteristics are judged more accurately than one would expect by chance. She also discovered that women judged age somewhat better than men. Her observers frequently reported that they based their inferences upon the similarity of the voice of some acquaintance to the voice heard on the radio.

Before describing our own experiments, it is essential to draw a certain distinction, suggested by Sapir, between *voice* and *speech*.[4] Our problem concerns only the psychodiagnostic significance of voice considered as an expressive agent. It excludes all other factors that go to make up the complex activity that we call speech. *What* a man talks about is a problem of speech, not of voice; whether he uses dialect, big words, long sentences or short, are also questions of speech, and

[2] T. H. Pear, *Voice and Personality*. London: Chapman & Hall, 1931.
[3] H. Herzog, "Stimme und Persönlichkeit," *Zsch. f. Psychol.*, 1933, 130, 300-379.
[4] E. Sapir, "Speech as a Personality Trait," *Amer. J. Sociol.*, 1927, 32, 892-905.

although these features are undoubtedly revelatory of personal traits, they must be excluded from an investigation interested exclusively in vocal quality. The requirement is the same that confronts the psychologist studying handwriting. If individual differences in *script* are the object of investigation, the context and subject matter, the quality of the stationery, mistakes in spelling, and the use of odd words must not be permitted to furnish an extra basis of judgment. Therefore, in order that our judges should have no basis for their opinions other than vocal expression, the speakers who participated in the experiments were required to read uniform material from typewritten texts. In this way differences in vocabulary, fluency of speech, grammatical accuracy, and subject matter were minimized. Except in the case of one speaker (a native of South Africa) there were no appreciable vocal differences that might be attributable to foreign culture rather than to individual variations within the standard American pattern.

Since it is the total pattern of vocal individuality that interests us, we have made no attempt to analyze voice into its constituent elements, as some writers have suggested.[5] To correlate pitch with one personal quality, timbre with another, and intensity with a third, would seem to us to make the whole problem atomistic. Such a study, like all others seeking correlations between artificial and meaningless fragments of expression and the well-structured qualities of personality, would be foredoomed to failure.[6] Here we are studying only the revelations of the unanalyzed, natural voice.

Throughout the experiments untrained voices were used. Professional announcers and actors are almost invariably individuals who have had vocal training either for the stage or for singing. They know how to place their voices, how to disguise them, and how to secure whatever effect they wish to produce. Our speakers, on the other hand, having no such training are more satisfactory for the purposes of these experiments. But the results obtained from untrained speakers should not be applied incautiously to professional broadcasters. In all probability trained speakers reveal *less* of their true personalities in their voices than do untrained speakers.

METHOD

In the main part of the investigation there were ten separate experiments: eight conducted in the laboratory, the other two from the broad-

[5] W. Michael and C. C. Crawford, "An Experiment in Judging Intelligence by the Voice," *J. Educ. Psychol.*, 1927, 18, 107-114: J. B. Sieffert, "Sprechtyphen," *XII Kongress der Ges. f. Psychol.*, 1931, 409-413.
[6] G. W. Allport, "The Study of Personality by the Experimental Method," *Character and Personality*, 1933, 1, 259-264.

casting studio of Station WEEI in Boston. In the eight laboratory experiments students acted as judges, the number in the different experiments ranging from 32 to 85. In the two WEEI experiments, the public was asked to send in judgments. From one of these appeals 190 replies were received; from the other 95. The total number of judges participating in these ten experiments was 655. The procedure in each of the laboratory experiments (I-VIII) and in the two studio experiments (IX-X) was practically identical.

Certain features of personality which could be reliably measured or otherwise objectively determined were selected for study. The features chosen ranged from such definite physical attributes as age and height to certain complex traits and interests of the "inner" personality. The following features were studied.

Physical and Expressive Features ("Outer" characteristics)

    1. age
    2. height
    3. complexion
    4. appearance in photographs
    5. appearance in person
    6. handwriting

Interests and Traits ("Inner" characteristics)

    7. vocation
    8. political preference
    9. extroversion-introversion
    10. ascendance-submission
    11. dominant values

Summary sketch

Of this list the meanings of the two semitechnical expressions (extroversion-introversion and ascendance-submission) were explained to the judges.[7]

Three speakers were selected for each of these ten experiments. There were twenty-four different speakers; eighteen participating in only one experiment and six in two. All speakers were male. In general a diversity of voices and personalities was sought, although extreme eccentricities or abnormalities were avoided. Objective information about each speaker was obtained before each experiment on all of the characteristics just listed. The objective criteria for the first eight

---

[7] An *extrovert* was defined as a realist, usually carefree and easygoing—the type who knows everybody, a hail-fellow-well-met. The *introvert* keeps to himself, tends to worry over little things, is sensitive and rather self-conscious.

An *ascendant* person was described as aggressive, forward, and domineering—the type of individual who can easily get rid of salesmen. A *submissive* person is docile and yielding and has difficulty in resisting a salesman.

features are obviously gathered from direct measurement, observation or questioning. The criterion for extroversion-introversion was the Heidbreder scale; for ascendance-submission, the Allport *A-S Reaction Study*; for dominant values, the Allport and Vernon *Study of Values*.

For experiments involving the matching of voice with handwriting or with photographs slides were made and projected on the screen for the duration of the experiment. Three photographs or three samples of handwriting remained upon the screen while the three voices took turns reading the standard passage. For the experiments involving a matching of voice with appearance in person simultaneous matching was impossible. After each reading all three of the speakers walked into the room where the audience was seated. An interval of perhaps half a minute elapsed between the voice and the appearance of the three speakers. The judges indicated their matchings by referring to a symbol which each speaker wore pinned to his coat.

At the beginning of each of the ten experiments there was one practice reading of the same passage by each of the three speakers to accustom the judges to the voices. The passages used in both the practice reading and in each portion of the experiment averaged approximately ten lines in length and were selected from Dickens, Lewis Carroll, or similar sources.

In Experiments I-VIII small record booklets were prepared for the judges, on each page of which the necessary information concerning one feature of personality was given. One page of the booklet, for instance, appeared as follows:

> Voice＿＿＿＿ very ascendant
> Voice＿＿＿＿ slightly ascendant
> Voice＿＿＿＿ very submissive

The subjects were instructed to match each of the three voices they were to hear (designated as Voice No. 1, Voice No. 2, and Voice No. 3) with the items of information given. The three speakers read the same passage in rotation. The judges entered beside each of the three items the number of the voice which the characterization seemed to fit best. The listeners were instructed to make independent judgments for each feature represented on the separate pages of the record booklet. In no case were they allowed to turn back or ahead.

The final part of each of these experiments consisted of matching the voices with three summary sketches giving all information available about each speaker. The last page of the record booklet in Experiment V, for example, read as follows.

> Voice＿＿＿＿ A teacher of physics who is interested in acquiring knowledge and in business, but who has little religious

interest. He is extremely submissive but neither extroverted nor introverted. He is 41 years old and six feet tall.

Voice_____ A supervisor of community centers who has social interest and likes power. He has very little artistic interest: is somewhat extroverted and slightly submissive. He is 51 years old and five feet, eight inches tall.

Voice_____ An electrical engineer who is interested in business and learning but is not religious. He is slightly introverted and slightly submissive. Thirty-one years old and five feet, ten inches tall.

In Experiments IX and X (from Station WEEI) this procedure had to be somewhat modified. The announcer first instructed the auditors how to fill out their own reply cards and then before each portion of the experiment gave the necessary information concerning the three speakers.

RESULTS

Table XVII presents the results obtained in these ten experiments. All figures indicate the reliability of the percentage of correct judgments. This reliability was determined by subtracting the theoretical percentage for chance matching (33 per cent) from the percentage of correct responses obtained from the judges. This difference was then divided by the probable error of the percentage (determined by the Yule formula, $PE = .6745\sqrt{\dfrac{pq}{n}}$).[8] All critical ratios (here represented by the symbol CR) which are four or over may be considered statistically "significant." All such ratios are italicized and are positive unless otherwise indicated.

It can be seen from Table XVII that 27 (39 per cent) of the coefficients are significantly positive; six (9 per cent) are significantly negative. Before drawing any conclusions, however, let us consider each result separately.

Age. Three of the four experiments in which age was judged yielded positive results. The greatest age difference between the speakers in VII (the exceptional experiment) was only seven years. In V and VIII the voices were quite successfully matched to the ages given. In IX the ages of the three speakers were merely estimated by the judges. The averages of the estimates were 25, 37, and 41, and the actual ages 27, 36, and 51 respectively. There

[8] G. U. Yule, *An Introduction to the Theory of Statistics* (8th ed.). London: Griffin, 1927, 337.

TABLE XVII

Results of Matching Various Features of Personality with Voice

Feature judged	Experiment Number									
	(Laboratory)								(WEEI)	
	I	II	III	IV	V	VI	VII	VIII	IX	X
Physical and expressive features										
1. age					9.9				+	
2. height			-3.3		4.3	-0.6	0.0	3.2	1.7	
3. complexion									4.6	
4. appearance in photographs	2.8	1.2	3.6	8.8	6.9					
5. appearance in person			-2.8	1.0	6.0	2.8				
6. handwriting	1.9		0.9	2.1	0.7	-2.2				
Interests and traits										
7. vocation	-2.8		-5.9	6.4	-1.3	0.4	-1.3	-4.8	24.5	8.2
8. political preferences	7.4		1.2	3.3						4.0
9. extroversion-introversion	14.0	15.0	-5.4	-3.1	-3.8	-0.8	3.2	14.4		19.2
10. ascendance-submission	13.5	14.5	17.0	8.8	-4.8		2.7	10.7	-8.7	
11. dominant values	7.4	6.0	-3.3	0.2	8.0	0.3	3.2	-6.7		
12. Summary sketch	14.7	13.5	-2.0	5.7	8.8	0.9	-0.6	3.1		
Number of judges	55	85	34	46	50	32	33	33	190	95
Voice number 1	A	A	D	G	K	N	Q	T	W	J
Voice number 2	B	B	E	H	L	O	R	U	X	H
Voice number 3	C	C	F	J	M	P	S	V	Y	M

was in each experiment a tendency to center the ages around a median of 35-40 corroborating the findings of Pear and Herzog.

Height. Herzog reported positive results in her study of the determination of height from voices. Only one of our four experiments on height seems to support her finding. The comparatively large percentage of correct answers (45 per cent) for this item in V was due primarily to the case of a short fat man whose voice was thick, mellow, and "chuckling." By 60 per cent of the listeners (instead of the 33 per cent expected by chance) this voice was judged correctly to belong to the shortest speaker.

Complexion. The only experiment which included this feature yielded somewhat significant results. No confidence can be placed in this finding, however, until it is confirmed by more extensive experimentation.

Appearance in Photographs. In all cases the results here are positive, and in two cases significantly so. The significant results in IV and V seem to be due chiefly to the distinctive appearance of one or two of the speakers in each experiment. For example, in IV, the photograph of speaker *H*, whose voice was correctly taken to be that of a poet, showed him with sideburns and a drawn, pointed face.

Appearance in Person. It seems illogical that the results here are not quite so positive as those obtained with photographs. This deficiency may be due to the time necessarily elapsing between hearing the voice and making the judgment, with the result that there was a fading out or confusion in the image of the voice before the matching could be made.

Handwriting. This matching has special significance for the problem of the consistency or harmony of an individual's expressive movements.[9] If the voice and handwriting are both expressions of personality, should they not be matched with each other? Wolff found that voices recorded by means of a gramophone were correctly matched with handwriting about one and a half times as frequently as would be expected by chance.[10] Although this matching was tried in five laboratory experiments, none of the results is significant. Four of the ratios are positive, however, and only one negative. The failure to obtain higher results may be due in part to the fact that untrained judges were employed, skilled in the judgment of neither voices nor handwriting.

Vocation. Three of the experiments yielded significantly posi-

[9] G. W. Allport and P. E. Vernon, *Studies in Expressive Movement.* New York: Macmillan, 1933.
[10] W. Wolff, "Ueber Faktoren charakterologischen Urteilsbildung," *Zsch. f. angew. Psychol.*, 1930, 35, 385-446.

tive ratios, while two were significantly negative. The largest coefficient of successful matching obtained in the entire series of experiments came from the judgments of vocation made by 190 listeners in Experiment IX. In this experiment one speaker was an artist, one a businessman, and one a professor. The coefficient of correct matching was 24.5. The negative results in III are also significant. Here one speaker was a professor of English, one a psychologist, and one a journalist. The psychologist, however, was a native of South Africa, had an "English accent" and was therefore consistently judged to be a professor of English. In Experiment VIII, the calm quiet voice of a businessman was consistently taken for that of a teacher. It is evident that the auditors have decided opinions concerning the kind of voice typical of each profession. Such presumptions are frequently, though by no means always, correct.

Political Preferences. Like the matching with photographs, the determination of political preferences from voice seems to be rather surprisingly successful. In the cases where significant results were obtained, however, there were present in each group of speakers at least one or two distinctive voices that made matching easy. The "poetic" voice of H, for example, was usually taken correctly as belonging to a socialist.

Extroversion-introversion. In four experiments this matching was accomplished with signal success. The strikingly significant results were clearly due to the loud, boisterous, carefree voices which in these three experiments happened to fit the extroverts, and the gentle, restrained voices which happened to fit the introverts. In the other experiments where slight negative results were obtained, these vocal characteristics were deceptive. This extremely irregular result, very unlike chance, is typical of all our findings and will be interpreted later.

Ascendance-submission. All but one of the results for these traits is significant, five markedly positive and two moderately negative. Here, as in extroversion-introversion, the distribution of results does not in the least resemble chance. The voice gives decided indications of traits, often correctly, but sometimes incorrectly. The degrees of ascendance-submission of the speakers in the first four experiments correctly fit into the picture of the forceful, aggressive voice as opposed to the passive, meek voice; in Experiment IX the great majority of the incorrect answers were due to the fact that the submissive professor had cultivated (for classroom purposes) a typically ascendant manner of speaking.

Dominant Values. In about half the experiments the results were clearly positive. In Experiment I two of the speakers were high in both aesthetic and religious interests (as measured by the *Study of Values*) and were often confused with each other. The positive result in this experiment is due, therefore, to the fact that these two speakers were scarcely ever mistaken for the third whose voice clearly betrayed his political and economic interests.

Summary Sketches. The single features just enumerated were summarized for the judges into one final thumbnail sketch of each speaker. The purpose of this final matching was to determine whether the voice reveals a *complex pattern* of personality better than a single feature. The results are positive. A pattern of qualities seems, on the average, to be more correctly matched with voice than does any single quality.

MATCHING FREE DESCRIPTIONS OF PERSONALITY WITH VOICE

In Experiments IV, V, IX, and X, the judges submitted free descriptions of the speakers to supplement their matchings. Many of these descriptions seemed even more accurate than the controlled judgments. The descriptions of six of the speakers were collated and arranged in the form of six brief sketches and employed in Experiment XI. All uncomplimentary and ambiguous items were deleted. Although such editing was to a certain extent arbitrary, each sketch was made to conform as faithfully as possible to the descriptions submitted. Qualities often mentioned were emphasized and conflicting characterizations were proportionately included. Following is one of the final sketches employed.

Mr. *A* is characterized by his ascendant, aggressive behavior. He has drive and initiative, knows what he wants and gets it. He has decided opinions and likes to express them. He is extroverted, easily resists salesmen, and cares little what others think about him. He is wealthy and aristocratic, and has an appreciation of good literature.

Experiment XI was divided into two parts. In *Part I* three of the speakers participated. The radio audience was instructed by the station announcer that three speakers (Voice A, Voice B, and Voice C) would read three descriptions (Descriptions 1, 2, and 3) intended to describe the speakers, and that the radio audience should decide which description best characterized each speaker. The three speakers then read Description 1, each speaker ending the passage with the question, "Does this describe me?" Then Description 2 was read by each speaker, and finally Description 3. *Part II* was identical with *Part I* except that three other speakers and their corresponding descriptions were employed.

The number of answers (25) returned by the listeners was unfortunately small (Amos 'n' Andy proving too great a competitor for science). The results, however, so far as they go, are significantly above chance in both parts of the experiment.

CR

Part I 4.4
Part II..................... 9.0

This experiment provides a kind of check upon the reliability of the impressions created by the six voices. Unlike Experiments I-X the judgments are not validated against objective criteria, but are compared with the judgments of other listeners who knew the speakers only by their voices. Whether the impressions are correct or incorrect, it is clear that they are essentially the same for *different* groups of listeners.

In a minor experiment (XII) the free descriptions of the speakers sent in by the judges in Experiment IX were listed. The three lists of brief characterizations ("moody," "nervous," "precise," "dapper," etc.) were then mimeographed on separate sheets. Copies were distributed to friends and acquaintances who were asked to decide which list best described the speaker or speakers they knew. Fifty-six judgments were received and 91 per cent of these were correct.

THE RADIO VOICE VERSUS THE NORMAL VOICE

To determine whether the mechanical transmission of voice reduces the ability of the judges to make correct matchings, several control presentations were introduced in some of the laboratory experiments. In these presentations, the speakers read behind a curtain in the same room where the subjects were seated. The same features matched with the radio voice were likewise judged in this situation.

Table XVIII shows that there is an average difference of about 7 per cent in favor of the normal voice. To control the effect of practice, the normal voice in some experiments was introduced before and in others after the voice had been heard over the radio. The order of presentation was found to make no difference.

This result has considerable theoretical and practical interest. From the theoretical point of view it may be said that listeners are quite successful in "hearing through" the inevitable burr which accompanies a mechanical transmission of the human voice. Adaptation to the change in the quality which a voice undergoes in such transmission seems to be remarkably rapid and thoroughgoing. Even the subtlest in-

TABLE XVIII

COMPARATIVE RESULTS OF MATCHING RADIO VOICE AND NATURAL VOICE WITH
VARIOUS FEATURES OF PERSONALITY

Feature judged	Radio voice % correct	CR	Normal voice % correct	CR
Experiment I[11]				
Photograph	41	2.8	59	9.1
Handwriting	38	1.9	44	3.6
Vocation	27	−2.8	44	3.6
Political preferences	53	7.4	51	6.0
Extroversion-introversion	67	14.0	70	13.6
Ascendance-submission	62	13.5	63	10.6
Dominant values	53	7.4	76	17.0
Summary sketch	70	14.7	64	10.9
Average	*51*		*59*	
Experiment II				
Extroversion-introversion	63	15.0	37	1.7
Ascendance-submission	62	14.5	75	23.0
Dominant values	46	6.0	64	15.5
Average	*57*		*59*	
Experiment V				
Height	46	4.3	50	5.9
Appearance	50	5.9	78	16.5
Ascendance-submission[12]	42	−4.8	63	2.9
Experiment VI				
Appearance	48	2.7	27	−1.2
Average (Exp. V, VI)	*46*		*55*	
Average in all exps	*51*		*58*	

flections may be successfully analyzed out from all extraneous sounds. The voice, as it were, becomes a distinct and well-identified figure upon the ground of subdued mechanical noise. (A very few people, however, seem incapable of negative adaptation to the ground and persistently complain of the distortion of the voices or musical instruments they hear. Such people usually dislike the radio.)

Even though the broadcaster can be assured that most people readily adapt to the figure-ground situation which radio creates, our experiments do show a slight loss in the accuracy of matching. On the average the natural voice is somewhat more revealing of personal qualities than is the radio voice. The loss represents perhaps only slight imperfections in transmission which mechanical improvements may in time remove.

[11] In Experiment I, 54 judges participated in the radio presentation and 45 judged the normal voice.
[12] Since two of the speakers obtained the same rating, the chance percentage for this feature is 55 rather than 33.

HOW WELL DO THE BLIND JUDGE PERSONALITY FROM VOICE?

It has often been said, and is usually believed, that blind people are supersensitive to the revelations of voice. One writer states the case in the following way: "Since social convention demands a greater control of visible expression than of voice modulation, the blind are keenly aware of the subjective mood, attitudes, and prejudices which they cannot detect from facial expression and manual gesture but which may be revealed in the voice."[13] Doubtless a blind person is often acutely conscious of a speaker's voice, but it does not necessarily follow that he is a better judge of personality from voice than is the individual with normal sight.

Two experiments (XIII and XIV) were conducted to compare the judgments of the blind with those of individuals having sight. Each experiment was performed on two groups of people: one consisting of 42 totally blind persons from the Perkins Institute for the Blind; the other, a control group, composed of 33 extension school students with normal vision.[14] The experimental groups were well matched in every particular, excepting sight. The only other ascertainable difference between the judges was age: the blind group was on the average three years younger than the control group. The procedure used with the blind was identical to that in Experiments I-VIII: three male speakers rotated in their reading of the same passage and the subjects were provided with record booklets containing the information concerning the personality characteristics of the three speakers. The booklets used by the blind were printed in Braille. The same six speakers were heard by both groups and the same instructions and explanations were given. The features of personality judged in each of these experiments were: vocation, age, ascendance-submission, extroversion-introversion, dominant values, and summary sketches. The comparative results are shown in Table XIX. A positive CR indicates that the blind were superior to the normals.

These results show in general that the blind are *not* superior in their judgments. On the contrary, 67 per cent of their judgments are less accurate than those of the control group. This finding, so at variance with popular belief, is probably accounted for by the fact that the blind have fewer opportunities to observe and to study personality. Their circle of acquaintance is more limited than the normal. Furthermore, they have no visual assistance in correcting their errors in judgment:

[13] T. D. Cutsforth, *The Blind in School and Society*. New York: Appleton, 1933, 104.

[14] Experiments VII and VIII reported above were the control experiments used in the investigation of the blind.

TABLE XIX

COMPARISON OF THE ABILITIES OF BLIND SUBJECTS AND SUBJECTS HAVING NORMAL
VISION IN JUDGING PERSONALITY FROM VOICE

Feature	% of blind correct	% of normal correct	P.E. diff.[15]	CR
Experiment XIII				
1. Vocation	25	20	2.74	1.34
2. Age	18	44	4.12	−6.31
3. A–S	63	83	3.87	−5.17
4. E–I	61	88	3.74	−7.48
5. Interests	26	16	3.74	2.70
6. Summary	22	43	4.00	−5.25
Experiment XIV				
1. Vocation	41	29	4.24	2.78
2. Age	25	33	4.35	−1.38
3. A–S	52	65	4.12	−3.16
4. E–I	29	44	4.24	−3.54
5. Interests	47	65	4.47	−4.03
6. Summary	37	31	4.36	1.38

they are denied the rich visual impressions of age, vocation, extroversion and all other personal qualities which in normal life serve to round out and to rectify the evidence revealed by voice. It is likely that the prevailing beliefs concerning the giftedness of the blind have grown up through stories about *exceptional* blind people.

In our experiments we have dealt almost entirely with physical and self-expressive characteristics rather than with moral and ethical ones. It *may*, of course, be true that the blind are more expert in detecting friendliness, tact, and trustworthiness from the voice than are people with normal vision, but on this matter our studies provide no evidence.

CONCLUSIONS AND INTERPRETATIONS

We are now in a position to answer the two fundamental questions with which all these experiments are concerned.

1. *Does voice convey any correct information concerning outer and inner characteristics of personality?* The answer is *Yes*. Not only are the majority of our coefficients positive (76 per cent), but 45 per cent are "significantly" so, often by large margins. If the judgments of the various features of personality were due entirely to chance we would, of course, expect an approximately equal number of positive and negative *CR's* and a much smaller percentage of "significant" results.

2. *Are there any characteristics of personality or any types of individuals that are always revealed correctly?* The answer is *No*. Exclu-

---

[15] The probable error of the difference between the two percentages was calculated by the formula $PE_{diff} = \sqrt{PE_1^2 + PE_2^2}$. (Cf. H. E. Garrett, *Statistics in Psychology and Education*. New York: Longmans, Green, 1930, 133.)

sively positive and significant results were obtained for no single feature except age and complexion (and our evidence here is too meager to be considered conclusive). Nor were the results for the personal characteristics of any one of our 24 speakers always positive and significant. On the average, the judgments are much more correct than would be expected by chance, but one cannot tell in advance what characteristic or what type of personality will be most accurately judged. The only generalization that can be made is that *many features of many personalities can be estimated correctly from voice.*

This general conclusion may be supplemented and interpreted by additional findings.

3. The fact that 54 per cent of our coefficients are "significant" (either positive or negative) and the fact that only 13 per cent fall within the range of 1 PE indicate that the judgments even when they are erroneous do not represent mere guesses. Although a voice may arouse a false impression, the impression is likely to be the same for a large group of listeners. *The uniformity of opinion regarding the personality of a radio speaker is in excess of the accuracy of such opinion.*

4. This discovery is evidence that stereotypes play an important part in the judgments. In everyday life we frequently hear people say, "He talks like a poet," "He sounds like a politician," "You can tell from his voice that he is timid." Likewise in the laboratory situation it appears that *for the various features of personality there is associated in the minds of the judges some preconception of the type of voice to which these features correspond.*

5. These preconceptions regarding the type of voice which "should" accompany various features of personality are not equally definite for each feature. The results show that *the more highly organized and deep-seated traits and dispositions are judged more CONSISTENTLY than the more specific features of physique and appearance.* In the group of characteristics which include physical features and handwriting, only 33 per cent of the matchings were "significant" (either correct or incorrect), while among the features classified as "interests and traits" twice as many (67 per cent) were "significant."[16]

[16] In an unpublished study, R. E. Woods asked eight listeners to describe spontaneously the personalities of eight radio announcers. The following tabulation shows that the more highly organized dispositions (traits) of personality seem to be most readily revealed by voice.

Previous vocation	4	General appearance	19
Morality	6	Interests	24
Age	7	Color of hair	26
Intelligence	9	Build	27
Education	11	Complexion	31
Specific habits	13	Personality traits	174
Feelings	13	Unclassified	7
Dress	17		

6. *Not only are the more highly organized traits and dispositions judged more consistently than such outer characteristics as physique and appearance, but they are also judged more CORRECTLY.* One-third of the judgments on "physical and expressive" features were significantly positive, whereas one-half of the judgments on "traits and interests" were positive and significant. This finding may be considered as support for the personalistic theory of expression which considers the highly organized qualities of the "inner" personality to be most closely associated with expression.[17]

7. *If a voice arouses a stereotype of the speaker, it is likely that several features of personality will be subsumed under that stereotype.* Thus in Experiment IX, speaker *W* was correctly judged to be the artist by 71 per cent of the listeners (only 3 per cent said he was the businessman.) But the stereotype of an artist's voice was not confined to vocation alone. Fifty-six per cent of the listeners said he was markedly submissive, 73 per cent thought he had a light complexion, and 44 per cent said he was tall. All of these judgments were significantly above chance and all of them were wrong. Likewise in the same experiment, speaker *X* was correctly judged by 72 per cent of the listeners to be the businessman. And 65 per cent believed (correctly in this case) that the businessman had a dark complexion. Since a stereotype regarding one feature of personality is so likely to be freighted with implications regarding other features, and since comparatively few people seem to correspond in their own natures to a given stereotype, our failure to obtain absolutely correct results with any one group of speakers is not surprising.

There is, therefore, a kind of totalizing effect that is prejudicial to accurate and detailed judgment. It is an aspect of the common tendency toward undue economy and simplicity described in recent studies on judgment and attitudes. In judging personality this tendency manifests itself almost as caricature.

8. The matching of voice with *summary sketches* was rather singularly successful. In general, *the more information given concerning the speaker, the more accurately is his voice identified.* Whereas the totalized stereotype is often prejudicial to correct estimates, the totalized portrait is helpful. This finding constitutes an argument against "segmental" and "atomistic" research upon arbitrarily isolated variables in personality. Studies which deal with the interplay and patterning of qualities are closer to the realities of organized vital processes and for that reason yield more positive results.

9. *The success of judgment is inevitably influenced by the hetero-*

[17] Cf. Allport and Vernon, *op. cit.*, 152-172.

geneity of the voices and personalities of the speakers. It seems clear that if any of our groups of three speakers included a captain of industry, a prima donna, and the village idiot, there would be almost no errors in matching. Too great a homogeneity among voices or personalities is equally prejudicial to representative results. The inconclusive findings in Experiment VI are to be explained by the lack of distinctive qualities in the three voices. The striking results of certain other experiments (e.g., IX and X) are due to the use of contrasting types. Our twenty-four speakers were of the same sex, and differed less than a random sampling of population in respect to age, educational status, and racial background. On the other hand, the use of the matching method required that the personalities be at least distinguishable by the objective tests and measurements employed as the criteria. All in all, it is probably true that our groups were neither unusually heterogeneous nor homogeneous, but represented reasonable variations in type.

10. It must be remembered that the criteria chosen for these experiments are all "objective," and are perfect neither in their reliability nor in their validity (except only records of physical characteristics). Those who are familiar with the complexities of the task of measuring personality will find it rather remarkable that the human voice can be so accurately matched with results obtained from the available tests for ascendance-submission, extroversion-introversion, and personal values. Such a degree of success with these objective criteria constitutes a peculiar kind of validation for the tests themselves and an encouragement to their further development. At the same time, since the criteria are imperfect, it must be borne in mind that the human voice may reveal even more concerning personality than our results indicate. *In our desire to keep the investigation objective and quantitative, we probably have minimized the degree to which the voice expresses personal qualities.*

11. When some of the experiments were repeated, using a curtain rather than the radio to conceal the speaker, the average results were approximately 7 per cent higher. This finding seems to indicate that *there is a slight distortion of the voice due to the background of mechanical noise.* Further improvements in broadcasting may reduce or eliminate this distortion.

12. Strong supporting evidence for several of our conclusions was obtained in two minor experiments (XI and XII) which demonstrated that *free descriptions of personality from voice were recognized by other listeners and by acquaintances of the speakers.* Whether the impression created by a voice is right or wrong, the *same* impression is aroused in different groups of listeners.

13. Two experiments with the blind showed them *to be less accurate in their judgment of personality from voice* than were people with normal vision. This is probably due to the fact that the limited experience of the blind provides them with less knowledge of personality and with no auxiliary visual associations.

Chapter VII

SEX DIFFERENCES IN RADIO VOICES

Summary. Why is it that most people would rather hear a man than a woman speak over the radio? Is the preference due to some mechanical factor in the transmission of voices or is it due to psychological considerations? Are there certain qualities in the male voice that account for its general appeal? Are men preferred for all types of material?

A group of eighty representative listeners, equally divided according to sex, were asked whether they preferred male or female announcers. Ninety-five per cent favored male. Later they rated five male speakers and five female speakers on various characteristics of voice when different types of material were read. Men were judged to be more natural and more persuasive than women, while women's voices were usually judged more attractive. Men were rated higher when the material was of a matter-of-fact variety (politics, news reports, etc.), and women when subtle or reflective material (poetry, abstract passages) was used.

The listeners' chief reason for preferring male announcers is that women seem to them affected and unnatural when they broadcast. Prejudice is shown to be a large factor in the case.

Most people would rather hear a man than a woman speak over the radio. Yet few listeners are able to explain this preference: they can tell neither how the sexes differ in their vocal appeal nor why. Even the supervisor of broadcasting at the studio can seldom give reasons why his announcing staff is entirely male. He may say that it is customary to hire men for such jobs, and therefore "only natural" that more men should serve as announcers. Or he may cite the preference of the listening public and argue that he cannot risk his station's reputation by hiring female announcers. Such answers, of course, beg the question. They do not in the least explain why women who are freely employed as singers or actresses on the radio are virtually barred as announcers.

What is the real reason for this preference? Is it due to mechanical factors affecting unfavorably the fidelity of transmission of the female voice? Are there specific psychological qualities in male and female voices that might explain the differences in appeal? Is the whole situation simply another reflection of the agelong social prejudice against women trying to enter professions where men have the first foothold? Or does the true answer involve the composite effect of all these factors?

Before the psychologist can work on the problem he must first analyze it into specific and accessible issues. He may ask, first of all, how widespread the preference for male voices really is: whether the preference is general, extending to every aspect of the voice and to every impression the voice creates, or whether it is limited to a few outstanding qualities. Important, too, is the question concerning the constancy of the preference. Is it always present, or does it vary with the type of material broadcast? Still another problem: do men and women have different attitudes toward male and female announcers?

METHOD

In many psychological experiments it is necessary to disguise the problem of investigation so the observer will give truthful answers. Otherwise he may try to make his successive reports consistent with each other or agreeable to his own preconceptions of the proper outcome of the inquiry. This precaution was particularly essential in the present investigation where the task involved the separation of prejudice and preconceived opinion from the natural, unbiased judgment of vocal qualities. The method adopted in these experiments achieved this purpose; all of the subjects testified at the conclusion of the sessions that they had no idea the problem of sex difference was under investigation.

For these experiments it was necessary first of all to obtain a truly representative radio audience. Accordingly eighty people were paid to take part. The group was equally divided according to sex, and represented various ages and occupations as well as different degrees of education. Professional men, day laborers, students, housewives, and clerks were included. The only common characteristic of the group was unemployment, which in a year of depression certainly created no selective factor that might influence our results.

These same subjects participated in some of the experiments reported in Chapters IX and X, and attended the sessions for a one-hour period for seven days. The three investigations in which they served were so arranged that during a single hour there was considerable variety of program. They had no opportunity to discover the exact purpose of any single experiment. The judges were repeatedly assured by the experimenter that there was no "right" answer to any of the questions asked. They were instructed to give their honest opinions as observant listeners—nothing more. They were, however, required to pay strict attention to the loud-speaker and to keep quiet during all the experiments. A five-minute rest period was allowed in the middle of each hour session. One experimenter gave directions from the front of the room while the other stood at the back and watched the subjects. The program was broadcast from another room in the laboratory. At each experimental session the subjects were given mimeographed booklets in which to record their judgments. As a combined result of the financial incentive, exhortation, and the interesting nature of the experiments, the cooperation of the subjects was at all times excellent.

Before the experiments began the judges were asked to answer the question, "In general when you are listening to radio broadcasting, do you prefer (find more pleasing and attractive) male or female announcers?" The replies to this question gave a vote of 95 per cent in favor of males. The next problem was to determine the detailed nature of the subjects' judgments given under experimental conditions.

Ten trained speakers from a nearby college of oratory participated, five men and five women. Since it was desirable that they should be of approximately equal training and ability, the selection was made by instructors at the college who knew them all. The use of five speakers of each sex would, of course, tend to cancel out chance differences in the appeal of individual voices.[1] Each speaker read a passage before the microphone and the subjects were required to give a rating for each voice in respect to five characteristics, as shown in the sample record sheet below.

Directions. In answering all questions, place a number under the column for the proper voice number.

Let 4 represent *extremely*
  " 3 " *very*
  " 2 " *fairly* (average)
  " 1 " *slightly*
  " 0 " *not at all*

Be sure you answer all five questions concerning each voice.

	Voice number
Questions	1 2 3 4 5 6 7 8 9 10

1. Was the voice persuasive?
2. Did the speaker seem interested in his material?
3. How well do you think you know the personality of the speaker from his (or her) voice?
4. How natural or genuine did the voice sound?
5. How attractive or pleasing was the voice?

These five characteristics were selected because they represented qualities significant to the psychologist and distinguishable by the untrained listener. The voices (male and female) spoke in random order, always specifying their assigned number (one to ten) before reading their script.

[1] In a preliminary experiment, the results of which are not reported here, ten other speakers participated. The results of this experiment were substantially the same as those reported in this chapter. It seems almost certain, then, that our findings are due to genuine differences in the appeal of the sexes and not to our sampling of speakers.

Seven experiments were conducted to determine whether or not the judgments were constant for different types of material. In each experiment a different type of material was read by the speakers. No speaker read the same passage, but all ten passages in any one experiment were selected for their equivalent interest and comprehensibility. The script was typical of professional broadcasting continuities. The seven experiments dealt with the following types of subject matter.

1. Exposition—extracts from elementary histories or radio educational talks.
2. Politics—portions of radio talks by Republican, Democrat, or Socialist candidates.
3. Advertisements—a. Ten typical advertising plugs of standard products of equal interest to both sexes (radio, coffee, mouthwash, shoes, etc.).
   b. To avoid any favorable or unfavorable opinion that might be aroused because of the association with well-known products, this experiment was repeated using fictitious ads.
4. Abstract material—theoretical passages of philosophy, psychology, physics, or biology.
5. Poetry—passages from Shelley, Keats, Millay, Browning, and other poets.
6. Weather reports—weather reports were written in the style of those regularly broadcast.
7. News reports—fictitious reports concerning local, national, or international news.

The experiments were conducted on different days and in each experiment the order of the speakers was changed.

RESULTS

Differential ratings on male and female voices. A summary view of the results of all the experiments is given in Table XX. The numerical values represent the significance of the differences between ratings by all subjects for the five female speakers and their ratings for the five male speakers.[2] All figures are positive unless otherwise indicated. Positive figures signify a higher rating for *male* voices; negative figures a higher rating for *female* voices. Differences at least twice their standard error are italicized.

The results shown in this table answer two of the questions asked at the beginning of the chapter.

1. *Is the preference for the voice of one sex general and uniform or is it limited to particular qualities?* The answer is that

[2] The significance of the difference was calculated by dividing the difference between the average ratings for male and female voices by the standard error of this difference. (Cf. H. E. Garrett, *Statistics in Psychology and Education.* New York: Longmans, Green, 1930, 121-125.)

TABLE XX

CRITICAL RATIOS OF THE DIFFERENTIAL RATINGS ON MALE AND FEMALE VOICES

Material	Persuasive-ness	Speaker's interest in material	How well personality known from voice	Natural-ness	Attrac-tiveness
Exposition......	2.1	1.7	0.5	3.2	1.1
Politics.........	4.8	4.7	2.4	5.4	3.4
Advertisements					
Real.........	2.5	1.2	0.8	3.3	0.0
Fictitious.....	−0.8	0.0	−0.1	1.4	−1.0
Abstract........	−1.1	−1.0	−0.7	0.2	−3.2
Poetry..........	−2.9	−4.2	−1.7	−0.6	−4.2
Weather reports.	5.3	6.6	0.3	5.2	1.8
News reports....	0.7	1.0	1.0	2.3	−2.3

women are rated higher in some qualities and men in others. In general *men* are judged to be more *natural* and more *persuasive*. Except in poetry and abstract passages, the listeners felt that men took more of an *interest in the material* they were broadcasting. In four out of seven experiments, *women's* voices were judged as more *attractive*. Since 95 per cent of the listeners had already stated before the experiments started, that *men's* voices were more attractive, this result shows a noteworthy difference between stereotyped and analytic judgments. It indicates that the preliminary judgment was based to a considerable degree upon mere prejudice. Finally, the listeners felt that men revealed their personalities most readily in political passages while the personalities of the women were best reflected in poetry.

2. *Is the preference constant or does it vary with the type of material broadcast?* The answer is that men are preferred for some types of material and women for other types. *Men* were rated considerably higher on every feature when *political* passages were read. They also received higher ratings in *exposition, weather reports,* and *advertisements*. Women were rated higher in every quality in the reading of *poetry* and were generally superior for *abstract* passages.

Adding together the ratios favoring men and comparing these with the ratios favoring women, it is possible to prepare a "masculinity-femininity" series for the various types of subject matter employed in these experiments.

	Political script (*most masculine subject matter*)
	Weather reports
favoring men	Expository script
	Real advertisements
	News

favoring neither   Fictitious advertisements

favoring women   Abstract script
Poetry (*most feminine subject matter*)

Comparison of the judgments of men and women on male and female voices. The comparison of the sex differences in the ratings of male and female voices may be divided into two different problems, each of which has practical and theoretical interest. The first question is: how do men and women compare in their judgments? For instance, do men think female voices are more attractive than women think they are? The second question is: do men think female voices are more attractive than male voices? Or do women think male voices are more persuasive than female voices? The two questions may be more clearly distinguished with reference to the following diagram:

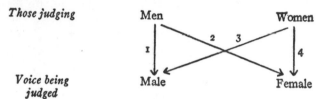

Those judging   Men   Women

Voice being judged   Male   Female

Here the first problem is to compare (1—3) with (2—4); the second problem to compare (1—2) with (3—4).

1. The difference between the ratings *by men and by women on male* voices and the ratings *by men and by women on female* voices. The determination of this difference involved the following calculations.

(a) the difference between the ratings by men and by women on *male* voices (1—3);

(b) the significance of this difference (dividing the obtained difference between the average ratings by its standard error);

(c) the difference between the ratings by men and by women on *female* voices (2—4);

(d) the significance of this difference.

The results shown in the following table include the figures obtained in steps (b) and (d). All figures are positive unless otherwise indicated. A *positive* figure signifies that *men give higher ratings* than women do.

Although many of these results, individually considered, cannot be regarded as statistically significant, their trend enables us to solve our first problem. We find that women are more charitably inclined in their judgments of the voices of both sexes than are men—they tend

TABLE XXI
Critical Ratios in Ratings Made by Men and by Women

	Significance of difference between ratings *by men* and *by women* on *male* voices	Significance of difference between ratings *by men* and *by women* on *female* voices
Persuasiveness		
exposition	0.4	−0.9
politics	−0.8	−1.1
real ads	−2.9	−3.0
fictitious ads	−3.4	−1.1
abstract material	−0.7	−1.0
poetry	−2.0	−2.7
weather reports	−1.4	−2.5
news reports	−1.5	−1.1
Speaker's interest		
exposition	−0.3	−3.0
politics	0.0	−1.8
real ads	−2.4	−4.2
fictitious ads	−2.2	−1.4
abstract material	−0.6	−2.2
poetry	−1.8	−3.1
weather reports	−1.2	−3.4
news reports	−1.9	−2.4
Knowledge of personality		
exposition	1.1	0.5
politics	−0.4	−2.7
real ads	−3.3	−3.1
fictitious ads	−4.5	−5.5
abstract material	−4.0	−5.4
poetry	−4.7	−5.7
weather reports	−3.0	−5.9
news reports	−2.5	−2.6
Naturalness		
exposition	−1.8	−1.3
politics	−2.2	0.7
real ads	−2.9	1.5
fictitious ads	−3.1	−0.2
abstract material	−3.1	−2.4
poetry	−2.9	−1.9
weather reports	−2.9	0.9
news reports	−1.8	0.2
Attractiveness		
exposition	0.5	−2.9
politics	−0.3	−0.7
real ads	−2.2	−2.0
fictitious ads	−1.8	−0.3
abstract material	−0.9	−2.6
poetry	−2.5	−2.5
weather reports	−0.7	−2.2
news reports	−0.7	−1.8

to rate both male and female voices higher than men rate them. This is especially true in the judgments of how well the personality of the speaker was revealed in his voice.

2. Comparison of the difference between *men's ratings on male and on female* voices and the difference between *women's ratings on male and on female* voices. This comparison involved the following calculations.

(a) the difference between the ratings by *men* on male and female voices (1—2);

(b) the significance of this difference;

(c) the difference between the ratings by *women* on male and on female voices (3—4);

(d) the significance of this difference;

(e) the difference between the obtained differences (1—2)—(3—4);

(f) the significance of this difference.

The results shown in Table XXII include the figures obtained in steps (b), (d), and (f). A *positive* figure in the first two columns signifies that *male voices are rated higher*. A *positive* figure in the third column signifies that individuals of one sex rate their own sex higher.

These results answer the questions involved in the second problem.

1. Column 3 of Table XXII shows that there is a slight tendency for judges of each sex to rate speakers of the *same* sex somewhat higher, except in the judgments of naturalness.

2. The ratings on *naturalness* are unique in the series. Both sexes tended to rate men as more natural (columns 1 and 2), but women rated male voices much higher on this quality than did men. Women, it seems, are credulous toward the voice of the male, at least they believe he is speaking with sincerity and conviction; whereas both sexes readily suspect affectation in female speakers.

3. In the judgments on *attractiveness*, men rated female voices higher in five types of material while women rated them higher in four.

4. Women felt they could tell more about the *personalities* of female speakers than of male speakers, and men felt that they could judge speakers of the male sex better.

5. Male voices were rated consistently higher by both sexes in *political* passages.

6. Female voices were generally rated higher by both men and women in *poetry* and *abstract* passages.

TABLE XXII

CRITICAL RATIOS IN THE RATING ON MALE AND FEMALE VOICES

	Significance of difference between *men's* ratings on *male* and *female* voices	Significance of difference between *women's* ratings on *male* and *female* voices	Significance of difference between men's ratings on male and female voices, and women's ratings on male and female voices
Persuasiveness			
exposition..............	2.2	0.7	0.9
politics.................	3.7	3.1	0.1
real ads................	1.8	1.8	0.1
fictitious ads...........	−1.8	0.7	−1.7
abstract material.......	−0.8	−0.9	0.2
poetry.................	−2.0	−2.1	0.2
weather reports.........	4.3	3.0	0.6
news reports...........	0.3	0.8	−0.4
Speaker's interest			
exposition..............	2.4	−0.4	1.9
politics.................	4.5	2.1	1.3
real ads................	1.7	0.0	1.2
fictitious ads...........	−0.3	0.5	−0.6
abstract material.......	−0.1	−1.5	1.0
poetry.................	−2.9	−3.1	0.5
weather reports.........	6.3	3.3	1.5
news reports...........	0.9	0.6	0.1
Knowledge of personality			
exposition..............	1.1	−0.5	1.1
politics.................	2.9	0.6	1.5
real ads................	0.4	0.6	−0.2
fictitious ads...........	0.2	−0.6	0.6
abstract material.......	0.1	−1.2	0.9
poetry.................	−0.9	−1.7	0.6
weather reports.........	1.4	−1.2	1.9
news reports...........	0.7	0.7	0.0
Naturalness			
exposition..............	2.1	2.3	−0.3
politics.................	2.7	5.0	−2.0
real ads................	0.3	4.6	−3.1
fictitious ads...........	−0.5	2.3	−2.1
abstract material.......	−0.6	0.8	−1.9
poetry.................	−1.1	0.3	−0.9
weather reports.........	2.2	5.2	−2.6
news reports...........	0.7	2.5	−1.5
Attractiveness			
exposition..............	2.5	−1.0	2.4
politics.................	2.7	2.1	0.3
real ads................	−0.1	0.2	−0.2
fictitious ads...........	−1.6	0.1	−1.1
abstract material.......	−1.8	−2.9	0.9
poetry.................	−3.3	−2.7	−0.1
weather reports.........	1.9	0.5	0.9
news reports...........	−1.2	−1.9	0.7

Listeners' reasons for preferring male voices. To secure more light on the matter of preferences, a questionnaire was devised and administered to the eighty subjects at the conclusion of the experimental sessions. In the questionnaire as it is here printed the average scores assigned by the subjects to each of the listed reasons are inserted in parentheses. The principal conclusion of the experiments is here borne out—the impression of affectation and unnaturalness is the chief source of the unpopularity of women's voices. But other interesting reasons are given that show the preference to be not altogether simple in its origins.

QUESTIONNAIRE

Below are a few reasons that have been given for the preference of male announcers. Rate each reason according to its importance in your own mind.

Let 4 represent *extremely* important
" 3 " *very* "
" 2 " *fairly* "
" 1 " *slightly* "
" 0 " *not at all* "

1. Female voices naturally do not carry over the radio as well as male voices (2.0)
2. Men seem to be more sure of their subject matter.................... (1.8)
3. Male voices show more interest in what they are saying.............. (1.6)
4. Men talk naturally and with little affectation over the radio, while women seem to "put on" a radio voice................................ (2.8)
5. Male voices are more persuasive.................................. (2.3)
6. The fact that the male voice is of a lower pitch than the female voice makes it more attractive.. (2.5)
7. Most announcers are men, therefore we are more used to them........ (1.9)
8. In general, men occupy more authoritative and important positions than women and so we are prejudiced in their favor.................... (1.4)
9. Female announcers are associated with advertisements of female interest such as recipes and therefore seem out of place when they talk on other subjects.. (1.8)
10. People are skeptical of women who do any kind of work usually done by men... (1.2)
11. Women usually announce the cheaper local programs and so we are prejudiced against them.. (1.0)
12. It is not simply the female voice which creates the prejudice but it is the selection of *poor* female voices that causes the preference for men... (2.2)

Additional reasons that you may care to give. (None were given that could not be subsumed under the twelve listed.)

CONCLUSIONS

The predilection for male voices is probably not due to mechanical factors in any appreciable degree. According to the statements of engineers, the voices of both sexes are transmitted with equal fidelity. To be sure, an inferior receiving set may distort women's voices relatively more than men's, but even when the best receiving sets are used the prejudice against women's voices remains. The problem, therefore, is not primarily one of mechanics but of psychology.

In a preliminary and uncontrolled report, 95 per cent of our subjects indicated their preference for male voices. In the course of the experiments it turned out that the chief basis for this preference lay in the rather constant impression of affectation and unnaturalness created by women's voices on the air. Along with this impression goes the judgment that men as a rule are more persuasive and more interested in the material they read. These findings, however, are only part of the story. It is also apparent that the prejudices are considerably greater than the analytical ratings of the judges seem to warrant, since for certain types of subject matter they actually favor women as speakers, and in respect to the attractiveness of voice women are regarded at least as equal to men. Judging from the objective results, therefore, it would seem that women might be entitled to a larger share of the work of announcers than is at present given them. For example, if they were employed to broadcast material that is poetic or reflective in nature, they should—according to our evidence—be quite popular with the listener.

The prejudice against women's voices may be due in part to the fact that sponsors and broadcasters are not careful enough to respect listeners' tastes in their selection of female announcers. "High-pressure" saleswomen are particularly objectionable to the average listener and his intense dislike of them may be indiscriminately transferred to other feminine voices. If in the future women are chosen whose voices are above reproach in respect to naturalness and if female announcers strive to overcome all suspicion that they are dressing up their speech for the occasion, prejudice against them should in time decline. There is, of course, no prejudice against women as musicians or actresses on the air. They may now safely broadcast whenever the nature of the program demands their services.

It should be recalled in this connection that contralto voices are greatly preferred (p. 100) for speaking as well as for singing. Just why the lower register is favored is not altogether clear. Popular comediennes, it will be noted, have voices that are not only low in pitch but likewise, as a rule, vulgar and uncouth in sound and the relaxed tones of the "torch" singer are greatly favored. On the other hand, women whose voice and speech create an impression of cultivation and refinement are not ordinarily popular. This observation suggests a deeper factor in the public's attitude. Radio, it seems, is regarded above all else as a medium of entertainment, on the level of vaudeville and the music hall. By ingrained tradition feminine refinement has no place in variety shows. The type of woman associated with such entertainments, therefore, is the type most welcome on the air.

Among the miscellaneous results of these experiments is the finding that women are more certain than men of their ability to judge personality from voice, especially the personalities of their own sex. Men believe they can judge other men from their voices better than they can judge women. Another fact of interest is that affectation is more readily suspected in the voice of one's own sex. Taken together, these results give some support to the common view that we understand better members of our own than of the opposite sex.

The harsher and deeper voice of the male is greatly preferred for matter-of-fact material—for politics, weather and news reports, and for advertisements. The comparatively softer voices of women are preferred for more reflective and subtle material. If men, as announcers, are considered more persuasive, interested, and natural, women at least are not unattractive and as actresses and musicians are decidedly popular. At some future date when they have learned better to adapt their voices to the requirements of straight broadcasting, and have battled a little longer against economic and social prejudice, they may also be successful as announcers.

CHAPTER VIII

SPEAKER *VERSUS* LOUD-SPEAKER

Summary. Two separate investigations were made to determine the differences between an individual's mental processes when he listens to a speaker personally present and when he listens to a loud-speaker. The first study compared various reactions of an audience listening before the radio to those of the same audience when face to face with the broadcaster. The experiments measured immediate memory, the subject's capacity for analysis, his comprehension, his ability to do mental arithmetic, his distractibility, the accuracy of his time estimation, his suggestibility, the nature of his mental associations, his ability to judge emotional expression, and finally the relative capacities of the speaker and the loud-speaker to compel the listener's attention. The second investigation involved a comparison of regular class lectures with radio lectures given to the same class by the usual instructors. After each lecture the students filled out a questionnaire, making specific comparisons between the two lecture situations.

Most of the differences obtained, taken individually, are not especially striking. Nevertheless, when combined they seem to show four intrinsic differences between face-to-face and radio presentations: (1) The radio situation is more solidly structured than the face-to-face situation, less easily analyzed and regarded less critically by the listener. (2) The radio situation is less personal and (3) less social than the face-to-face situation. (4) Finally, the radio situation seems to have a slight dulling effect upon certain of the higher mental processes.

It is a recognized principle of social psychology that an individual's mental processes are affected to some degree by the social situation in which he finds himself. The solitary man does not think or behave in quite the same way as he does in a group or in a crowd. It makes a difference, too, whether the group is cooperative or competitive, whether or not it has a leader, whether it is large or small, whether it is coacting or face-to-face.[1] The radio, with its immense scattered audience, with its spatial separation of listener and speaker, creates a unique social condition and we must, according to all precedents, expect corresponding peculiarities in the thought and behavior of members of the radio audience.

In the report of the religious revival in Chapter I, it was pointed out that the overflow congregation, unable to see the evangelist and hearing him only through a loud-speaker, displayed virtually no crowdish behavior. This audience gave little to the collection, sang scarcely at all, supplied no penitents, and depolarized rapidly at the end of the service. The congregation that could *see* the evangelist behaved in a typically emotional, crowd-like manner. But in two respects this episode of the revival was not typical of the social situation existing for

[1] F. H. Allport, *Social Psychology.* Boston: Houghton Mifflin, 1924, ch. XI.

139

ordinary radio audiences. In the first place, it involved a large throng of listeners sitting together, whereas radio audiences are seldom of the congregate nature and the members are deprived of any opportunity to influence one another. In the second place, the program was emotional, its purpose being to secure immediate expression of strong personal feelings. The radio, on the other hand, is seldom used to arouse immediate, concerted, passionate behavior. It would probably fail in its purpose if it were so used, unless a remarkable degree of preparation for concerted action existed in the listeners. In times of political crises where a large faction is ready for some direct action, the commands of the leader over the air could undoubtedly precipitate an emotional outbreak already planned. But the radio is ill-adapted for producing unpremeditated crowd behavior. The case of the evangelist and the overflow meeting, then, does not adequately represent the conditions found in normal radio programs and in normal radio audiences.

If, however, with the aid of experimental methods the conditions of the usual radio audience are duplicated and if the mental measurements taken under such conditions are compared with those taken under conditions of a face-to-face relationship between speaker and listener, the findings should have significance.

On the theoretical side, a peculiarly interesting issue is involved. The psychologist would like to know what happens when he interrupts the normal visual-auditory pattern of stimulation by taking away the visual impression of the speaker. Let us assume for a moment that the auditor in the congregate assembly normally receives as many units of visual stimulation as auditory. Would the removal of the visual stimuli in the radio situation reduce his mental responses by exactly one-half? Obviously not, the reader will reply. We certainly do not find our attentiveness, our comprehension, our memory, and our interest reduced by fifty per cent simply because half the stimulus elements are removed. And yet, in the case of the evangelist's audience, the removal of the visual effects seemed to reduce the emotional responsiveness far *more* than half. Crowdish effects require an unbroken, unified, visual-auditory configuration of stimuli. Intellectual activities, on the other hand, apparently are not greatly affected when from this total configuration all visual elements are subtracted. Under ordinary conditions of listening to the radio, our attention and understanding *seem* to us to be normal. And yet are they? May there not be a slight though usually unrecognized impairment in our mental efficiency when we are denied a view of the speaker? Or, may the answer perhaps lie in quite the opposite direction: are our mental functions to some extent actually sharpened by the stimulation of the radio?

ANTECEDENT EXPERIMENTS

Several studies, designed and executed by other investigators, have been concerned with these questions and have employed methods that seem, on the whole, to be fairly well controlled and to resemble those employed in the present chapter.

Gaskill[2] discovered that two regular 21-minute talks on Psychology and Athletics broadcast at a one-week interval were comprehended significantly better by college students when the talks were heard over the radio than when heard in the studio. While the difference in the scores made by the studio and radio groups was small, every subject achieved a higher score on the radio examination than on the studio test.

Ewbank[3] reports a study carried out at the University of Wisconsin in which students listened to formal and informal speeches given face-to-face and over the radio. A formal speech was defined as "a strict presentation of facts, few personal pronouns to be used, the speaker assuming a disinterested, impersonal attitude"; an informal speech as "a presentation of facts through the use of many personal pronouns, the speaker assuming an intimate, personal manner." Each talk lasted for ten minutes and was then followed immediately by a completion test. The order and manner of presenting the speeches were reversed by employing two audiences. In the case of the *formal* speeches, the average score achieved by the auditors who saw the speaker was significantly higher than that made by the radio audience, but with the *informal* speeches the average of the radio audience was higher than that of the group who saw the speaker. The majority of individuals indicated a preference for platform speaking in contrast to the radio situation.

Wilke[4] used three different techniques to present the same propaganda material: a face-to-face speech, a broadcast, and a printed text. Twelve groups of students participated. The experiment was repeated with four different topics, each speech lasting ten minutes and each group receiving material only once by the same technique. Attitudes were measured before and after the presentations and it was found that the face-to-face address had the most positive effect, the loud-speaker less, and reading least of all.

[2] H. V. Gaskill, "Research Studies Made at Iowa State College," *Education on the Air*, 1933, 322-326.

[3] H. L. Ewbank, "Exploratory Studies in Radio Techniques," *Education on the Air*, 1932, 234-236.

[4] W. H. Wilke, "An Experimental Comparison of the Speech, the Radio, and the Printed Page as Propaganda Devices," *Archives of Psychology*, 1934, No. 169.

The apparent conflict between the results of Gaskill and Wilke indicate that the mental function aroused by the presentation is an important variable in comparing a speaker and a loud-speaker: Gaskill studied the *comprehension* of factual material while Wilke was chiefly concerned with the effects of *suggestion* and *argumentation*. Ewbank's finding that the ability to recall a radio address depends upon its construction suggests that an informal and intimate style is necessary to compensate for radio's inherent impersonality.

In the first study reported below, a series of experiments compared the mental processes of an audience listening before the radio with those of the same audience when face-to-face with the broadcaster. In the second study, the psychological differences between radio lectures and regular class lectures were investigated. The procedure of the first study involved a rigid conformity to the technique of the laboratory; the second took place in the more natural setting of the classroom. Although each investigation is reported separately, the conclusions to be derived from them will be considered together. The original problem is identical in both cases; the studies vary only in their methods of approach.

COMPARISON OF THE MENTAL PROCESSES OF AN AUDIENCE LISTENING
BEFORE THE RADIO AND OF THE SAME AUDIENCE LISTENING IN
THE PHYSICAL PRESENCE OF THE BROADCASTER[5]

General procedure. The experiments were given simultaneously to two equivalent small audiences consisting of from four to seven persons each. One group formed the radio audience (R group) and the other group, in the presence of the speaker, formed the face-to-face audience (F group). While the speaker was addressing the audience in the "studio" his words were broadcast to the other audience which was in a similar room in another part of the laboratory.

The subjects in the experiments were male college students. The broadcaster who presented all the instructions, directions, and material used in the experiments was always the same person, a young man trained in public speaking. The subjects were seated in two rows in front of the speaker or the loud-speaker. They were instructed to take the same seats in all experiments and to keep their eyes fixed on the speaker or the loud-speaker when not engaged in writing on their record sheets. The controls were so regulated that the intensity of the voice was essentially the same in the two experimental rooms.

[5] Most of these experiments were conducted by Mr. George Houghton, the remainder by Mr. M. Sherif. Mr. Houghton analyzed the data and computed all the results.

Each experimental session lasted one hour, with a five-minute rest period halfway through. There were three series of experiments, each consisting of six to eight one-hour sessions. The sessions were so arranged that there was an alternation of audiences. The group forming the radio (R) audience in the first session of each series became the face-to-face (F) audience in the second session of that series, (R) in the third, (F) in the fourth, (R) in the fifth, and (F) in the sixth. Each group, for each series of experiments, served an equal number of times as listener in the studio and as listener before the loud-speaker. The same individuals served as subjects throughout each series of experiments. Twelve was the average number of subjects in a series. In all, thirty-six subjects took part.

Experiments were devised to compare the following mental processes in the two situations: (1) immediate memory, (2) capacity for analysis, (3) comprehension, (4) ability to do mental arithmetic, (5) distractibility, (6) time estimation, (7) suggestibility, (8) association, (9) judgment of emotional expression, (10) affective spread. A further experiment (11) compared the radio and the "real" voice in respect to their capacities for compelling the attention of the listener. In all these experiments, excepting (7) and (11) whose nature made the procedure impossible, the method of reversing the groups and of repeating the experiments equalized the effects of practice, of novelty, and of individual differences in ability.

Comparisons of the results obtained in the two situations were made by (1) calculating the average score in the F and in the R situations of each subject for all experiments testing each mental function, (2) combining the scores pertaining to each mental function for all subjects in the F situation and also for the R situation, (3) obtaining the differences between the average scores in the F and R situations for each experiment, (4) determining the probable error of the differences obtained,[6] and (5) calculating the ratio of the obtained differences to the probable error of the difference, the critical ratio (CR). It will be seen that all scores under the F situation and the R situation are based on identically the same individuals, thus eliminating the troublesome variable of individual difference in ability and performance. The separate experiments follow.

(1) *Immediate Memory.* Three types of material were used in the

[6] Since the same subjects participated in each experiment in the two situations, the formula used to calculate the probable error of the difference was $PE_{m_1 - m_2} = .6745 \sqrt{\sigma_{m_1}^2 + \sigma_{m_2}^2 - 2r(\sigma_{m_1}\sigma_{m_2})}$. This takes into account the consistency of the same individual in the R and F situations (cf. T. L. Kelley, *Statistical Method*. New York: Macmillan, 1924, 182).

memory experiments: connected meaningful material, lists of words and digits, and paired associates.

a. Memory for connected meaningful material. Passages of prose and poetry (three or four lines in length) were read to the subjects who were asked to reproduce as much of the material as possible after each selection was finished. For purposes of scoring, the prose passages were broken up into words and the poetic passages into phrases, each of which counted as a unit. The number of units *omitted* constituted the subject's score.

The results were as follows:

	Number omitted	
	Prose	Poetry
F situation	3.53	3.50
R situation	3.83	3.08
$PE_{m_1-m_2}$	.18	.43
$\dfrac{m_1-m_2}{PE_{m_1-m_2}}$ or CR	1.61	0.98

The face-to-face situation was slightly superior to the radio situation for the memory of prose, while the R situation was slightly superior to the F situation for the memory of poetry. The R group tended to reproduce poetry more as an organic whole, preserving the meter and rhyme, while the F group tended to reproduce scattered phrases.

b. Memory for unconnected material. Series of words (the names of telephone exchanges) and series of digits varying in length from four to six units were presented, the subjects being instructed to reproduce each list as soon as it had been read. The number of errors or omissions per series was scored.

Results were as follows:

	No. of errors per series	
	Words	Digits
F situation	2.21	1.46
R situation	2.26	1.42
$PE_{m_1-m_2}$	.19	.14
CR	.26	.28

The extremely low critical ratios obtained in these experiments justify no interpretations of the obtained differences.

c. Memory for paired associates. This experiment was based on the "right associates" method of Jost and G. E. Müller. Pairs of words were presented and the subject was asked to write down the second word in each pair after the series was completed. The number of wrong associates was scored.

	Average no. of wrong associates
F situation	1.70
R situation	2.34
$PE_{m_1-m_2}$	.22
CR	2.84

Memory for paired associates was considerably better in the F situation.

(2) *Analysis.* Two investigations of analysis were conducted: one involving the counting of certain specified words in a prose context, the other involving an analysis of arguments.

a. Analysis of words. Passages were read by the speaker; the subjects were instructed in some of the experiments to count the number of times the word "and" occurred and in other experiments to count the number of times "of" occurred. The score consisted of the number of "ands" and "ofs" the subject failed to count.

	No. of "ands" omitted	No. of "ofs" omitted
F situation	2.94	5.62
R situation	4.18	6.23
$PE_{m_1-m_2}$	.61	.54
CR	1.86	1.12

These results show analysis to be somewhat better in the F situation.

b. Analyzing arguments. Advertising script was read and the students were told to list the arguments used in the advertisement.

	Average no. arguments listed
F situation	10.50
R situation	10.43

Although these results are in the same direction as those of the other analysis experiment, the difference is too slight to be considered.

(3) *Comprehensibility.* Several difficult passages of legal, philosophical, and psychological writing were read to the subjects who were instructed to rate their comprehension of these passages on a scale ranging from seven to zero, seven representing perfect comprehension.

	Average rating
F situation	3.80
R situation	3.88
$PE_{m_1-m_2}$	.13
CR	.79

The difference is slight and unreliable.

(4) *Mental arithmetic.* The broadcaster spoke a number and then directed the subjects to add to it a second number, subtract a third, multiply by a fourth, divide by a fifth, etc. (e.g., $4 + 5 - 3 \times 7 \div 3 + 4 - 2 + 12 \div 4 = ?$). All the arithmetic was done mentally; only the final answer was written down by the subject.

	Average no. errors
F situation	2.74
R situation	3.42
$PE_{m_1-m_2}$	.38
CR	1.81

On the whole mental arithmetic was done somewhat more correctly by the F group.

(5) *Distractibility.* In each of two sessions a task lasting about two minutes was set for the subjects. While they were working a story was read to them. The quantity of the work done, the quality of the work, and the amount of the distracting story that could be recalled at the close of the experiment were measured.

In the first experiment the subjects added and subtracted printed figures while the speaker read them a story. In the second experiment, they were handed a printed series of tied letters such as bleakesalcheerousnetralchecketedoglocpoemjubijenoutilisedimnpenpernap . . . and

TABLE XXIII
EFFECTS OF DISTRACTION

Quantity of work done	Adding and subtracting	Underlining words	Grouping 17s
(Total units accomplished)			
F situation	51.8	53.6	22.7
R situation	52.6	50.3	21.4
$PE_{m_1-m_2}$	1.91	3.84	.91
CR	.42	.86	1.43
Quality of work done			
(No. of errors)			
F situation	2.63	28.6	3.19
R situation	2.20	27.9	3.16
$PE_{m_1-m_2}$	.37	2.53	.36
CR	1.14	.27	.08

Recall of distracting story
(Scoring method based on number of lines reproduced meaningfully)

F situation	2.03
R situation	1.93
$PE_{m_1-m_2}$	.15
CR	.67

were told to underline all adjacent letters forming English words. The third experiment involved the use of a printed series of numbers with instructions to underline all adjacent numbers which, when added together, totaled 17.

The results of these three experiments are shown in Table XXIII.

The *quantity* of work done under distraction was somewhat greater in the F group in two experiments and slightly greater in the R group in another experiment. The *quality* of the work was slightly better in the R group in all three experiments, but the F group recalled more of the distracting story. On the whole, subjects in the R group seemed better able to inhibit the distraction.

(6) *Time estimation.* The subjects were asked to estimate in seconds the time interval between two taps. The intervals ranged from 4 to 60 seconds. The experiment was repeated in four different sessions with a total of 40 judgments from each subject. The results below indicate the average error in the estimations. A minus sign before a number indicates *under*estimation.

$$
\begin{aligned}
&\text{F situation.} \ldots \ldots \ldots \ldots \quad -2.9 \\
&\text{R situation.} \ldots \ldots \ldots \ldots \quad -1.5 \\
&\text{PE}_{m_1-m_2} \ldots \ldots \ldots \ldots \ldots \quad .77 \\
&\text{CR.} \ldots \ldots \ldots \ldots \ldots \ldots \quad 1.80
\end{aligned}
$$

Within the ranges used the time seemed shorter to the F group.

(7) *Suggestibility.* These experiments were designed to test the efficacy of suggestion in the two situations. Two experiments employed indirect suggestion and three direct suggestion.

a. *Indirect* suggestion: the acceptance of leading questions relating to nonexistent facts. This experiment was adapted for radio use from Binet's *Aussage* tests and Verendonck's testimony tests. A story was read and immediately afterwards the subjects were questioned. Some of the questions related to matters not mentioned in the story. The percentage of such fictitious questions which the subject answered gave his score for suggestibility.

$$
\begin{aligned}
&\text{F situation.} \ldots \ldots \ldots \ldots \quad 58\% \\
&\text{R situation.} \ldots \ldots \ldots \ldots \quad 58\%
\end{aligned}
$$

An equal number of suggestions was accepted by both groups.

b. *Indirect* suggestion: influencing time estimation. The false suggestion was made by the speaker that most people tend to overestimate the duration of time intervals and that the subjects should, therefore, allow for this tendency in their judgments of the duration between the taps in the experiment that would follow. The average error of each subject in estimating time was computed from his time estimations in the experiment just reported. If the subject estimated the time intervals under his *usual* judgments, he was regarded as having followed the suggestion. The results below indicate the deviation of all the subjects' estimates from their normal estimates and not from the absolute time interval. A minus sign indicates that the suggestion was followed.

F situation............... −10.75
R situation............... 0.46

The F group followed the suggestion and the R group reacted somewhat negatively to it.

c. *Direct* suggestion: acceptance of statements contrary to fact. Downey's method was employed. A list of twelve words was read three times. At the conclusion of the reading, fourteen printed statements concerning the words just read were given the subjects, each statement to be marked true or false. Such statements would read "The first word in the list was 'chair' " or "Three words were adjectives." When the subjects had marked all the statements, they were told that seven were true and seven false and that they might now correct their papers accordingly. (All of the statements were true.) The figures below indicate the percentage of subjects who followed this suggestion.

F situation............... 83%
R situation............... 100%

The R group accepted the suggestion more readily.

d. *Direct* suggestion: acceptance of statements contrary to fact. The procedure differed only slightly from that just described. The statements judged true or false were based on a short story rather than on a series of unrelated words. The figures indicate the percentage of subjects who followed the suggestion.

F situation............... 50%
R situation............... 100%

Again the R group accepted the suggestion to a greater extent than the F group.

e. *Direct* suggestion: muscular contractions. A speaker skilled in hypnosis gave certain suggestions often used to induce the hypnotic state. The subjects were told that their eyes would become so heavy they could not open them, that their feet could not be lifted from the floor, etc. After the experiment, the subjects graded the effectiveness of the suggestion on a three to zero scale, three indicating that the suggestion was fully accepted and that the contractures occurred. The average rating in the two situations was as follows:

F situation................. 0.67
R situation................. 1.10

Here again, according to the subjects' own reports, the R group was more suggestible.

In all the cases of direct suggestion, where the instructions took the nature of commands, the R situation was more effective. Of the two experiments where the suggestion was indirect, one favored the F situation and one was equivocal. If these findings are confirmed, it will mean that subtle suggestions depend more upon the personal presence of a speaker than do outright commands. Since the nature of the tasks made it impossible to repeat these experiments without weakening the force of the suggestion, the F and R groups were not reversed and the effects of individual differences accordingly were not held constant. In other words, the scores here recorded are not those of the *same* subjects in the F and R situations but of different subjects in these two situations. However, since the composition of the groups varied in these experiments on suggestibility, it is unlikely that the results could be influenced greatly by the chance presence of highly suggestible subjects in the R group.

(8) *Free Association.* Fifty words of the Kent-Rosanoff free association test were given when one group was in the F situation and one group before the loud-speaker. The other fifty words were given when the groups were reversed. Scoring the average number of "most frequent responses" (according to the Kent-Rosanoff tables) the results are:

$$
\begin{aligned}
&\text{F situation} \dots \dots \dots \dots \quad 10.5 \\
&\text{R situation} \dots \dots \dots \dots \quad 10.9 \\
&PE_{m_1-m_2} \dots \dots \dots \dots \dots \quad .80 \\
&CR \dots \dots \dots \dots \dots \dots \quad .37
\end{aligned}
$$

If "individual responses" (those not appearing at all in the Kent-Rosanoff tables) are recorded, the following figures are obtained.

$$
\begin{aligned}
&\text{F situation} \dots \dots \dots \dots \quad 11.3 \\
&\text{R situation} \dots \dots \dots \dots \quad 10.8 \\
&PE_{m_1-m_2} \dots \dots \dots \dots \dots \quad 1.03 \\
&CR \dots \dots \dots \dots \dots \dots \quad .51
\end{aligned}
$$

Although the critical ratio is small in either case, there is a slight tendency for the R group to give more uniform, less individualistic responses.

(9) *Judgment of emotional expression.* The subjects were given a printed check-list of names of emotions or feeling states. They were told to try to identify the emotion expressed in each of the passages read by the speaker. Several short dramatic or poetic passages of two

or three lines taken out of unfamiliar contexts were then read expressively by the broadcaster who knew from acquaintance with the context what emotion was represented. He employed facial expression and some gesture along with his vocal interpretation. The results indicate the average number of errors in selecting the appropriate emotion expressed in the passages.

$$
\begin{aligned}
&\text{F situation}\ldots\ldots\ldots\ldots\ldots\quad 0.83\\
&\text{R situation}\ldots\ldots\ldots\ldots\ldots\quad 1.50\\
&\text{PE}_{m_1-m_2}\ldots\ldots\ldots\ldots\ldots\ldots\quad .21\\
&\text{CR}\ldots\ldots\ldots\ldots\ldots\ldots\quad 3.19
\end{aligned}
$$

Clearly more errors are made in the R group.

(10) *Emotional reaction.* This experiment was based on the *Pressey X-O Test.* A list of words was read and the subjects were asked to make a record of each word that was unpleasant to them. The average number of words checked is indicated below.

$$
\begin{aligned}
&\text{F situation}\ldots\ldots\ldots\ldots\ldots\quad 22.25\\
&\text{R situation}\ldots\ldots\ldots\ldots\ldots\quad 20.17\\
&\text{PE}_{m_1-m_2}\ldots\ldots\ldots\ldots\ldots\ldots\quad 1.95\\
&\text{CR}\ldots\ldots\ldots\ldots\ldots\ldots\quad 1.07
\end{aligned}
$$

There is a slight tendency for those in the F situation to check more words as unpleasant.

(11) *Conflict of speakers.* In two experiments all the subjects were seated in the loud-speaker room. Two stories of approximately equal interest and length (one page) were read to them simultaneously, one by a speaker over the radio and one by a speaker present in the room with the subjects. The speaker in the room endeavored to keep the intensity of his voice equal to that of the broadcaster. In one experiment the speaker in the room with the subjects stood in front of them, in the other experiment he stood in back while they fixed their eyes on the loud-speaker in front. At the close of the reading the subjects were asked to write the story they remembered better. The results were as follows.

	Story remembered		
	That read by speaker	That heard over radio	Parts of both
Speaker in front of room...............	35	1	4
Speaker in back of room...............	20	0	0

These experiments clearly show that the voice of the speaker who is personally present (whether visible or not) is much more attention-demanding than the radio voice.

DIFFERENCES BETWEEN A RADIO LECTURE IN THE CLASSROOM AND THE USUAL TYPE OF LECTURE

In order to compare the effects of the radio situation with those of the face-to-face situation in a somewhat more natural setting, eight radio lectures were given by the writers to their classes in social psychology. These lectures came to the classroom through a loud-speaker. They were not announced in advance. Two of the lectures were given in 1931, two in 1932, and four in 1933. At the end of each lecture the students were asked to fill out questionnaires designed to compare the radio lecture with the usual type of lecture by the same instructor. Since the majority of students had already taken several courses in psychology, it was felt that their introspections would be more reliable than any obtainable from the general public.

Only the data from the last four lectures are presented in Table XXIV. The results from the first four lectures are, however, in substantial agreement. These last four lectures were given to the same students in the same semester, each instructor giving two radio lectures. Approximately 140 questionnaires were collected. A student observer sitting in the rear of the classroom recorded the overt behavior of the other class members.

The topics discussed in these four radio lectures were especially chosen for variety. The first lecture was on "Crowds." The principles of crowd formation were profusely illustrated by the tactics of a popular evangelist then in Boston and whom many of the students had heard. This lecture was of particular interest to them and provided considerable humor. The second lecture was on the "Origin of Language." It was difficult and dull. "The Psychology of Laughter" was third in the series. Various theories of laughter were illustrated by jokes or amusing incidents. The fourth lecture on "The Psychology of Dress" reviewed in a monotonous and repetitious way the theories of the origin of clothes.

The questions and answers received in all four lectures are shown below. All figures are in terms of percentage.

The more important trends to be noted in this table of results are as follows:

    1. Surprisingly few clear-cut differences were found between the two lecture situations. On the whole the two types were found equally interesting, equally important, equally convincing, and equally agreeable. The students felt as much at ease in one lecture as in the other. Very few had trouble in adjusting themselves to

TABLE XXIV

COMPARATIVE JUDGMENTS BY STUDENTS OF RADIO LECTURES AND
ORDINARY CLASSROOM LECTURES

Questions	Answers	Lecture				
		1	2	3	4	Average
1. How did your attention to the loud-speaker compare with your usual attention to the lecturer?	More attentive to loud-speaker	55	31	36	33	39
	Less attentive to loud-speaker.	11	17	8	18	13
	Same......................	34	52	56	49	48
2. Were you more aware of your neighbors than in the usual situation?	Yes........................	5	26	26	24	20
	Less aware than usual........	58	29	23	24	34
	Same......................	37	45	51	52	46
3. Did irrelevant stimuli (such as noises outside, etc.) distract your attention?	More than usual.............	8	17	14	15	13
	Less than usual..............	71	54	39	46	53
	Same......................	21	29	47	39	34
4. Do you think the same lecture would be more easily understood if given in the usual way?	Yes........................	26	31	20	24	25
	No, less easily understood....	50	20	33	21	32
	Same......................	24	49	47	55	43
5. As you were listening to the lecture, did you find that you had more difficulty in relating each remark to the subject matter as a whole than you would have had in the same lecture given in the usual way?	Yes........................	10	17	11	9	12
	No, less difficulty than usual..	40	31	28	22	31
	Same......................	50	52	61	69	57
6. Do you think you understood the *factual* material in the lecture better than you would have in a regular lecture?	Yes........................	34	29	19	21	26
	Less......................	3	8	6	3	5
	Same......................	63	63	75	76	69
7. Do you think you understood the abstract or theoretical material in the lecture better than you would have in a regular lecture?	Yes........................	27	14	22	15	20
	Less......................	5	20	6	15	11
	Same......................	68	66	72	70	69
8. If there were any parts of the talk which seemed amusing, do you think they were more amusing over the loud-speaker than if presented in the usual way, less amusing than usual, or about the same?	More over loud-speaker......	34	26	8	18	22
	Less " "	45	43	67	53	52
	Same......................	21	31	25	27	26
9. Did you have visual imagery of the speaker?	Yes........................	75	69	64	56	66
	No.........................	25	31	36	44	34
Was your imagery vivid or slight?	Vivid......................	31	16	15	11	19
	Slight.....................	69	84	85	89	81
Was your imagery constantly present or infrequent and fleeting?	Constant...................	37	27	23	17	27
	Infrequent.................	63	73	77	83	73
10. Did the lecture seem more important than it would have if given in the regular way?	Yes........................	38	29	19	13	25
	Less important..............	27	31	11	31	25
	Same......................	35	40	70	56	50
11. Did the lecture seem more convincing than it would have if given in the regular way?	Yes........................	35	9	22	15	21
	Less convincing..............	24	37	22	30	28
	Same......................	41	54	56	55	51
12. Did the speaker seem to talk faster than usual?	Yes........................	22	49	42	45	39
	Slower.....................	43	29	28	27	32
	Same......................	35	22	30	28	29
13. Was it more difficult than usual to take notes?	Yes........................	26	37	28	36	32
	Less difficult...............	47	40	42	36	42
	Same......................	27	23	30	28	26
14. Was it more difficult than usual to get the main points?	Yes........................	5	14	8	9	9
	Less difficult than usual......	58	49	42	42	48
	Same......................	37	37	50	49	43
15. Did you miss the illustrations that might have been put on the blackboard?	Yes........................	34	49	22	33	35
	No.........................	66	51	78	67	65
16. Did the lecture seem any less personal?	Yes........................	58	66	67	73	66
	No.........................	42	34	33	27	34
17. Check one of the following features of the speaker's movements which you missed most.	Facial expressions...........	49	55	61	48	53
	Gestures with hands.........	18	19	12	10	15
	Change of posture...........	33	26	27	42	32

TABLE XXIV (*continued*)

Questions	Answers	1	2	3	4	Average
18. Did the speaker seem more interested in his lecture than usual?	Yes	45	14	14	3	20
	Less interested	8	14	11	21	13
	Same	47	72	75	76	67
19. Do you feel that in a radio lecture more repetition is necessary than in an ordinary lecture?	Yes	26	46	33	36	35
	Less necessary	32	11	22	15	20
	Same	42	43	45	49	45
20. Do you think this lecture required more concrete examples than if it had been given in the usual way?	Yes	37	35	25	36	33
	Less than usual	29	21	28	15	23
	Same	34	44	47	49	44
21. Did the speaker's sentences seem longer than usual?	Yes	8	6	22	15	13
	Shorter than usual	36	34	22	36	32
	Same	56	60	56	49	55
22. Did you feel more at ease than in a regular lecture where the speaker is present?	Yes	32	40	25	29	31
	Less at ease	16	20	22	23	20
	Same	52	40	53	48	49
23. Did the speaker's voice reflect his personality?	Very much	13	3	3	0	5
	Considerably	63	60	20	37	45
	Slightly	21	29	69	63	45
	Not at all	3	8	8	0	5
24. Did the lecture seem more monotonous than it would have in the regular lecture situation?	Yes	22	40	42	42	36
	Less monotonous	54	37	33	27	38
	Same	24	23	25	31	26
25. Did you find it difficult to adjust yourself to the radio situation?	Yes	5	12	11	18	11
	No	95	88	89	82	89
26. Was the total effect of the radio lecture agreeable, disagreeable, or indifferent?	Agreeable	79	37	42	36	49
	Disagreeable	0	11	8	18	9
	Indifferent	21	52	50	46	42
27. Would you prefer a course of lectures given entirely over the radio?	Yes	18	11	11	9	13
	Should prefer it less	71	77	71	75	74
	Same	11	11	18	16	13

the radio situation; a small minority missed the illustrations that would ordinarily have been put on the blackboard. The student observer reported no more whispering than usual. No one left the room.

2. Although in the first lecture the majority of students paid more attention to the loud-speaker than they usually did to the speaker and although they were less aware than usual of their neighbors and of distracting stimuli, adaptation soon set in; behavior and attention became more normal in later lectures.

3. Note-taking habits were distorted: some found it more difficult to take notes before the loud-speaker and some found it easier. Less than a third reported that it made no difference.

4. Factual material seemed slightly better understood over the radio than did abstract material.

5. Although there was a tendency to find that each situation required about the same amount of repetition and concrete illustration, those who did note any difference felt that more repetition and more concrete examples were required over the radio.

6. Two-thirds of the students had visual imagery of the speaker.

7. The majority of students thought the speakers' voices reflected their personalities to some extent. The voice of the first

speaker (lectures 1 and 2) was felt to be more revelatory than that of the second speaker.

8. In the most difficult and abstract of the four lectures (No. 2), a larger proportion of the students missed the blackboard illustrations, felt the speaker was talking faster than usual, and believed more repetition was needed. More restlessness (such as stretching and shuffling) was reported during this lecture.

9. One outstanding quantitative result concerned humorous parts of the lectures. These were generally judged less amusing over the radio than they would have been with the speaker present. This was especially true in the lecture on laughter (No. 3) where numerous anecdotes were related. The observer in the lecture room reported that there was usually complete silence after each joke. In none of the lectures was there any group laughter, although occasional private chuckles were elicited.

10. When the students' answers to the separate questions are reviewed they seem by no means to be unfavorable to the radio. The responses for the most part indicate few significant differences between the radio and the regular lecture situation and in several respects actually favor the radio. On the other hand, as their final judgment, only 13 per cent of the students state that they would prefer a course of lectures given entirely over the radio; 74 per cent would like it less. The only foundation evident in our questionnaire for this negative decision seems to lie in the common judgment that the radio lecture is "less personal." The students seem to miss particularly the facial expressions of the lecturer, and the occasional humor is brighter and more enjoyable in the personal situation. Mere habit may be a factor in their choice, as well as the absence of opportunities for discussion and argument. Considering the students' tastes in the matter, it does not seem that a university of the air would be a serious competitor for colleges of brick and stone and for teachers of flesh and blood.

11. From the lecturer's point of view it should be added that, in spite of all attempts to keep the two types of lectures equivalent, the delivery of the radio lecture was inevitably slower, more precise, and more emphatic. These changes were an automatic compensation for the lecturer's inability to obtain guidance in his talk from the audience itself. Unconsciously the speaker prepares himself better and orders his material more compactly for radio delivery. Some of the superiorities that the students observed in the radio lectures may have been due to this improvement in the speaker's style.

INTERPRETATIONS

Only when the results of these numerous experiments are combined do any clear-cut tendencies emerge. Taken individually the single experiments yield slight and usually indecisive results. Our first and most general interpretation, therefore, must be that while the radio affects certain higher mental processes *on the average* in ways that are appreciable, these effects are not especially striking. Individual auditors under special conditions of interest and alertness may secure much more from a radio discourse than from the ordinary face-to-face address. The attitude of the listener is highly important. Nevertheless, tracing through the responses of many auditors under repeated conditions, using controlled material and controlled measurements, there do appear by and large certain differences that must be laid to the intrinsic properties of radio communication as such.

1. *Psychologically considered the radio situation is more of a "closed whole" than is the face-to-face situation.* Although the physical presence of the speaker makes the face-to-face situation more complete and more normal, the radio situation seems to be more solidly structured. Perhaps it is the gestures and facial expressions of the speaker that tend to divide the total situation into smaller configurations, freeing the auditor's attention, as it were, for more rapid and efficient change. The radio delivery seems more consecutive and more monotonous in its appeal to one and only one sensory channel, giving little relief to attention and permitting fewer perceptual patterns to be discriminated. Here is the evidence:

a. The analytic dismemberment of a prose context was superior in the F group.

b. In the two experiments on distraction (5 and 11) subjects found it relatively easy to exclude (inhibit) the radio presentation as a whole from consciousness.

c. Mental arithmetic, requiring alert fluctuations in attention, was slightly better in the F situation.

d. In reproducing poetic passages, the R group tended to remember meter and rhyme whereas the F group recalled scattered words.

e. The memory for paired associates, calling for discrimination and grouping, was better in the F situation.

f. Abstract or theoretical material which demands analysis was less well understood when presented in radio lectures.

g. Students felt that repetition and illustration are necessary to overcome the handicaps of radio delivery.

h. The fact that listeners are inclined to give more uniform mental associations and the fact that they are somewhat more suggestible to direct command over the radio indicate likewise the solid, well-structured character of a broadcast.

2. *The radio situation is less personal than the face-to-face situation.* Words coming from the lips of a speaker spatially distant are devoid of their personal setting and seem to the listener to be psychologically as well as physically distant. The inevitable result is that radio presentation suffers wherever the factor of personal relationship is an important one in the delivery.

a. Radio lectures even when delivered by a familiar person (the class instructor himself) seemed to the students to be less personal and less desirable.

b. When subjects heard two stories simultaneously, one coming over the loudspeaker and one read by a speaker in the room with them, almost all of them recalled only the story read by the speaker physically present. This was true even when the speaker stood in the back of the room and was unseen by the subjects. The mere knowledge that certain words "belong" to a speaker personally present is enough to direct attention to them.

c. When work was done under distraction, more of the distracting story was recalled in the F group which had, as it were, been forced to pay attention against its will to the speaker physically present.

d. The subjects in the F group judged more words unpleasant. This might be accounted for by the personalization of feeling tone resulting from the physical presence of the speaker.

e. The common occurrence of imagery may mean that the students listening to radio lectures try unconsciously to make the situation seem more personal by visualizing the speaker.

3. *The face-to-face situation has more of the characteristics of a social situation.* The subtle rapport between speaker and audience is obviously greater in the F group.

a. Laughter, notably dependent on a social setting, is less intense in all radio audiences; likewise, students regard humor as far more enjoyable when the lecturer is present.

b. Social facilitation is greater in the F situation as shown by the quantity of work accomplished.

c. Subjects in the F group were more accurate in their judgments of emotional expression from the speaker's delivery.

d. In the F situation time intervals were estimated as of shorter duration than in the R situation. This result, though based on short intervals, bears out the common experience that time passes more swiftly in company than in solitude. Looking at a loud-speaker is boredom itself compared with watching a human face.

4. Summing up, *radio seems to have a slightly dulling effect upon higher mental processes.* In the radio situation the listener is on the whole less analytical, less alert, less involved personally and socially, and more passively receptive than he is in the face-to-face situation. This statement must, of course, be qualified by the admission of individual variation among auditors and by allowance for special types of programs and special conditions that may reverse this general average tendency. The evidence for this general conclusion is derived from the following experimental results:

a. In radio lectures, factual material was somewhat better understood than abstract material. The former demands passive receptance; the latter, active analysis.

b. Mental arithmetic was slightly better in the F situation.

c. Distractions coming from the radio are more easily inhibited than distractions emanating from a person physically present. The radio may be more easily excluded from consciousness; it seems in a sense to be less "real"; certainly it is less compelling to the attention.

d. Fewer individualized word associations were given in the R group, suggesting that the listener is in a somewhat conventional frame of mind in facing the loud-speaker.

e. Humor is less appreciated and greeted with less laughter in the radio audience.

f. Unfilled time seems somewhat longer in the R group, probably because the listener's mind is less occupied with watching the broadcaster.

g. The finer shadings of emotional expression are missed by the radio audience.

h. Neither arguments nor prose passages are as efficiently analyzed into units in the R group.

i. Radio talks seem to require more concrete illustration and more repetition, apparently because the listener's mind is not acting as creatively as in the face-to-face situation.

j. The R group seems somewhat more amenable to direct suggestion. Suggestibility, of course, is synonymous with the dulling of critical faculties.

k. Radio is a one-way method of communication. It is not fully social in its effects. The listener may be as unresponsive as he chooses: he does not feel in active contact with the speaker. The impersonal situation does not create in him a sense of responsibility for understanding and responding to the communications he receives.

Chapter IX

LISTENING *VERSUS* READING

Merton E. Carver, Ph.D.

University of Richmond

Summary. Although the relative value of reading and hearing the same material is a problem that has often been studied, the results have not been clear-cut nor immediately applicable to radio. Earlier experimenters failed to recognize many of the variables that enter into the situation, and few of them have directly employed the radio as their medium for auditory presentation. In the present experiment the rôles played by four variable conditions were studied: (1) the difficulty of the material presented, (2) the type of material employed, (3) the mental functions aroused, and (4) the educational background of the subjects. The method was one of group comparison with equivalent sets of material: one group heard what the other read. By reversing the groups it was possible to compare the auditory and the visual performance of a single group for equivalent sets of material.

The chief results may be summarized in relation to the four experimental variables. (1) *Difficulty of the material.* The effectiveness of auditory presentation tends to vary inversely with the difficulty of the material presented. (2) *Type of material.* The effectiveness of auditory presentation is limited to meaningful material, and tends to be superior for subject matter that is concrete and serial in nature. (3) *Mental functions.* If other conditions are kept constant, the mental functions of recognition, verbatim recall, and suggestibility seem more effectively aroused in listening; whereas critical attitudes and discriminative comprehension are favored by reading. The human relationship involved in the auditory situation is of value for certain types of communication (e.g., aesthetic and humorous) where the personal factor customarily plays a rôle. (4) *Educational background.* The higher the cultural level of the listener the greater is his ability to profit from auditory presentation.

For many years educators have been asking the question, "Which is the more efficient method of presenting material to students, by ear or by eye?" Thanks to radio, the possibilities of reaching the ear are now vastly extended and the question has assumed greater practical and theoretical importance than ever before. Not only educators, but likewise advertisers, politicians, news editors, and all manner of speakers and writers are turning to the psychologist for advice. "Do people understand what they hear better than what they read?" they ask. "Do they remember it better?" "Do they find it as interesting?" "Are they more critical toward it?" Categorical answers to these questions are desired, but categorical answers are difficult to give.

Studies comparing the effectiveness of visual and auditory presentations antedate the radio by a good many years. Already in 1912 there appeared an extensive review of the studies published prior to that date. Since then the amount of literature has rapidly increased.[1] In general, three approaches to the problem are represented: the pedagogical, the introspective, the practical. *Pedagogical* studies have focused attention on the relative effectiveness of visual and auditory presentation as it varies with age and with the type of material received. Several investigators have shown that auditory presentations have the advantage when young schoolchildren are tested for their memory of the material; other stud:es have found that the superiority of auditory presentation disappears with increasing age, visual presentation being more effective when the ability to read has been definitely acquired. Investigations on the memory and learning of adults yield conflicting results on the comparative advantages of the two methods of presentation. *Introspectionists* have held that the solution to the problem can come only when the characteristic mental processes aroused by each method of presentation are thoroughly understood. It is argued that the effects of a given type of presentation will differ with individuals according to their habits of perception and the type of imagery customarily employed. In general these introspective studics split hairs too finely. It is not possible to translate the modes of sensory presentation into modes of imaginal retention. The most one can do is to compare a visual presentation (allowing its naturally associated motor and imaginal concomitants to be what they may) with an auditory presentation (and all of its motor and imaginal accompaniments). It is the *stimulus-situation* as it functions in everyday life (through the press and the radio) that is the subject of interest for social psychologists. They see in radio a new device for persuading, educating, and entertaining the public and are naturally curious to find out exactly how radio compares with newspapers, magazines, and books as an agency for fashioning public opinion. In a few instances radio has been taken into the psychological laboratory to compare its effects with those of the printed page. Generally the comparisons have favored radio as a device for enhancing suggestibility and interest, and aiding recall and recognition. Yet contrary findings have also been reported and doubts arise.

The majority of previous investigators have attempted to settle the problem of visual versus auditory presentation once and for all through the use of coarse procedures. Studies have been made under such a variety of circumstances that results are scarcely comparable. The failure to distinguish the influence exerted by neglected conditions is the chief reason why the findings so often contradict one another. To

---

[1] It is fully reviewed by the writer in *A Study of Conditions Influencing the Relative Effectiveness of Visual and Auditory Presentations* (Cambridge: Harvard College Library, 1934). A less complete but more accessible survey of the topic is contained in Chapter VII of H. L. Hollingworth's *Psychology of the Audience* (New York: American Book Co., 1935).

remedy this situation, a series of experiments was designed to study the influence of four selected variables: (1) the type of material presented, (2) the difficulty of the material, (3) the mental functions involved, and (4) the cultural level of the subjects. No account was taken of the imagery patterns resulting from the stimulation of separate modalities. Imagery and motor responses were allowed to function freely and in this respect our procedure approximated the conditions of radio listening and of reading as they occur in everyday life.

Method. The method was one of group comparison with equivalent sets of material. In each experiment two groups of subjects took part. Form A of one set of material was presented visually to Group I and the same form aurally to Group II; Form B, on the other hand, was presented aurally to Group I and visually to Group II. With this method it was possible to compare both the performance of equivalent groups of subjects, and the performance of a single group of subjects for equivalent sets of material. Two large groups were employed during some of the experiments, while a number of smaller groups ranging from two to four persons participated in other phases of the investigation.

In the visual presentation, the subjects usually read the material in typewritten form at their own rates of speed, *once* only. The auditory presentations were made by an invisible speaker—always the same individual—usually over the radio, but in certain experiments from behind a curtain. In this way the personal element, totally absent in reading, was reduced to a minimum in hearing. Listening, of course, is *inevitably* a social activity; it requires that the voice of another person be brought actively and contemporaneously to our attention. Since this is true, it will never be clear that the differences between reading and listening—whatever they may be—are due solely to the receptive attributes of the eye and the ear; the difference may be due in large measure to the contrast between the social conditions of listening and the solitary conditions of reading. Nevertheless, in a study devoted to the psychological characteristics of radio listening it was obviously necessary to use the type of auditory presentation found in broadcasting, not the full-bodied social situation where the listener is attentive to the face of the speaker as well as to his words.

Subjects. The experiments were conducted both with college trained subjects and with those without such training. One group, known as the "urban population," was composed of 52 adults. This population (part of the population described in Chapter VII) was divided into two groups of 26 subjects each, and will be referred to as Groups I and II. These two groups were kept entirely separate. The second, "college population," was composed of 39 male undergraduates. In terms of training, cultural background, and general ability, our subjects represent a typical urban population on the one hand and a typical college population on the other.

Materials. Various types of material were used including narrative, descriptive, explanatory, and abstract passages; series of directions; short selections of prose, poetry, and humorous stories; vocabularies of 25 difficult words; and lists of nonsense syllables, digits, and words.

The *mental functions* studied were: (1) immediate recall; (2) recognition; (3) comprehension; (4) judgments for the aesthetic value of prose and poetry; (5) judgments for humor; (6) criticalness; and (7) discrimination. Some additional data concerning interest and suggestibility were obtained.

EXPERIMENT I: RECALL OF DISCONNECTED MATERIALS PRESENTED VISUALLY AND AURALLY

Method. Six series of nonsense syllables, numbers, and words, containing ten members each were used in this experiment. Each type of material was arranged in equivalent pairs for each of three levels of difficulty (very difficult, intermediate, least difficult). Care was exercised in selecting the nonsense syllables so that the lists given would be as fair to the auditory as to the visual mode of presentation.[2] The six series of numbers and of words were secured and arranged in lists with the help of five judges. Additional memory material was employed in the form of sentences, including five short and five long *specific* statements, five short and five long *general* statements. All of the sentences used were easy and typical of everyday conversation.

All instructions were given orally by the writer. The subjects were always told in advance what the mode of presentation would be. When an auditory presentation was concluded the announcer always said, "The end." The subjects were instructed in advance to write down immediately the items they were able to recall or otherwise to react to the material in some specified manner. The experimental schedule was arranged to introduce variety and interest during the hour.

In the experiments with college subjects, the nonsense syllables, digits, and words were presented (1) visually, (2) auditorily from behind a curtain (designated as "aural" presentation), and (3) auditorily over the radio ("radio" presentation). The "aural" and "radio" presentations were used to determine whether or not the mechanical or

[2] This material was available in the requisite levels of difficulty from the studies of J. A. Glaze ("The Association Value of Nonsense Syllables," *J. Genetic Psychol.*, 1928, 35, 255-269) and J. A. McGeoch ("The Influence of Association Value upon the Difficulty of Nonsense Syllable Lists," *J. Genetic Psychol.*, 1930, 37, 421-426).

social factors involved in radio transmission affect the auditory-visual comparison.

By dividing the total number of college subjects into three groups (Groups III, IV, and V) of 11 members each, a program was arranged so that two groups always received similar lists of material in the same manner. The scores of these groups were combined and *n* was then taken as 22 for purposes of comparison. The comparisons made were: visual-aural, visual-radio, and aural-radio. The methods of presentation together with the different comparisons possible for each of the equated sets of material may be illustrated as follows:

	Group III	Group IV	Group V
Set A........	visual	aural	radio
Set B........	aural	radio	visual

This procedure was employed for all comparisons within a given level of difficulty and for each of the three types of material employed.

The results obtained with nonsense syllables, numbers, and word lists were scored for the number of items absolutely correct, partially correct, and wholly incorrect. On this basis a composite score was worked out for each individual, for each group, and for the three types of material presented. Two points were allowed for all items of a series correctly recalled and one point for all items partially correct. A deduction of one point was made for each item wholly incorrect. The sentences were scored for correctness of meaning, the total number of words used, and the number of words used correctly.

The statistical procedure was one of evaluating differences between means. The means and their standard deviations were obtained in the usual manner. The standard error of the difference between the means was determined by the formula

$$\sigma_{\text{diff}} = \sqrt{\sigma_1^2 + \sigma_2^2}$$

in all cases where it was not possible to take account of the correlation between the scores of the same individuals on two tests. When such a correlation could be made, the following formula was used:[3]

$$\sigma_{\text{diff}} = \sqrt{\sigma_1^2 + \sigma_2^2 - 2r_{12}(\sigma_1\sigma_2)}$$

The reliability of the differences (reliability coefficient or "critical difference ratio") between the mean group scores was then calculated by dividing the obtained difference by the standard error of the difference.

Results. 1. *Nonsense syllables.* Visual presentation with nonsense syllables is superior to aural and to radio presentation for all levels of

[3] T. L. Kelley, *Statistical Method.* New York: Macmillan, 1932, 182.

TABLE XXV

MEMORY SCORES FOLLOWING VISUAL, AURAL, AND RADIO PRESENTATION OF NONSENSE SYLLABLES

	1st Level (Least difficult)						2nd Level (Intermediate)						3rd Level (Most difficult)					
	Vis	Aur	Vis	Radio	Aur	Radio	Vis	Aur	Vis	Radio	Aur	Radio	Vis	Aur	Vis	Radio	Aur	Radio
Mean..........	8.91	5.41	8.91	4.73	5.41	4.73	4.73	3.91	4.73	3.45	3.91	3.45	5.23	3.09	5.23	2.09	3.09	2.09
σ (dis.)......	2.71	2.79	2.71	2.91	2.79	2.91	2.96	3.64	2.96	2.81	3.64	2.81	2.45	2.89	2.45	3.22	2.89	3.22
Diff.........	3.50		4.18		.68		.81		1.27		.45		2.14		3.14		1.00	
σ diff.......	.85		.87		.88		1.02		.88		1.00		.83		.88		.94	
Diff. / σ diff.	4.12		4.81		.77		.79		1.43		.45		2.58		3.55		1.06	
Superior......	Vis		Vis		Aural		Vis		Vis		Aural		Vis		Vis		Aural	

difficulty and for all groups. The results obtained with the college groups are summarized in Table XXV. The number of nonsense syllables which can be immediately recalled is greatly influenced by the relative difficulty of the material irrespective of the mode of presentation. The influence of the difficulty of material on the accuracy of recall is least with visual and greatest with radio presentation. The table also shows that aural presentation (from behind a curtain) is somewhat superior to the radio presentation, showing that certain mechanical factors may interfere with the intelligibility of nonsense material, or that the social factor created by the presence of the invisible speaker has some influence upon retention.

2. *Numbers.* Series of numbers given over a loud-speaker are recalled somewhat better than they are when presented directly from behind a curtain or visually (Table XXVI). The differences taken individually are not significant statistically but radio presentation is consistently superior to both visual and direct aural with the exception of one comparison on the intermediate level. The visual and the direct aural presentation are about equal in effectiveness. The differences are less significant on the intermediate level than on either the easy or the difficult level.

3. *Words.* Visual presentation is consistently superior to both forms of auditory presentation when difficult word lists are presented (Table XXVII). On the other hand, both forms of auditory presentation are more effective (to about the same degree) than visual when lists of easy words are given.

4. *Sentences.* Regardless of the type of sentences presented, accuracy in immediate recall is significantly greater for auditory presentation than for visual. Whether the sentences were long or short, general or specific, appeared to make little difference. The results are summarized in Table XXVIII.

The amount of verbiage indicated in the table is the relation of the number of words used by the subjects in reproducing the sentences to the number of words actually contained in the sentences. It is apparent that there is a distinct tendency to use more words following an aural than a visual presentation.

EXPERIMENT II: RECOGNITION OF MATERIAL PRESENTED TO THE EYE AND TO THE EAR

Experimenters seem to agree that material once heard is ordinarily recognized more swiftly and accurately than material once seen. This finding squares with everyday experience. We may often re-read pages

TABLE XXVI

MEMORY SCORES FOLLOWING VISUAL, AURAL, AND RADIO PRESENTATION OF DIGITS

	1st Level (Least difficult)						2nd Level (Intermediate)						3rd Level (Most difficult)					
	Vis	Aur	Vis	Radio	Aur	Radio	Vis	Aur	Vis	Radio	Aur	Radio	Vis	Aur	Vis	Radio	Aur	Radio
Mean	10.14	9.59	10.14	10.45	9.59	10.45	8.18	8.86	8.18	8.59	8.86	8.59	4.41	4.00	4.41	5.23	4.00	5.23
σ (dis.)	2.49	2.33	2.49	2.33	2.33	2.33	2.62	2.34	2.62	2.81	2.34	2.81	2.39	3.37	2.39	2.49	3.37	2.49
Diff.	.55		.32		.86		.68		.41		.27		.41		.82		1.23	
σ diff.	.74		.74		.72		.77		.84		.80		.90		.75		.91	
Diff./σ diff.	.73		.43		1.20		.89		.48		.34		.45		1.09		1.34	
Superior	Vis		Radio		Radio		Aur		Radio		Aur		Vis		Radio		Radio	

TABLE XXVII

MEMORY SCORES FOLLOWING VISUAL, AURAL, AND RADIO PRESENTATION OF WORDS

1st Level (Least difficult)

	Vis	Aur	Vis	Radio	Aur	Radio
Mean	12.23	13.14	12.23	12.78	13.14	12.78
σ (dis.)	2.07	2.60	2.07	3.33	2.60	3.33
Diff.	.91		.55		.36	
σ diff.	.72		.85		.92	
Diff./σ diff.	1.25		.64		.39	
Superior	Aur		Radio		Aur	

2nd Level (Intermediate)

	Vis	Aur	Vis	Radio	Aur	Radio
Mean	11.91	11.60	11.91	11.36	11.60	11.36
σ (dis.)	3.12	2.37	3.12	2.64	2.37	2.64
Diff.	.31		.55		.24	
σ diff.	.85		.80		.77	
Diff./σ diff.	.27		.61		.29	
Superior	Vis		Vis		Aur	

3rd Level (Most difficult)

	Vis	Aur	Vis	Radio	Aur	Radio
Mean	10.45	9.00	10.45	9.73	9.00	9.73
σ (dis.)	2.54	2.75	2.54	3.48	2.75	3.48
Diff.	1.45		.72		.73	
σ diff.	.82		.94		.97	
Diff./σ diff.	1.78		.77		.75	
Superior	Vis		Vis		Radio	

TABLE XXVIII

MEMORY SCORES FOLLOWING VISUAL AND RADIO PRESENTATION OF SENTENCES

	Specific short sentences				General short sentences				Specific long sentences				General long sentences			
	Verbiage		Accuracy		Verbiage		Accuracy		Verbiage		Accuracy		Verbiage		Accuracy	
	Vis	Radio	Vis	Radio	Vis	Radio	Vis	Radio	Vis	Radio	Vis	Radio	Vis	Radio	Vis	Radio
Mean............	.67	.78	.56	.67	.71	.77	.59	.69	.62	.79	.50	.69	.31	.55	.24	.42
σ (dis.)........	.18	.16	.16	.15	.18	.14	.14	.15	.23	.14	.19	.17	.19	.23	.16	.17
Diff............	.11		.11		.06		.10		.17		.19		.24		.18	
σ diff.........	.05		.04		.05		.04		.05		.05		.60		.46	
Diff./σ diff.	2.24		2.52		1.30		2.53		3.20		3.77		4.04		3.96	
Superior......	Radio		Radio		Radio		Radio		Radio		Radio		Radio		Radio	

of printed material without a clear sense of recognition, whereas we usually have an unmistakable feeling of familiarity when a communication is heard twice.

Method. The material for this experiment consisted of two series of sentences. The first was designated as the *original series*, the second as the *test series*. The original series contained a list of 17 commonplace sentences of varying lengths. The test series contained 15 sentences, always presented to the subjects in printed form. In the test series certain sentences were repeated exactly as they had been given in the original series, certain sentences were omitted altogether, some new sentences were added, and in some sentences one single important word was altered. A few of the original sentences, and a portion of the test series are presented by way of illustration.

(*Original Series*)

My friend was waiting on the corner.
A growing child is constantly forming more bone, more muscle, and more blood.
She wore a blue dress and her sister wore a white one.

(*Test Series*)

Do you think each of the sentences below is similar to any sentence you have just read (or heard)? Check your opinion. If only one word in the sentence has been changed UNDERLINE that WORD.
A growing child is constantly in need of more food, more exercise, and more fresh air.

_____ exactly the same
_____ same idea worded differently
_____ not read before

She was a night-school student.

_____ exactly the same
_____ same idea worded differently
_____ not read before

My friend was waiting on the corner.

_____ exactly the same
_____ same idea worded differently
_____ not read before

The visual presentation was made by having the subjects read the original series of sentences once. When they had finished, by previous instruction they turned to the test series. The auditory presentation was given over the radio. The sentences were spoken at a uniform rate with an even emphasis. A short pause occurred between sentences. When the series was concluded, the announcer said "the end" and the subjects turned immediately to the test series.

The same tests were given to all groups. The method was one of group comparison with equivalent forms of the test. In scoring the results, a maximum credit of two points was given for each correct response in each of the fifteen recognition situations of the test series. The highest possible score on the test was 30 points.

Results. The tabulations of numerical values in Tables XXIX and XXX show that the auditory mode of presentation is significantly superior to the visual for all groups and for both forms of the recognition test. The difference in favor of listening is not quite so marked with the college population as it is with the urban population. In general, these results are in complete agreement with those of other investigators. Recognition is a mental function definitely favored when the material to be recognized is heard rather than read.

TABLE XXIX

RECOGNITION: COMPARISON OF AUDITORY AND VISUAL PRESENTATION OF SIMILAR MATERIAL TO THE SAME GROUP

	Gp I Form $\begin{Bmatrix} A=Aud \\ B=Vis \end{Bmatrix}$		Gp II Form $\begin{Bmatrix} A=Vis \\ B=Aud \end{Bmatrix}$		Gp III Form $\begin{Bmatrix} A=Aud \\ B=Vis \end{Bmatrix}$		Gp IV Form $\begin{Bmatrix} A=Vis \\ B=Aud \end{Bmatrix}$	
	Aud	Vis	Aud	Vis	Aud	Vis	Aud	Vis
Mean	22.50	17.73	20.77	16.62	19.31	17.31	22.88	17.18
σ (dis.)	3.39	4.42	5.00	5.07	4.66	3.67	4.09	3.33
Diff.	4.77		3.85		2.00		5.70	
σ diff.	.88		1.09		1.06		1.06	
Diff./σ diff.	5.41		3.54		1.88		5.39	
Superior	Aud		Aud		Aud		Aud	

TABLE XXX

RECOGNITION: COMPARISON OF AUDITORY AND VISUAL PRESENTATION OF SAME MATERIAL TO DIFFERENT GROUPS

	Form A		Form B		Form A		Form B	
	Gp I Aud	Gp II Vis	Gp I Vis	Gp II Aud	Gp III Aud	Gp IV Vis	Gp III Vis	Gp IV Aud
Mean	22.50	16.92	17.73	20.77	19.31	17.18	17.31	22.88
σ (dis.)	3.39	5.07	4.42	5.00	4.66	3.33	3.67	4.09
Diff.	5.58		3.04		2.13		5.57	
σ diff.	1.22		1.33		1.46		1.39	
Diff./σ diff.	4.57		2.28		1.46		4.00	
Superior	Aud		Aud		Aud		Aud	

EXPERIMENT III: COMPREHENSION OF CONNECTED MEANINGFUL MATERIAL

In this experiment an attempt was made to answer the following questions: (1) Is material that is read comprehended better than similar material that is heard? (2) Does the degree of comprehension vary with the type of material presented, e.g., narrative, explanatory, descriptive, and abstract material? (3) Are directions understood better when given visually or auditorily? (4) Does the advantage of a given mode of presentation vary with the difficulty of the material? (5) Does the advantage of either mode vary with the educational background of the subject?

Method. Paired samples of connected meaningful passages together with sets of directions were selected with the help of judges. This collection included passages of a narrative, descriptive, abstract, and explanatory type. There were comparable adventure stories; paired descriptions of a date palm and of a banana plantation; short essays on theoretical, legal, and historical subjects.

To test the subjects' comprehension, an objective test (true-false or completion) was employed in many instances. At other times short essay tests were used. The results of the essay tests were scored by five judges, generally agreeing well in their scores. In addition to the test, each sample of the material was accompanied by a questionnaire on which the subject was asked to indicate how well he understood the passage just presented and how interesting it was to him.

The materials necessary to the experiment were arranged in booklets. When the presentation of a given selection was visual, the selection was included in the booklet followed by the questionnaire and then the test. For the radio presentations, only the questionnaire and the test were included in the booklet. The subjects were told in advance of a given sample of material what mode of presentation would be employed, what type of material would be given, and how many pages to answer in the booklet immediately after reading or hearing the selection. All auditory presentations were given over the radio. No time limit was imposed for any of the tests. The director simply noted when everyone had finished a given exercise. In the meantime the other subjects waited quietly and were warned not to look back or ahead in the booklet. Monotony was avoided by interspersing these experiments on comprehension with others of a different type.

Results.[4] Although in many of the comparisons the differences are slight, certain general trends of a consistent order seem to emerge (Table XXXI).

1. The *difficulty of the material* is an important variable.[5] The easier the material, the greater is the likelihood that auditory presentation will be more effective than visual. Materials of average difficulty tend to give equivocal results; whereas, in general, material that is intrinsically difficult is better comprehended if presented to the eye.

[4] It should be pointed out that more time was spent by all groups in listening than in reading, but since the excess of auditory time over visual was essentially constant, it should not be expected to affect the comparisons made in this experiment.

[5] Table XXXI presents only the results obtained from material of a difficult level. The conclusions here stated are based on more complete data contained in an unpublished manuscript by M. E. Carver, *A Study of Conditions Influencing the Relative Effectiveness of Visual and Auditory Presentation* (Cambridge: Harvard College Library, 1934).

TABLE XXXI

COMPREHENSION: COMPARISON OF URBAN AND COLLEGE POPULATIONS ON DIFFICULT HISTORICAL MATERIAL

| | Urban population | | | | College population | | | |
| | Form A | | Form B | | Form A | | Form B | |
	Gp I Vis	Gp II Aud	Gp I Aud	Gp II Vis	Gp III Vis	Gp IV Aud	Gp III Aud	Gp IV Vis
Mean........	5.63	4.78	3.99	5.28	6.45	7.29	6.41	6.00
σ (dis.).......	2.51	3.03	2.71	3.00	1.58	1.19	1.58	2.33
Diff...........	.85		1.29		.84		.41	
σ diff.........	.79		.81		.53		.75	
Diff./σ diff....	1.08		1.60		1.59		.55	
Superior......	Vis		Vis		Aud		Aud	

2. The results indicate that the *cultural level* of the subjects is an important variable influencing comprehension. The higher the cultural level the greater the capacity to respond to auditory presentation as compared to visual. In other words, a college population is able to demonstrate a more successful response to increasingly difficult auditory presentations than is the population at large. Beyond a certain stage in the scale of difficulty, the general population will do better to read the material. Even with a college population, however, a point is reached where the factor of difficulty in the material outweighs the relative advantage of auditory presentation. Table XXXI indicates the differences in performance of the two populations for relatively difficult paired historical passages. This table may be considered typical of the findings for material of a fairly complex order.

3. There is a positive correlation between the degree of comprehension and of interest of the material. The urban population was generally more interested in the material read, the college population in the material heard. All groups rated the degree of comprehension higher when *directions* were heard than when they were read, although by objective tests this superiority was not always established.

EXPERIMENT IV: PREFERENCE FOR PROSE AND POETRY WHEN READ AND WHEN HEARD

This experiment was designed to determine whether or not equivalent passages of prose or poetry are preferred in visual or auditory form by the majority of people.

Method. Six paired passages of short prose were selected. The style, choice of words, figures of speech, as well as the subject matter, were such as might be expected to appeal to the imagination and to contemplative attitudes. The passages possessed rhythmic and musical qualities. Ten equivalent passages of poetry were also used, including paired stanzas from the same poem, in order that subject matter and rhythm might be held constant.

The auditory presentations were expressively rendered, then the visual presentation of the other sample immediately followed. The subjects read the material at their natural speeds. At the bottom of the page containing the visual sample the subjects were asked to check which of the two passages they enjoyed more:

Passage just heard _____
Passage just read _____

Results. Short literary prose passages presented auditorily are more enjoyable. Poetry, on the other hand, reveals no trend of preference in favor of either mode of presentation. This result, so far as it goes, brings into question the general belief that poetry must be heard to be appreciated. It does not affect the other common contention that poetry must be read aloud by the subject himself to be fully appreciated. No important differences due to cultural factors are found for either poetry or prose passages. The preferences shown in Table XXXII are stated in percentages.

TABLE XXXII

VISUAL-AUDITORY PREFERENCES FOR PROSE AND POETRY

	Prose		*Poetry*	
	Vis	Aud	Vis	Aud
Group I	26	74	37	63
Group II	46	54	52	48
Group III	36	64	53	47
Group IV	43	57	46	54
Total	38	62	54	46

EXPERIMENT V: COMPARISON OF RATINGS FOR HUMOROUS STORIES PRESENTED VISUALLY AND AUDITORILY

This experiment was designed to determine whether or not humorous stories are more appreciated when read or when heard.

Method. Two sets of five "after dinner" jokes were prepared. Five jokes were presented over the loud-speaker and then without any delay the subjects were asked to read five more jokes and to indicate (1) which series of jokes they enjoyed more:

Jokes just heard _____
Jokes just read _____

and (2) whether they would rather read a funny story or hear it over the radio. The material was given to Groups I and II only, the sets of jokes being reversed in the usual manner. The number of preferences given for auditory and for visual presentation were separately tabulated for each group and expressed as ratios to the total number of judgments made by a group on a given set of materials.

Results. Unfortunately, the two sets of jokes did not prove to be sufficiently equivalent; when the two samples were reversed the preponderance of judgments in favor of a given mode of presentation also tended to reverse. Nevertheless, a slight advantage in favor of auditory presentation appears. The expressions of opinion or general preference indicated that 60 per cent of the subjects preferred to hear funny stories over the radio than to read them. There was more laughter when stories were heard than when they were read.

EXPERIMENT VI : CRITICAL ATTITUDES IN LISTENING AND READING

Two questions prompted this experiment: (1) Are people more discriminating in their judgments of grammatical constructions when material is read or when it is heard? (2) Is the average person more critical of material that he reads or that he hears?

Method. Twelve illustrative sentences were selected from authoritative textbooks of English grammar. Six of the sentences were grammatically incorrect, three were awkward and displeasing, and the remaining three were correct in every way. Two such series of sentences were compiled. For purposes of the actual test a chart was constructed, a portion of which, along with a portion of the material used in one form of the test, is given below.

Read each of the following sentences at your natural speed. As you finish each sentence, indicate your opinion of its construction by checking the proper column below.

1. The only ones absent were his brother and him.
2. He drunk only water.

Sentence Number	Grammatically Incorrect	Awkward and Displeasing	Approved in Every Way
1			
2			

In the visual presentation this chart was placed directly below the sentences. In the auditory presentation a sheet containing the chart only was given to each subject.

The instructions for the visual presentation have been indicated above. The subjects were again impressed that they should read each sentence only once. In the auditory presentation the instructions were: *"As you hear* each sentence place a check mark in one of the columns below indicating whether you approve or disapprove of its construction. The number of each sentence will be given; be sure you check the proper sentence number." The sentences were read clearly and at a constant tempo by the announcer. Five seconds intervened between sentences. This experiment was conducted with Groups I and II only; the order of presentations was reversed for the two groups.

The scoring and treatment of results were as follows: (1) to secure a measure of accuracy in detecting correct, incorrect, and awkward sentences, the tests were scored in terms of the number of judgments correct for each type of sentence. (2) In order to determine whether or not there was any tendency for individuals to be more critical toward material presented in one manner than in another, the checks occurring in each of the three columns (correct, incorrect, and awkward) were totaled regardless of whether the responses were right or wrong. It was assumed that any tendency to be more critical of material presented auditorily, for example, would be indicated by a larger number of checks in the "incorrect" or "awkward and displeasing" columns for auditory presentation and a lesser number of checks in the same columns with visual presentation. If there was a tendency for individuals to be more critical toward visual material and less critical toward auditory, the reverse relationship should appear. (3) The mean scores and their standard deviations were determined for each column

TABLE XXXIII

ACCURACY OF GRAMMATICAL JUDGMENT

	Grammatically incorrect		Awkward and displeasing		Correct in every way	
	Vis.	Aud.	Vis.	Aud.	Vis.	Aud.
Mean.......	5.17	4.25	1.67	1.54	1.79	1.69
σ (dis.)......	1.28	1.14	1.25	1.25	.69	.67
Diff.........	.92		.13		.10	
σ diff.......	.19		.29		.12	
Diff. / σ diff........	4.81		.47		.78	
Superior.....	Vis.		Vis.		Vis.	

TABLE XXXIV

MEASURES OF CRITICALNESS

	Grammatically incorrect		Awkward and displeasing		Correct in every way	
	Vis.	Aud.	Vis.	Aud.	Vis.	Aud.
Mean.......	5.96	5.25	2.71	2.75	3.46	4.13
σ (dis.)......	1.49	1.54	1.79	1.40	1.39	1.48
Diff.........	.71		.04		.67	
σ diff.......	.22		.32		.22	
Diff. / σ diff........	3.28		.12		3.07	
Superior.....	Vis.		Neither		Aud.	

of the combined tests and for each mode of presentation. The visual and auditory means for each column were then compared statistically.

Results. Table XXXIII shows that greater accuracy in the discrimination of correct, incorrect, and awkward sentences is obtained when presentation is visual rather than auditory. This is most marked for sentences grammatically incorrect and least noticeable for awkward and displeasing sentences. Table XXXIV indicates that individuals tend to be more critical of grammatical faults in material read than in material heard. Whether or not this criticalness extends to matters other than grammar and style is not, of course, established by this single experiment.

EXPERIMENT VII: "COMPREHENSION" OF MEANINGFUL AND FICTITIOUS WORDS

What degree of meaning and familiarity do words have when read and when heard out of context? Is there any tendency for individuals to ascribe meaning to fictitious words presented visually and auditorily, thus revealing suggestibility as a function of the mode of presentation? Lastly, do results obtained with material of this type vary with cultural differences in subjects?

Method. Two lists of words were prepared. Each list was composed of twenty meaningful words and five nonmeaningful or fictitious words (jokers) which were made to appear as plausible as possible.

The instructions for visual presentation were as follows: "(1) Beside each of the following words make *one* check mark if you think you have seen the word before. (2) Make *two* check marks if you think you could define the word. (3) Make *three* check marks if you *are sure* you could define the word. You may be asked later to define the words you have checked three times." The subjects were further told to indicate first judgments and not to labor over any one word or to go back over the list. No time limit was imposed but most of those taking part succeeded in doing the test within a period of two minutes.

In the auditory presentation the subjects were given the same instructions, except they were told that they would hear a list of twenty-five words read to them over the radio. All words were carefully pronounced. Four seconds intervened between words. All four groups participated in the experiment and the two forms of the material were reversed in the usual manner.

In treating the results, the following rules were observed: (1) The number of single, double, and triple checks given by each subject for the twenty real words were added separately and tabulated in their respective columns. (2) The "jokers" or fictitious words were treated in the same manner but kept separate from the other words. (3) A composite score was derived for each subject by weighting the sum of the triple checks by three, the double checks by two, and the single checks by one. (4) The same weighting scale was applied to the fictitious words. (5) The visual scores of one test were combined with the visual scores of the other for Groups I and II and for Groups III and IV. The auditory scores were likewise combined. (6) The means were then statistically compared and evaluated.

Results. Three tendencies are revealed in Table XXXV.

TABLE XXXV
SUMMARY OF RESPONSES GIVEN TO MEANINGFUL AND FICTITIOUS WORDS

	Meaningful words				Fictitious words			
	Urban population		College population		Urban population		College population	
	Vis.	Aud.	Vis.	Aud.	Vis.	Aud.	Vis.	Aud.
Mean...	34.17	33.87	42.60	41.33	.77	1.46	.70	1.00
σ (dis.)..	14.53	13.82	9.30	11.35	1.38	1.91	.90	1.03
Diff.....		.31		1.27		.69		.30
σ diff....		1.33		2.10		.25		.20
$\dfrac{\text{Diff.}}{\sigma\ \text{diff.}}$...		.23		.60		2.79		1.47
Superior.		Vis.		Vis.		Aud.		Aud.

1. Words of more than average difficulty seem more meaningful to the subjects when read than when heard. The differences are not statistically significant in any single comparison, but the direction of the difference in favor of reading is constant for all groups.

2. Fictitious words are judged as authentic when heard more often than when read. In other words, individuals seem to be less critical and more gullible toward spoken material. The sound of fictitious words seems to be more suggestive of meaningful associations than the sight of such words. Similar tendencies toward the acceptance of erroneous forms of expression were revealed in the experiments on grammatical constructions.

3. College students are more critical of fictitious words than are noncollege subjects.

SUMMARY AND CONCLUSIONS

The chief results may be summarized in relation to the four principal variables.

1. *Difficulty of the material.* The relative effectiveness of visual

presentation varies directly with the difficulty of the material. Conversely, the effectiveness of listening is greater when the material is simpler. Materials of intermediate difficulty tend to give nonsignificant or equivocal results.

2. *Type of material.* The effectiveness of auditory presentation is limited to familiar and meaningful material; it is markedly inferior when strange or meaningless material is used.

3. *Mental functions.* When the factors of difficulty of material and cultural level of subjects are kept constant, the mental functions of recognition, verbatim recall, and suggestibility (noncriticalness) are more successfully exercised when listening. Comprehension, criticalness, and discrimination seem by and large to be facilitated by reading. Auditory presentation is significantly preferred for aesthetic prose passages and for humor. Selections of poetry give equivocal results.

4. *Cultural level.* The higher the cultural level, the greater the capacity to profit from auditory presentation.[6] There is, however, a point reached where the factor of the difficulty in the material outweighs the relative advantage of cultural training and the advantage of auditory presentation is lost in favor of the visual.

A brief analysis of the differences between the experience of listening and that of reading may facilitate the interpretation of these results. In the *reading* situation, printed words, although spatially separated, are experienced more as related items in larger groupings than as isolated units. Every reader, unless he is a beginner or unless a passage is unusually difficult, makes word-groupings of some kind, although, to be sure, the number of words included within a single perceptual grouping will vary with his attitude, with his familiarity with the material, and with his general reading habits. While reading one is also able to fit a word into the immediate context of words which *follow* it as well as those which have just preceded it, a factor of particular importance in the comprehension of difficult material. In short, the reader to a large extent determines the range and tempo of his own perceptual experiences. Varying his speed, grouping words and phrases, and studying contexts, he extracts from the visual stimulus-situation as much meaning as he possibly can.

In the *listening* situation, on the other hand, words are separated in time and must necessarily be experienced more as isolated units. To be sure, elisions and pauses tend to group neighboring words into phrases. But such groupings are comparatively stereotyped and are produced by the *speaker*. The listener does not make his own groupings; they are made for him. In addition, the listener has an oppor-

[6] A similar conclusion is reached by Hollingworth who reports that visual aids are of value chiefly to unsophisticated audiences (*Psychology of the Audience*, 106).

tunity to fit a word or group of words into the context only in so far as he is able to remember the previous words. In ordinary discourse this process presents no difficulties, but it becomes difficult when the words and contexts lose their familiarity.

These differences between the perceptual experiences in reading and listening may be represented diagrammatically. The sentence below was selected from an abstract passage used in one experiment and represents material of more than average difficulty which was comprehended better when read than when heard. The connecting lines indicate possible perceptual groupings which an individual might make in the reading situation.

Visual presentation

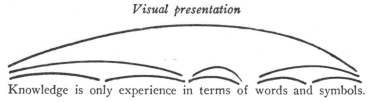

Knowledge is only experience in terms of words and symbols.

(The reader may perceive the printed words in bunches, swiftly grasp contexts, form larger groupings, and obtain the meaning of the whole sentence as his eyes play about the words in the normal process of reading.)

Auditory presentation

Knowledge
    is only
        experience
           in terms of
                words and
                    symbols

(The words are experienced more as isolated units except where elisions occur. Grouping is possible only in so far as the listener remembers words that have already been heard and the meaning of the whole sentence is grasped only if all successive words can be related to those preceding. This is difficult to achieve for abstruse material, although easy enough in ordinary discourse.)

A number of our results seem to be explained by this intrinsic difference between the patterns of auditory and visual perception. We find, for example, that mental activity requiring analysis, critical discrimination, the handling of unfamiliar or nonsense material is markedly favored by visual presentation. On the other hand, the understanding of familiar statements, the sense of recognition, the recall of easy word lists, series of numbers, and simple directions, all demonstrate the superiority of the "stepwise" auditory presentation as contrasted to the "interlocking" visual presentation.

But besides the basic differences in the mode of perceiving visual and auditory material, there are distinctions of an affective order that undoubtedly play an important part. Listening is a friendly activity, usually more enjoyable and more interesting than reading. It depends upon other human beings. We are usually sympathetic when we listen; at least we are on our good behavior. Through long training we have learned to listen patiently: the plethora of platitudes reaching our ears during the day would be unbearable if we encountered them in print. And so it is that whatever is human, personal, or intimate seems favored by auditory communication—humor, for example, and suggestibility. The listener seems as a rule to be friendly, uncritical, and well disposed toward what he hears. The reader, on the other hand, tends to be more analytical and more critical, and in the long run probably more accurate in his knowledge and better informed.

CHAPTER X

EFFECTIVE CONDITIONS FOR BROADCASTING

Summary. Experiments were designed to answer certain questions frequently asked by radio speakers. (1) *Is it better for a broadcaster to prepare his script in such a way that general statements will predominate, or should his ideas be presented concretely, or is some combination of the two methods superior?* In these experiments it was found that passages in which a general idea was followed by a specific reference or concrete illustration were in every case more interesting and better recalled than either an entirely general or an entirely specific passage. (2) *Is it better to use long or short sentences in broadcasting?* When the material has no intrinsic interest or is of a highly factual nature, short sentences increase its memory value. The greater effectiveness of short sentences disappears as the material becomes more interesting and more unified. (3) *What is the optimum speed for broadcasting different types of material?* The majority of broadcasts are most comprehensible and most interesting when the speed is not less than 115 nor more than 160 words per minute. Factual or difficult material (directions, abstract passages) can be broadcast slower without losing its interest, but material readily comprehended (news, narrative) loses its interest and is consequently less well understood if broadcast slower than 120 words per minute. (4) *What is the value of repetition in broadcasting various types of material?* In general, repetition facilitates comprehension and aids memory, although it runs the risk of making a broadcast less interesting. (5) *How do broadcasts of different lengths on the same subject compare in effectiveness?* In this investigation we were unable to reproduce all types of talks at all possible lengths but the findings indicate that the listener's loss of interest in long talks tends to counterbalance any intrinsic effectiveness gained by an expansion in length. Although there are distinct exceptions to the general rule, for ordinary educational, political, factual, or news broadcasts the most suitable length seems to be around fifteen minutes.

Almost everyone who faces a microphone for the first time asks certain questions concerning the most effective methods of broadcasting. How fast should one talk? How much repetition should one use? Should there be many illustrations or few? In what part of the discourse should they come? If financial considerations are of no concern, the speaker will also wonder what the optimum length of time may be for his particular type of message.

Experienced speakers and continuity writers have already discovered approximate answers to these questions. By trial and error they have learned how to give the most effective expression of their own personal styles. Because they have been primarily interested in their *own* effectiveness, the advice they are able to give others often seems vague or inappropriate. In his compilation of empirical rules drawn from the experience of broadcasters, Koon points out that the speaker "must cooperate closely with the station manager," that he must "pronounce correctly," "articulate distinctly," and "avoid extraneous noises."[1] Such rules are self-evident and easy to follow. Others, however, are more difficult. The speaker is told to "organize his subject matter to conform to the requirements of the medium." He wonders exactly what this means. He learns, too, that he should "make the radio broadcast compact and concise so that the line of thought will be easy to follow," and that he should "make only a few points and illustrate them simply." How concise, exactly, should he be? When is illustration ample and when is it redundant? He learns also that he should "vary the rate of delivery according to [his] own style and the thought being expressed." But he is not told what the proper rate of delivery may be for the thought he is trying to express. Mr. Koon himself realizes that more exact help might be given the speaker if some of these problems were submitted to experimental inspection. "Microphone technique," he concludes, "must be made the subject of a scientific investigation rather than be left to the empirical maxims of practitioners themselves."

Thus far there have not been many experimental studies to determine the optimum conditions for broadcasting. A few investigators, to be sure, have concerned themselves with the proper rate of speech. Ewbank, for example, had speakers broadcast at three different speeds.[2] A completion test based on the factual material contained in the speeches revealed that some speakers were more effective at a slow speed (around 172 syllables per minute), while others were more effective at a faster speed (around 222 syllables per minute). In all cases, however, since more material was crowded into broadcasts at the most rapid rates (around 312 syllables per minute), listeners learned more facts per minute at fast speeds, although retaining a smaller percentage of the total material broadcast. Lawton[3] had students rate what they considered the proper speed and found a delivery of 135-140 words per minute optimum. Borden[4] found that 165 words per minute was the best speed, approximating the 170-word average of NBC announcers.[5] Lumley[6] analyzed various radio talks and found

[1] C. M. Koon, *The Art of Teaching by Radio*. Washington: U. S. Government Printing Office, 1933.
[2] H. L. Ewbank, "Exploratory Studies in Radio Techniques," *Education on the Air*, 1932, 231-239.
[3] S. P. Lawton, "Principles of Effective Radio Speaking," *Quar. Jl. of Speech*, 1930, 16, 265-277.
[4] R. C. Borden, "The Principles of Effective Radio Speaking," *Modern Eloquence* (2nd suppl. vol.), 1927, 9-17.
[5] A. N. Goldsmith and A. Lescarboura, *This Thing Called Broadcasting*. New York: Holt, 1930, 134.
[6] F. H. Lumley, "Rates of Speech in Radio Speaking," *Quar. Jl. of Speech*, 1933, 19, 393-403.

that educators average 160 words per minute, news reporters 191, politicians 107, and preachers 171.

Other studies have related the effectiveness of talks to the vocabulary employed. Dale[7] and Lumley[8] have urged that simple words be used in educational talks. Some educators have tried to estimate the number of general ideas that can be broadcast to children in a single program. Worcester[9] found that many school broadcasts were of questionable value because too many general ideas and too few illustrations were used. Dale[10] has suggested that one or two ideas amply illustrated are enough for a single school broadcast.

Most of these studies have been made by educators interested in the immediate problem of classroom teaching. The majority of them based their findings upon actual radio talks and were, therefore, unable to vary the conditions for experimental purposes. In the investigations reported in this chapter both the conditions of broadcasting and the type of material used were varied.

PROCEDURE AND RESULTS

In this investigation the method of two equivalent audiences described in Chapter IX was again employed. One group of listeners heard a message under one condition while the second group heard the *same* message under a varied condition. There was sufficient repetition so that the two types of presentation could be judged an equal number of times by each group. Five separate conditions were studied, each condition independent of all the others. Thus when condition C was the object of investigation, conditions A, B, D, and E were held as constant as possible.

All of the passages were read by the same announcer. The subjects recorded their answers in the record booklets provided them at the beginning of each experimental session. The pages of these booklets were so arranged that no subject could know in advance of each broadcast what questions he would be expected to answer concerning it. The order of the experiments was varied, and since these experiments were interspersed with those reported in Chapters VII and IX, the subjects were never aware of their exact purpose.

[7] Edgar Dale, "The Vocabulary Level of Radio Addresses," *Education on the Air,* 1931, 245-253.
[8] Lumley, *op. cit.*
[9] D. A. Worcester, "What People Remember from Radio Programs," *Education on the Air,* 1932, 220-228.
[10] Edgar Dale, "Preparing Radio Talks for Children," *Education on the Air,* 1932, 105-115.

1. *Is it better to present ideas in a general way, in a specific way, or is some combination of general presentation followed by specific illustration superior?* Since the radio talk is addressed to an unseen audience, the speaker is unable to detect signs of bewilderment that would ordinarily provoke him to give more illustration; nor can he detect signs of boredom that might warn him to progress more rapidly from one idea to another. He must know, then, certain guiding rules that define a safe, average procedure.

Method. Three types of presentation were compared: (a) passages written completely in general terms, (b) passages written entirely in specific terms, and (c) passages where a general idea was followed by a specific example. Each type of material presented to one group in one way (e.g., all general terms) was presented to the other group in another way (e.g., all specific terms). The passages broadcast to the two groups in each experiment were identical in their ideational content. If the particular experiment involved a comparison of general and specific presentation, a *general* idea expressed in one passage was given *specifically* in another passage, if the comparison was between general presentation and a presentation in which a general idea was followed by a specific reference, each *general* idea contained in a passage heard by one group was heard by another group but *followed by the specific reference*. The example below is illustrative of the method employed.

(*All general terms*) Mr. L. has all the homely virtues generally associated with a conservative, law-abiding citizen of the lower middle class. He is intensely religious and has set up for himself and family an almost puritanical code of morals. Although most of his friends are well-off or hold responsible positions, Mr. L. is quite content with his lot and has no ambition to gain power or wealth. He has had little formal schooling but is a wide reader and is well informed.

(*All specific terms*) Mr. L. is a clerk in a large city. He enjoys riding a bicycle to work and teaches a Sunday School class in a Baptist church. His favorite reading is *The National Geographic Magazine* and religious periodicals. L. believes dancing and smoking are sinful. He spends his evenings at home. Mr. L.'s grammar is flawless and he enjoys correcting the grammar of friends, most of whom are doctors and executives.

Seven experiments were conducted on this problem and four different types of material were used. The presentation was so arranged that all possible comparisons were made and that each group received the same number of passages representing the different types of material. The following order of the experiments shows both the type of presentation used and the material broadcast.

Group I	Group II
General (Weather report A)	*Specific* (Weather report A)
General (Weather report B)	*General-specific* (Weather report B)
Specific (Personality A)	*General* (Personality A)
Specific (Psychology)	*General-specific* (Psychology)
General-specific (Personality B)	*General* (Personality B)
General-specific (History B)	*Specific* (History B)
	(Control)
General-specific (History A)	*General-specific* (History A)

The subjects were instructed to listen to the passage as they would to any similar talk over the radio. When the broadcast was finished they answered the following questions found on their record sheets:

1. How well do you think you understood the talk?

  _____ extremely well
  _____ very well
  _____ fairly well (average)
  _____ slightly
  _____ not at all

2. How interesting was the talk?

  _____ extremely
  _____ very
  _____ fairly (average)
  _____ slightly
  _____ not at all

After the broadcast of the personality sketches the questions "How well do you think you understand the person described?" and "Was this sketch vivid?" were substituted for the above questions.

On the day following the presentation of each type of material, the experimenter read aloud a single leading sentence from the particular passage the group had heard the day before and asked the subjects to write in their booklets as much as they could remember of the topic suggested by the sentence. In this way were obtained a subjective rating on the comprehensibility of the passage and an objective score on the amount recalled.

Results. The mean ratings on the comprehensibility and interest of the passages were obtained by weighting an answer of "extremely" with four, "very" with three, "fairly" with two, "slightly" with one, and "not at all" with zero. The amount which the subjects recalled of the passage heard the previous day was graded by assigning one point to each idea correctly reproduced. Each item in the general and specific presentations was taken as a unit while each general idea and each specific illustration in the general-specific presentations was regarded as a half-unit since twice as many items were contained in this type of presentation. The total possible score that might be obtained varied with the material presented. Thus a score of 26 was possible on one of the history passages while the maximum score on one personality sketch was only 12. The mean scores obtained by one group of subjects as shown in Table XXXVI should be compared, then, only with the mean scores obtained by the other group for the *same type* of material.[11] The comparison is always between *methods of presentation* and *not* types of material.

TABLE XXXVI

MEAN RATINGS AND SCORES OBTAINED WHEN PASSAGES VARY
IN THE GENERALITY OR SPECIFICITY OF STATEMENT

Type of presentation	Material	Group	How well subjects thought they understood the passage	How interesting the passage was	Amount of passage recalled following day
General	Weather	I	2.41	1.66	1.23
Specific	report A	II	2.66	1.57	1.09
General	Weather	I	2.55	1.84	0.57
General-specific	report B	II	2.72	2.28	0.73
Specific	Personal-	I	2.72	2.27	2.05
General	ity A	II	2.60	2.15	3.17
Specific	Psychology	I	2.53	2.47	1.22
General-specific		II	2.26	2.60	1.60
General-specific	Personal-	I	2.72	2.27	2.82
General	ity B	II	2.60	2.15	1.64
General-specific	History B	I	2.56	2.60	4.04
Specific		II	2.60	2.37	3.83
General-specific	History A	I	2.79	2.43	3.26
General-specific		II	2.83	2.40	3.20

A comparison of the obtained means is justified only if the two groups are equivalent. Although the attempt was made to divide the subjects as equally as possible, Group I tended to give higher ratings and to do better on the objective tests. It was, therefore, necessary to "correct" the obtained results for this discrepancy between the groups. The figures in the table represent the results obtained after correcting for the 7 per cent higher rating customarily given by Group I for

[11] We should be unjustified in reducing all scores for different types of material to a common unit, since the number of items recalled would vary with the length and difficulty of the material.

comprehension, its 8 per cent higher rating for interest, and its 20 per cent superiority shown on all the objective tests.

1. Although a passage written in specific terms is sometimes felt to be more comprehensible and more interesting than the same context written entirely in general terms, the latter is always more correctly recalled. In many cases the specific items which the subjects wrote in their booklets were illustrative of the correct general idea but were wrong in their specific contents. It seems that specific illustrations build up a correct general impression which the subject remembers well. When the subjects in turn try to give specific instances of this correct general impression their illustrations are often fictitious.[12]

2. The *passages in which a general idea was followed by a specific reference were in every case more interesting and better recalled than either an entirely general or an entirely specific passage.* This result clearly shows to the broadcaster the didactic value of crystallizing a general idea with an illustration immediately following.

2. What is the comparative effectiveness of short and long sentences?

Method. In these experiments one group of listeners received a passage written in short sentences while the other group heard the *same* passage written in long sentences. The following material is typical:

Short sentences. To reach the Yacht Club, proceed as follows: From Gifford Square, go north on Sterling Avenue. At Cumberland Street, bear left. Follow the car track for a mile and a half. Cross the railroad at Harbor Island station. A quarter mile beyond, watch for a flashing traffic signal. Turn right on gravel road. Go left at end. Follow the beach road to the Yacht Club.

Long sentences. To reach the Yacht Club, go north on Sterling Avenue from Gifford Square, bearing left at Cumberland Street and following the car track for a mile and a half to Harbor Island station, where you cross the railroad tracks. Turn right on a gravel road at a flashing signal a quarter mile beyond and when you get to the end of this road, turn left and follow the beach road to the Yacht Club.

Three different types of material were used: directions, lost and found ads, and simple exposition. There were six examples of each

[12] This finding is in keeping with the psychological principle that *general* attitudes and *general* meanings play a preëminent rôle in adult mental life. (Cf. Hadley Cantril, "General and Specific Attitudes," *Psychol. Monog.,* 1932, 42, No. 192.) It is evident that in broadcasting it is not primarily factual items that are retained by the listener. It is rather the *pattern* of his consciousness that is affected.

type of material (except in exposition, where only four examples were used). The presentation was so arranged that each group received the same number of passages written with short and long sentences. The experiments were scattered over several days and interspersed with experiments of a different nature. The order of presentation was as follows:

Group I	Group II
Short (Directions A)	*Long* (Directions A)
Long (Lost-found ad A)	*Short* (Lost-found ad A)
Short (Exposition A)	*Long* (Exposition A)
Long (Directions B)	*Short* (Directions B)
Short (Lost-found ad B)	*Long* (Lost-found ad B)
Long (Exposition B)	*Short* (Exposition B)
Short (Directions C)	*Long* (Directions C)
Long (Lost-found ad C)	*Short* (Lost-found ad C)
Short (Exposition C)	*Long* (Exposition C)

After hearing a passage, the subjects were instructed to answer the following questions in their record booklets:

1. (*For all types*) How well do you think you understood the directions?

_____ extremely well
_____ very well
_____ fairly well (average)
_____ slightly
_____ not at all

2. (*For exposition only*) How interesting was this presentation?

_____ extremely
_____ very
_____ fairly (average)
_____ slightly
_____ not at all

After answering these questions the subjects were instructed to turn to the next sheet in their record booklets where they found questions based on the passage they had just heard. For example, after the reading of the passage given above, the following questions were given:

(a) Do you go north or south at Sterling Avenue?
(b) How far do you follow the car tracks?
(c) What do you look for one-quarter of a mile beyond the Harbor Island station?

Results. The mean ratings on the comprehensibility and interest of the passages were obtained by weighting the answers as in the experiment previously reported. The completion tests used in the comparison of the two presentations for the *same* type of material were always identical. The number of items on the test, however, varied with the type of material and the mean scores obtained by one group on the tests (as shown in Table XXXVII) should be compared only with the mean scores obtained by the other group for *the same type* of material. Group I again tended to rate the passages higher in comprehensibility and to do better than Group II in the completion tests. The figures represent the results obtained after correcting for the 7 per cent higher rating of Group I on comprehension and its 7 per cent superiority on the tests.

TABLE XXXVII

MEAN RATINGS AND SCORES OBTAINED FOR SHORT AND LONG SENTENCES

Length of sentences	Material	Group	How well subjects thought they understood the passage	How interesting the passage was	Scores on completion tests
Short	Directions	I	0.82		1.72
Long	A	II	0.86		1.41
Long	Directions	I	2.79		3.26
Short	B	II	2.77		3.17
Short	Directions	I	1.31		1.59
Long	C	II	1.38		1.26
Long	Lost-found	I	2.45		10.56
Short	ad A	II	1.66		10.97
Short	Lost-found	I	2.55		9.96
Long	ad B	II	2.26		9.63
Long	Lost-found	I	2.63		7.57
Short	ad C	II	2.55		8.00
Short	Exposition	I	2.33	2.18	1.79
Long	A	II	2.69	2.31	2.09
Long	Exposition	I	2.41	2.32	3.07
Short	B	II	2.21	2.15	3.03

The general tendencies in Table XXXVII may be summarized as follows:

1. Passages of *exposition* are more interesting when *long* sentences are used.
2. *Directions* were more accurately remembered in two experiments out of three when they were broadcast in *short* sentences. In the third experiment the difference is slightly in favor of long sentences.
3. *Lost and found ads* were in every case more correctly remembered when the presentation was in the form of *short* sentences.
4. Exposition was recalled more accurately when presented in *long* sentences.

General conclusion. When the material presented has no intrinsic interest and is of a highly factual nature, the use of short sentences increases its memory-value. The greater effectiveness of short sentences disappears as the material becomes more interesting and more unified.

3. *What is the optimum speed for broadcasting different types of material?* Almost all previous investigations of this problem have compared the speeds of ordinary public broadcasts with listeners' judgments of the effectiveness of these broadcasts. In such studies it is impossible to control other factors (e.g., difficulty and interest) that may also affect the ratings. Only by the use of experimental broadcasting can these disturbing factors be controlled.

Method. The announcer read the same passage slowly to one group and rapidly to the other group. Since four examples of each type of material were used in different experiments, it was possible to test the effectiveness of eight different speeds (four "fast" and four "slow") for the same type of material. The time taken for each reading was recorded.

Six types of material were broadcast: theoretical passages (psychology, philosophy, etc.), arguments (political, economic, etc.), factual material (history, etc.), directions, news, and narratives. The four samples of each type of material were of approximately the same length and the same degree of difficulty. The different *types* of material, however, varied considerably in their interest and comprehensibility; viz., the theoretical passages were more difficult than the arguments, while the arguments were more difficult than the news or narratives. Both groups received two examples of each type of material at a fast speed and two examples at a slow speed. The order of presentation is indicated below.

Group I	Group II
Slow (Theoretic A)	*Fast* (Theoretic A)
Fast (Argument A)	*Slow* (Argument A)
Slow (Factual A)	*Fast* (Factual A)
Fast (Directions A)	*Slow* (Directions A)
Slow (News A)	*Fast* (News A)
Fast (Narrative A)	*Slow* (Narrative A)
Fast (Theoretic B)	*Slow* (Theoretic B)
Slow (Argument B)	*Fast* (Argument B)
Fast (Factual B)	*Slow* (Factual B)
Slow (Directions B)	*Fast* (Directions B)
Fast (News B)	*Slow* (News B)
Slow (Narrative B)	*Fast* (Narrative B)
Slow (Theoretic C)	*Fast* (Theoretic C)

Fast (Argument C)	*Slow* (Argument C)
Slow (Factual C)	*Fast* (Factual C)
Fast (Directions C)	*Slow* (Directions C)
Slow (News C)	*Fast* (News C)
Fast (Narrative C)	*Slow* (Narrative C)
Fast (Theoretic D)	*Slow* (Theoretic D)
Slow (Argument D)	*Fast* (Argument D)
Fast (Factual D)	*Slow* (Factual D)
Slow (Directions D)	*Fast* (Directions D)
Fast (News D)	*Slow* (News D)
Slow (Narrative D)	*Fast* (Narrative D)

At the end of each reading the subjects answered the following questions:

1. (*For all types of material*) How well do you think you understood the material presented in this talk?

    _____ extremely
    _____ very
    _____ fairly (average)
    _____ slightly
    _____ not at all

2. (*For all types of material*) In your opinion was the passage read too fast _____, too slowly _____, or at just the right speed _____?

3. (*For all types except directions*) How interesting was the material?

    _____ extremely
    _____ very
    _____ fairly (average)
    _____ slightly
    _____ not at all

4. (*For arguments only*) How convincing was the argument?

    _____ extremely
    _____ very
    _____ fairly
    _____ slightly
    _____ not at all

After the *directions* and *factual material* the subjects were also tested for their knowledge of the material read.

Results. The figures in Table XXXVIII indicate the mean ratings of the subjects on the comprehensibility, interest, and persuasiveness of the passages. Comparisons of the results on the completion tests should be made only between the presentations of the *same* material. The maximum possible score on each is three. All figures have been corrected for the 3 per cent higher rating of Group I on comprehensibility, its

TABLE XXXVIII

MEAN RATINGS AND SCORES OBTAINED FOR DIFFERENT SPEEDS OF BROADCASTING

Speed (words per minute)	Material	Group	How well subjects thought they understood passage	How interesting passage was	How convincing passage was	Scores obtained on completion tests
Slow 84	Theoretic A	I	1.97	2.15		
Fast 222		II	1.40	1.66		
Fast 198	Theoretic B	I	1.62	1.12		
Slow 120		II	1.74	1.57		
Slow 84	Theoretic C	I	1.29	1.34		
Fast 162		II	1.09	1.32		
Fast 156	Theoretic D	I	1.25	1.26		
Slow 84		II	1.09	1.21		
Fast 192	Argument A	I	2.43	2.43	2.13	
Slow 96		II	3.14	2.63	2.31	
Slow 126	Argument B	I	2.11	2.02	1.58	
Fast 186		II	2.37	1.91	1.21	
Fast 180	Argument C	I	2.61	2.14	1.57	
Slow 108		II	2.45	2.12	1.64	
Slow 102	Argument D	I	1.85	1.52	1.43	
Fast 192		II	1.67	1.55	1.45	
Slow 90	Factual A	I	2.69	2.62		1.72
Fast 168		II	2.43	1.97		1.66
Fast 192	Factual B	I	1.97	1.80		0.71
Slow 120		II	2.37	2.03		1.29
Slow 84	Factual C	I	2.63	2.01		1.60
Fast 138		II	2.26	2.00		1.21

TABLE XXXVIII—Concluded

MEAN RATINGS AND SCORES OBTAINED FOR DIFFERENT SPEEDS OF BROADCASTING

Speed (words per minute)	Material	Group	How well subjects thought they understood passage	How interesting passage was	How convincing passage was	Scores obtained on completion tests
Fast 156	Factual E	I	2.49	2.12		1.02
Slow 84		II	2.22	1.94		1.15
Fast 222	Directions A	I	1.27			0.92
Slow 114		II	2.21			0.97
Slow 114	Directions B	I	2.66			1.68
Fast 216		II	2.00			1.23
Fast 138	Directions C	I	2.00			1.50
Slow 84		II	2.21			1.91
Slow 90	Directions D	I	2.52			2.20
Fast 254		II	2.13			1.88
Slow 120	News A	I	2.81	2.46		
Fast 210		II	2.17	2.14		
Fast 210	News B	I	2.38	1.80		
Slow 120		II	2.63	2.03		
Slow 90	News C	I	2.88	2.31		
Fast 138		II	2.42	2.09		
Fast 192	News D	I	2.69	1.90		
Slow 84		II	2.70	1.82		
Fast 240	Narrative A	I	2.51	1.42		
Slow 126		II	3.26	1.40		
Slow 120	Narrative B	I	2.26	1.78		
Fast 216		II	1.97	1.71		
Fast 180	Narrative C	I	2.31	1.51		
Slow 114		II	2.62	1.79		
Slow 60	Narrative D	I	2.27	1.08		
Fast 120		II	2.52	1.94		

5 per cent higher rating on the interest of the passages, and its 8 per cent higher average on the completion tests.

The subjects' opinions of the various speeds are shown in Table XXXIX. The figures represent percentages of the total number of subjects listening to the broadcasts (approximately 80).

The main tendencies revealed in Tables XXXVIII and XXXIX are summarized below. The optimum speed for broadcasting a particular type of material was considered to be that speed at which the comprehensibility and interest of a passage and the subjects' opinion of the speed, considered together, were maximum.

Theoretical (abstract) material

1. These passages are well understood within a wide range of speeds. When the passages are unusually difficult to comprehend, the majority feel that even such a slow speed as 84 words per minute is not too slow, while if the material is comparatively easy to understand, the speed may safely be increased to 160 words per minute.
2. A relatively slow speed tends to make the passages more interesting.
3. The *optimum speed* for broadcasting theoretical material seems to be around 110 to 130 words per minute.

Arguments

1. Arguments are judged to be more convincing if they are given slowly (from 96 to 126 words per minute).
2. Although a slow speed seems to make for greater convincingness, when the comprehensibility and interest of the passage and the subjects' opinions of the speed are also considered the *optimum speed* for broadcasting argumentative material seems to be around 140 to 170 words per minute. This comparatively fast time is satisfactory probably because arguments gain in unity if the various points they contain are swiftly related.

Factual exposition

1. Comprehension is good between the speeds of 90 and 160 words per minute.
2. The interest of factual material varies with its comprehensibility.
3. The scores on all the completion tests were higher after the broadcasts at slow speeds.
4. The *optimum speed* for broadcasting factual material of the type used seems to be around 120 to 140 words per minute.

TABLE XXXIX

LISTENERS' OPINION OF DIFFERENT RATES OF SPEED IN BROADCASTING

Type of material	Speed (words per minute)	Too fast	Just right	Too slow
Theoretic	84	0	67	33
	84	0	77	23
	84	3	59	38
	120	0	91	9
	156	57	43	0
	162	3	97	0
	198	77	23	0
	222	94	6	0
Argument	96	0	46	54
	102	0	63	37
	108	0	45	55
	126	0	64	36
	180	17	83	0
	186	51	49	0
	192	52	45	3
	192	92	8	0
Factual	84	0	53	47
	84	3	74	23
	90	3	62	35
	120	3	76	21
	138	27	73	0
	156	51	49	0
	168	51	49	0
	192	87	13	0
Directions	84	0	73	27
	90	0	94	6
	114	0	90	10
	114	6	85	9
	138	40	60	0
	216	79	21	0
	222	85	15	0
	254	71	29	0
News	84	0	12	88
	90	0	34	66
	120	0	63	37
	120	0	74	26
	138	30	61	9
	192	69	31	0
	210	52	48	0
	210	72	28	0
Narrative	60	0	11	89
	114	0	37	63
	120	0	54	46
	120	21	79	0
	126	0	71	29
	180	33	64	3
	216	76	24	0
	240	92	8	0

Directions

1. The ratings on comprehensibility were always greater for the slow broadcasts.
2. The completion tests show a consistent superiority for the slower broadcasts.
3. The *optimum speed* for broadcasting directions seems to be around 90 to 115 words per minute.

News

1. The combined ratings on both comprehensibility and interest are higher for the relatively slow speeds.
2. The *optimum speed* for broadcasting news reports seems to be around 120 to 140 words per minute.

Narrative

1. Comprehensibility is rated higher for the slower speeds, although the interest in narratives is maintained even if the speed is as high as 240 words per minute.
2. The *optimum speed* for broadcasting narratives seems to be around 120 to 150 words per minute.

General conclusions. Broadcasts are usually felt to be more comprehensible and more interesting if given at relatively slow speeds. Completion tests show that material containing definite facts is better remembered when broadcast slowly. The effectiveness of difficult passages (certain theoretical material and directions) is not greatly decreased even if the speed is reduced to 84 words per minute, while material which is readily comprehensible (news, narratives) rapidly loses its interest and is consequently less well understood if broadcast too slowly (less than 120 words per minute). Although the best speed for broadcasting depends upon the clarity of the speaker's diction, the difficulty of the material, and the attentiveness of the listener, still, if a rough rule is desired, the speaker may place his rate within the ranges suggested.

4. *What is the value of repetition in broadcasting?* In his book on the audience, Hollingworth concludes that "among the special devices usable in oral delivery by way of emphasis, the most effective, though not the most economical, is repetition, to the extent of three or more assertions."[13] Whether or not this conclusion holds for the radio audience as well as for the assembled audience remains to be determined.

Method. One audience received a passage written without any repe-

[13] H. L. Hollingworth, *The Psychology of the Audience.* New York: American Book Co., 1935, 107.

tition while the other audience heard the same passage with the main points repeated. Six types of material were used: theoretical passages, factual passages, advertisements, lost and found ads, exposition, and news items. Each type of material was represented by four passages, two texts written in two different ways. The following pair of passages is typical.

(Factual straight)

Seattle is the largest city of the Pacific Northwest. It is the county seat of King County, Washington, and is located on the east side of Puget Sound. Its harbor is one of the largest and deepest landlocked ports in the United States. In 1916 the Washington customs district became second to New York in the value of foreign trade and Seattle commerce then amounted to over half a billion dollars annually. Seattle handled over 50 per cent of the entire Pacific Coast foreign commerce. Because of its location it is the nearest United States port to China, Japan, the Philippines and Siberia and is the gateway to Alaska. Direct steamship lines, both freight and passenger, are maintained to these countries. In 1900 the population of Seattle was 80,671; since then the population has nearly quadrupled. In 1920 it was 315,000. Besides its maritime activities, Seattle has many industries, including shipyards, foundries, mills, meat packing and fish canning. The chief exports are coal, lumber, meat, fruit, wheat and hops.

(Factual repeat)

Because its harbor is one of the largest and deepest landlocked ports in the United States, Seattle, the county seat of King County, Washington, is the largest city of the Pacific Northwest. Seattle is the nearest United States port to China, Japan, the Philippines and Siberia, and is the gateway to Alaska. Seattle is situated on the east side of Puget Sound. The population of Seattle has nearly quadrupled since 1900, and it is now the largest city of the Pacific Northwest. The 1920 population was 315,000. The development of Seattle was due to its location. Few cities in the United States have access to larger or deeper protected harbors. Direct steamship lines, carrying passengers as well as freight, are maintained between Seattle and Siberia, the Philippine Islands, China and Japan, for which countries Seattle is the nearest seaport in the United States. In 1918 Seattle became second to New York as a port, its commerce amounting to over half a billion dollars annually, and consisting of more than 50 per cent of all the Pacific Coast trade. Besides being important as a shipping center, carrying freight and passengers by regular steamship lines to and from the Orient, and serving also as the gateway to Alaska, Seattle has many industries, including shipyards, foundries, mills, meat packing and fish canning. The population of Seattle in 1900 was only 80,671; in 1920 it was 315,000, so that it has nearly quadrupled since the beginning of the century. The chief exports are coal, lumber, meat, fruit, wheat and hops. Together with imports, the value of this trade has risen steadily to over 50 per cent of all the trade of the Pacific Coast. The commerce of Seattle was valued in money at more than a half billion dollars in 1918; and Seattle became second in importance to New York as a port. The inhabitants of Seattle, numbering only 80,671 in 1900, maintain shipbuilding and canning industries, work in mills and foundries, and pack meat for export. Other agricultural products, such as fruit, hops and wheat are exported, and much coal and lumber passes through the city. Seattle is located on the east shore of Puget Sound and is the county seat of King County, Washington.

The order of the experiments was so arranged that each group received both a simple and a repetitive passage for each type of material.

Group I	Group II
Straight (Theoretical A)	Repeat (Theoretical A)
Repeat (Factual A)	Straight (Factual A)
Straight (Advertisement A)	Repeat (Advertisement A)
Repeat (Lost-found A)	Straight (Lost-found A)
Straight (Exposition A)	Repeat (Exposition A)
Repeat (News A)	Straight (News A)
Repeat (Theoretical B)	Straight (Theoretical B)
Straight (Factual B)	Repeat (Factual B)
Repeat (Advertisement B)	Straight (Advertisement B)
Straight (Lost-found B)	Repeat (Lost-found B)
Repeat (Exposition B)	Straight (Exposition B)
Straight (News B)	Repeat (News B)

At the completion of each passage the subjects answered the following questions:

1. (*For all types*) How well do you think you understood this passage?

    _____ extremely well
    _____ very well
    _____ fairly well (average)
    _____ slightly
    _____ not at all

2. (*All types except lost and found ads.*) How interesting was this passage?

    _____ extremely
    _____ very
    _____ fairly (average)
    _____ slightly
    _____ not at all

3. (*For all types*) Do you think there was too much repetition?

    Yes _____   No _____

4. (*For all types*) Would you have understood this broadcast better if there had been more repetition?

Yes _____   No _____

After the *factual* material, *exposition, lost and found ads,* and *advertisements,* the subjects also answered a short completion test on the passage just heard. For example, the test for the passage cited above was:

a. What was the value of the commerce handled in Seattle in 1918?
b. What was the population of Seattle in 1900?
c. Seattle is the county seat of what county?

Results. The ratings on the comprehensibility and interest of the passages were obtained as in the above experiments. Each completion test contained a different number of items to be answered and a test score should be compared only with the mean score of the other group on the *same* passage. All of the figures in Table XL have been corrected for the higher rating of Group I on comprehensibility (7 per cent), on interest (9 per cent), and for its general superiority in the tests (8 per cent).

TABLE XL

MEAN RATINGS AND SCORES FOR THE EFFECT OF REPETITION

Presentation	Material	Group	How well subjects thought they understood passage	How interesting the passage was	Scores on completion tests	Was there too much repetition? Yes	No	Was more repetition desirable? Yes	No
Straight	Theoretic A	I	2.27	1.77		27	73	25	75
Repeat		II	2.46	1.43		85	15	5	95
Repeat	Theoretic B	I	2.40	2.00		17	83	8	92
Straight		II	2.26	1.91		0	100	9	91
Repeat	Factual A	I	2.57	1.88	1.69	84	16	13	83
Straight		II	2.60	2.23	1.58	3	97	9	91
Straight	Factual B	I	2.03	1.56	1.27	3	97	33	67
Repeat		II	2.15	1.69	1.84	72	28	9	91
Straight	Advertisement A	I	3.02	1.85	0.29	5	95	3	97
Repeat		II	3.00	1.37	0.43	55	45	0	100
Repeat	Advertisement B	I	2.87	1.70	0.32	16	84	5	95
Straight		II	2.91	1.91	0.00	3	97	15	85
Repeat	Lost-found ad A	I	2.74		4.91	29	81	16	84
Straight		II	2.31		4.36	3	97	39	61
Straight	Lost-found ad B	I	2.66		2.22	0	100	30	70
Repeat		II	2.91		2.64	42	58	6	94
Straight	Exposition A	I	2.29	2.08	2.13	5	95	25	75
Repeat		II	2.57	2.26	2.23	48	52	6	94
Repeat	Exposition B	I	2.32	1.94	2.29	33	67	16	84
Straight		II	2.15	2.03	1.97	3	97	14	86
Repeat	News A	I	2.85	1.98		45	55	10	90
Straight		II	2.86	2.14		0	100	6	94
Straight	News B	I	2.88	2.04		0	100	5	95
Repeat		II	2.79	2.09		60	40	3	97

Table XL reveals the following tendencies.

1. In 67 per cent of the cases, the passages which contained *repe-*

tition were judged to be *more comprehensible*. This was especially true in the *theoretical* passages and the *lost and found ads*. The other 33 per cent of the comparisons show small differences. *News* broadcasts give the impression of being equally well understood in either method of presentation.

2. Sixty per cent of the passages were judged to be more *interesting* if they contained *no repetition*.

3. All of the mean scores on the *completion tests* were higher when the passages broadcast contained repetition.

4. In general, the subjects felt that the passages containing repetition were *too* repetitious. This was especially true for factual material, news, and advertisements.

5. Repetition was held most useful in the lost and found ads, factual material, and exposition. In news reports and advertising it was felt to be undesirable.

General conclusion. Repetition tends to make a broadcast uninteresting. The majority dislike it, and feel that it does not help them understand the broadcasts better. Nevertheless, the ratings obtained on the comprehensibility of the passages as well as the scores on the completion tests prove that repetition facilitates comprehension and aids memory.

5. *How do broadcasts of different lengths on the same subject compare in effectiveness?*

Method. In these studies only two different time intervals were compared and it was impracticable to employ long broadcasts. One audience heard a talk lasting three minutes and the other audience heard the same talk expanded into ten minutes. The prepared passages were of approximately the same interest and degree of difficulty. Three types of material were used: factual, argumentative, and simple exposition (elementary chemistry or physics). Two samples of each type of material were used. Each sample was written so that the same material consumed three minutes when presented to one group and ten when presented to the other group. The broadcasts were so arranged that each group heard one ten-minute passage and one three-minute passage devoted to each type of material.

Group I		Group II	
3 min.	(Exposition A)	10 min.	(Exposition A)
10 "	(Factual A)	3 "	(Factual A)
3 "	(Argument A)	10 "	(Argument A)
10 "	(Exposition B)	3 "	(Exposition B)
3 "	(Factual B)	10 "	(Factual B)
10 "	(Argument B)	3 "	(Argument B)

After each broadcast the subjects answered the following questions:

1. How well do you think you understood the passage?

_____ extremely well

_____ very well

_____ fairly well (average)

_____ slightly

_____ not at all

2. How interesting was the talk?

_____ extremely

_____ very

_____ fairly (average)

_____ slightly

_____ not at all

3. Do you think this talk was about the right length_____, too long_____, or too short_____?

A completion test was given after the *factual* material had been broadcast. All figures in Table XLI have been corrected for the 8 per cent higher rating of Group I on comprehensibility, 5 per cent higher rating on interest, and 9 per cent better performance on the completion tests. The judgments of the subjects on the lengths of the passages are expressed in percentages.

At the end of these experiments the subjects were asked to give their opinions regarding the proper length for talks on various subjects.

TABLE XLI

MEAN RATINGS AND SCORES OBTAINED FOR BROADCASTS OF DIFFERENT LENGTHS

Length	Material	Group	How well subjects thought they understood passage	How interesting the passage was	Scores on completion tests	Too long	Just right	Too short
3 min.	Exposition A	I	2.63	2.85		3	82	15
10 min.		II	2.80	3.14		12	82	6
10 min.	Exposition B	I	2.79	2.86		22	22	2
3 min.		II	2.64	2.48		0	76	24
10 min.	Factual A	I	2.16	1.76	5.31	65	35	0
3 min.		II	2.06	2.09	4.51	39	55	6
3 min.	Factual B	I	2.31	1.98	6.03	18	79	3
10 min.		II	2.30	2.06	6.82	47	53	0
3 min.	Argument A	I	2.45	2.43		0	88	12
10 min.		II	2.57	2.34		64	33	3
10 min.	Argument B	I	2.66	2.44		68	32	0
3 min.		II	2.67	2.36		3	88	9

Interpretation of Table XLI:

1. The ten-minute talks were judged to be more comprehensible than the three-minute talks in 67 per cent of the comparisons. The passages of exposition were rated consistently higher when

broadcast in the ten-minute length. Only small differences were found between the ratings on the two lengths for arguments and factual passages.

2. There was a slight tendency to rate the ten-minute talks as more interesting. This was especially true for the passages of exposition.

3. Factual material was better remembered if it was expanded to ten minutes rather than broadcast in a three-minute length.

4. The docility of most listeners is shown in their tendency to be satisfied with whatever length is employed.

TABLE XLII

OPINIONS OF OPTIMUM LENGTH FOR VARIOUS TYPES OF RADIO TALKS

(*Percentage of judgments*)

Type of material	3 min.	5 min.	10 min.	15 min.	30 min.	1 hr.	
Political talks......	7	11	26	29	11	16	100
Educational talks...	3	16	26	34	13	8	100
News reports.......	13	13	34	34	3	3	100
Drama...........	4	1	6	21	51	14	100
Religious talks.....	6	16	19	25	11	23	100
Stories...........	3	4	18	35	25	15	100

Table XLII gives the opinions of the listeners on the proper length for broadcasts of various types. If these judgments are pooled for each type of material, we find that the lengths best suited to the group as a whole are:

News reports...........12 minutes
Educational talks.......17 minutes
Political talks..........21 minutes
Religious talks.........24 minutes
Stories................24 minutes
Drama................28 minutes

General conclusion. Although we cannot assume that the listener's attitude in the laboratory is the same as his attitude in the home, and although in this investigation we could not reproduce all types of talks at various lengths, we were able to determine the extent to which comprehensibility and interest were affected when different types of material were compressed into a three-minute length or expanded into ten minutes. The experimental findings and the listeners' opinions concerning the lengths of the laboratory broadcasts and the optimum lengths for regular radio talks point to the same general conclusion, namely, that although a long radio talk allows for greater elucidation of the topic under discussion, the fact that the listener tends to lose interest in longer talks may counterbalance any intrinsic effectiveness gained by an expansion in length. If interest can be maintained (as in drama) or if the listener is already favorably disposed to the talk (as are some persons toward sermons), then an increase in length will enhance the effectiveness. If the speaker is not unusually interesting, if the topic under discussion is not vital to the listener, or if he is not enthusiastically predisposed to the type of material to be broadcast, then greater effectiveness is achieved if the talk is relatively short. The optimum length of time for ordinary educational, political, factual, or news broadcasts is probably from ten to twenty minutes. Even as popular a radio speaker as President Roosevelt chooses, probably wisely, to confine his fireside chats on political topics to approximately twenty minutes.

The interdependence of interest and comprehensibility apparent in this experiment and in other studies reported in this chapter is of considerable theoretic significance. It shows the futility of studying learning or comprehension when the interest of the material is "held constant" by the use of nonsense syllables. In everyday life people deal only with meaningful material, some of which interests them and some of which does not. If even the simplest material is found to be uninteresting, it will probably be absorbed slowly if at all. The classical laboratory experiments on learning made by Ebbinghaus, Meumann, Radossawljewitsch, and others are hopelessly inadequate in the study of learning as it occurs in everyday life. The village simpleton may be found to know all the season's baseball scores; the college professor, on the other hand, could learn them only with considerable effort unless he himself were a baseball fan. Eisenberg found that the radio programs children remember are generally the same as those they prefer.[14] Similarly in a study of moving pictures, Holaday and Stoddard found that if a movie is interesting, a child will remember a great deal; if it is dull, he remembers little or nothing.[15] The effectiveness of any method of presentation depends, therefore, above all else on the interest aroused in the listener by the subject matter.

The experimental results reported in this chapter should not, of course, be followed blindly. Every broadcast has its special purpose and its characteristic requirements. The broadcaster interested in applying these results should refer to the next four chapters, where the experience of studios and informal studies of listeners' reactions are combined with our experimental findings to help in the solution of certain practical problems.

[14] Azriel L. Eisenberg, *Children and Radio Programs.* New York: Teachers College Bureau of Publications, 1935.

[15] P. W. Holaday and G. D. Stoddard, *Getting Ideas from the Movies.* New York: Macmillan, 1933.

PART III

PRACTICAL INTERPRETATIONS

Chapter XI

BROADCASTING

NOT all of the practical problems of radio have as yet been brought into the psychological laboratory; many of them never will be. The experiments reported, for example, deal exclusively with spoken material and not at all with music; even the spoken material we have employed has been perforce relatively simple and straightforward—no drama, no interviews, no exhortation, no political speeches, and no variety programs. At the present time such broadcasts have too complex a structure for experimentation.

Incomplete though they are, our studies contain some lessons of practical significance for the announcer, the program maker, the advertiser, the actor, the educator, and the listener. In the present chapter and in the three immediately following we shall discuss these practical applications and in so doing shall draw not only upon our own experiments, but upon discoveries of other investigators, and upon the everyday experience of broadcasters and listeners.

THE BROADCASTER

The profession of broadcasting has great fascination for the public. Stations are besieged by untrained aspirants hoping to make an entrance. A retail merchant in Boston sponsored an amateur hour, and 2,200 candidates appeared at the studio clamoring for a chance to be heard. Since only 26 could be given time at the microphone, the experiment was repeated the following week in a downtown theater crowded with spectators. This time the number of applicants was 3,000! Thereafter, the program became a weekly feature. One amateur singer in a similar program in New York City received 2,206 telephone calls of congratulation at the studio over specially installed lines. But one has only to listen to the dreadful attempts of most amateurs to realize the great gulf that separates them from professional broadcasters who possess native gifts and sound training. First-rate talent is rare; only a negligible fraction of the aspirants possess even the elementary qualifications for success. Each year one network holds announcer's auditions for approximately three hundred applicants of whom not more than ten are finally employed. These ten, it turns out, almost invariably have had previous vocal training either for the stage or for singing.

There are several psychological considerations—seven, to be exact—

that should interest anyone who is seriously concerned with the qualifications of successful announcers.

(1) First of all, we know that the average listener prefers male speakers. To a certain degree this preference may be due to the lower pitch of the male voice which makes it more agreeable in mechanical transmission. The higher frequencies of the sound waves, particularly of the partials, produced by the feminine voice create difficulties for all but the finest devices involved in recording, transmitting, and receiving. But since the mechanics of the process have already been fairly well perfected, most of the preference is due not to mechanical factors, but to various forms of antagonism and prejudice (pp. 136ff.). The outstanding complaint against women is that they "put on" a radio voice and therefore seem self-conscious and affected.

In favor of feminine announcers we find that their voices, though not usually judged to be as persuasive or as natural as men's are nevertheless regarded as higher in aesthetic value and are preferred for the reading of poetry and other material of an artistic and reflective nature. Men's voices are favored for material of a matter-of-fact variety—for news and weather reports, political speeches, and lectures. When women take part as singers, commentators, or actresses, the contralto voice is almost always preferred to the soprano (p. 102). Some advertisers featuring cosmetics and household appliances prefer feminine announcers, but apart from the specific demands created by the program there are few exceptions to the general rule that broadcasting is a masculine profession.

(2) From the listener's point of view affectation is the unpardonable sin of broadcasting. Both men and women agree that the female announcer more often sounds affected than the male, but women are more critical of this trait in their own sex than are men. Although men dislike affectation in a woman's voice, they are even quicker to condemn the same quality in the male voice. In other words, insincerity is never welcome, but when it appears in an announcer's voice it is viewed somewhat more tolerantly by members of the opposite sex.

(3) Actually it is only the *impression* the voice conveys that matters to the listener, and it is for this reason that the trained voice is almost always more successful than the untrained. Curiously enough, an insincere actor is often able to create more of an impression of honest conviction than an earnest but untrained speaker. A voice well in control, one that has had to simulate many parts and express all manner of uncongenial ideas, is best adapted to the varied demands of the radio. Although he may possess conviction and authentic emotion, the untrained speaker before the microphone is likely to fall into a variety

of errors, often attempting to adopt what he thinks is the proper vocal expression, and for his pains he is considered affected.

(4) Although the trained speaker can mask his voice and produce almost any effect he chooses, it may still be possible for the listener to detect certain of his personal traits. But the detection is much more successful in the case of untrained speakers. Traits such as dominance, introversion, professional and social interests are on the whole judged more correctly than such physical features as height (cf. Chap. VI).

Age is judged with fair accuracy over the air; less successfully in the cases of very young or very old speakers. Stations, of course, have no interest in the true ages of the actors they employ, but they realize none the less that voice does betray age. In their dramatic programs they almost always (probably in 90 per cent of the cases) employ actors who are within ten years of the age of the character they portray. There are, of course, a few striking exceptions in instances where adults have extraordinarily flexible or eccentric voices, as in the case of the fat man whose specialty is crying like a baby.

The majority of listeners wonder what sort of person the announcer is; they frequently create for themselves an imaginary picture of his physical appearance and his personal traits. Although a fair proportion of these judgments is correct, they are almost certain to result in a stereotyped portrait conforming to various preconceived ideas of what "type" of voice goes with what "type" of person. For example, the listener may correctly detect from voice that a certain speaker has marked aesthetic interests, but he may then erroneously extend this judgment to include an image of a slender, blond, pale, and delicate individual with communistic leanings and sideburns. Such stereotyped additions are more likely to be wrong than right. Purely imaginary attributes (unfortunately not recognized by the listener as imaginary) cluster about a core of sound judgment, and form portraits only partially reliable.

(5) Broadcasters know that they should match the voice to the message. In other words, they know that the stereotype created by the voice (whether a true representation of the speaker or not) should harmonize with the program. The sponsors of a certain yeast hour choose a speaker whose voice suggests the dignity and authority of a physician. A sensational newspaper selects an announcer whose voice sounds emotional, restless, tense with confidences to be revealed. A sedate newspaper, on the other hand, employs an unperturbed, precise speaker who creates an impression of conservatism and incorruptibility. And who could be better chosen than Mother Schumann-Heink to present the merits of a patented baby food?

(6) Standard diction and accurate pronunciation are required of every announcer. Dialect, foreign or regional accent, ungrammatical speech are permitted only if they are deliberate importations to fit the needs of a special program. Broadcasters must have an alert interest in linguistic standards and in the art of speech; they must also have an education better than average, particularly if they are called upon to frame impromptu messages. Proper names are especially exacting, and the way in which they are announced tells a subtle tale about the speaker's cultural background, and indirectly reflects upon his employer. Here are some of the telltale names commonly mispronounced:

> La Follette
> Zuider Zee
> Saint-Saëns
> Roosevelt
> Van Loon
> Chopin
> Goebbels
> Wagner (composer)
> Tschaikowsky

Musical terms are often fatal tongue twisters for the announcer. Without musical sophistication and flexible speech he would almost certainly have trouble with:

chorale	chanson
concerto	cachucha
pizzicato	aria di bravura
cantabile	bourrée
maestoso	mazurka
chaconne	Konzertstück
capriccio	

Some of the most popular numbers in musical programs cause difficulty; for example

Scheherazade	La cathédrale engloutie
Kamennoi Ostrow	L'oiseau de feu
Träumerei	Kinderszenen
Passacaglia	Götterdämmerung
Ständchen	Malagueña
La Marseillaise	Åse's Tod
Petrouchka	

Although each station has its method of trying out the voice and speech of applicants, the audition for announcers consists generally of script involving just such terms and titles, drawn from commercial, news, and musical continuities.

Sometimes announcers are employed whose voices are highly individualistic and deviate from the accepted standard. Judging from fan mail, such voices elicit strong affective responses of one sort or another. Some listeners like the voice for its originality, for its refinement or its "interesting" quality; others condemn it out of hand for its affectation and eccentricity. Generally speaking, unusual voices of any type are hazardous unless, of course, the nature of the program demands them.

(7) Speakers other than professional announcers differ strikingly in their ability to attract and to hold the radio audience. Many admirable orators, trained to address exacting audiences, feel lost (and sound lost) before the microphone. The elder La Follette relied so largely upon gestures and upon inspiration from visible auditors that he was virtually helpless in broadcasting.

By contrast, there is the tremendously successful Fireside Chat instituted by President Roosevelt. His manner is informal, intimate and sincere, paternal and reassuring; he seems simultaneously to be both master and servant of the people. Such at least is the report that many listeners give. Dos Passos has described the effect:[1]

There is a man leaning across his desk, speaking clearly and cordially to youandme, painstakingly explaining how he's sitting at his desk there in Washington, leaning towards youandme across his desk, speaking clearly and cordially so that youandme shall completely understand that he sits at his desk there in Washington with his fingers on all the switchboards of the federal government, operating the intricate machinery of the departments, drafting codes and regulations and bills for the benefit of youandme, worried about things, sitting close to the radio in small houses on rainy nights, for the benefit of us wage earners, us homeowners, us farmers, us mechanics, us miners, us mortgagees, us processors, us mortgageholders, us bankdepositors, us consumers, retail merchants, bankers, brokers, stockholders, bondholders, creditors, debtors, jobless and jobholders. . . Not a sparrow falleth but. . . He is leaning cordially towards youandme, across his desk there in Washington, telling in carefully chosen words how the machinations of chisellers are to be foiled for youandme, and how the manycylindered motor of recovery is being primed with billions for youandme, and youandme understand, we belong to billions, billions belong to us, we are going to have good jobs, good pay, protected bank deposits, we edge our chairs closer to the radio, we are flattered and pleased, we feel we are right in the White House.

When the cordial explaining voice stops, we want to say: Thank you, Frank; we want to ask about the grandchildren and that dog that had to be sent away for biting a foreign diplomat. . . . *You have been listening to the President of the United States in the Blue Room.* . .

[1] John Dos Passos, "The Radio Voice," *Common Sense*, February, 1934, 17.

HOW TO BROADCAST

Preparing the Script. The speaker must realize at the outset that he is going to talk to people and not to a microphone, and that people, unlike microphones, have feelings and prejudices which he must respect. If, wittingly or unwittingly, he offends his listeners even in a minor part of the program, they are likely to reject or resent the program in it entirety. This fact creates a serious dilemma for every broadcaster, for there are innumerable, and in part unpredictable, prejudices represented by the listening public. The speaker must either water down his script until it is both innocuous and colorless, until it cannot for any reason offend any person, or else he must run the risk that the vigor, spice, or partisanship of his message will repel some of his auditors. Most speakers seem to choose the colorless method, but as a penalty they suffer reproaches for their indecisiveness and inanity. And the moral of *that* is that broadcasters should not hope to please all of the people all of the time. They might just as well risk a script that is vigorous and decisive as play safe with one that is namby-pamby. A broadcast never suits all listeners.

A dull beginning is particularly fatal, for the listener knows that the air is filled with music to be had for a slight turn of the wrist. One group of representative listeners estimated that they turned off 85 per cent of all spoken programs (excluding drama and news) before the end! In preparing his script, therefore, the speaker should not be satisfied with a talk that is only mildly interesting. Even a famous person must realize that his prominence and prestige do not give him the advantage on the air that they do in a public assembly. Every message must be compelling in its own right; it may not rely on borrowed glory.

The conventions of the spoken language rather than those of the written language must prevail. This is true even though speeches and continuity are as a rule carefully written out. Radio has hastened the demise of the old-fashioned cannonading style of oratory. Transplanted from its historic setting in the congregate crowd to the calm atmosphere of the home it usually sounds silly. Except in rare instances where definite enthusiasms prevail, appeals to emotion and prejudice are distasteful. Only clever demagogues, capitalizing on definite preëxisting attitudes and widespread discontent, can successfully use inflated oratory. Stilted speech, long and involved sentences, and a recondite vocabulary have no place on the air. Lumley has shown that the effectiveness of educational talks by radio is in inverse ratio to the number of unusual and difficult words employed.[2] What is true of educational talks is even more true of informal programs. Words should be common, though not necessarily short. Sentences should be looser and less periodic than those meant for print. The script should be written with only slight punctuation so the speaker will be free to group the words according to his own style of delivery. *Employ a conversational approach.*

Only rarely does the radio speaker choose the length of time during which his discourse shall last. Neither his wishes nor the nature of his message can offset financial considerations or the conventional units of time. However, if he has any choice in the matter at all, he should remember that time generally passes more slowly for the radio listener than for the listener who is facing the speaker, and that the listener tends to lose interest in long presentations even though they result in greater clarity of comprehension (pp. 200ff.). A speaker of great popularity and prestige, President Roosevelt, finds a period of about twenty minutes most satisfactory. All other speakers, of course, are required to observe the conventional units of time and to end their talks within the narrow limits of the assignment.

The amount of material covered in the assigned time depends upon the speaker's normal speed. In order to determine his own rate he must rehearse his script several times. Material that is readily understood may sometimes be effectively broadcast as fast as 240 words per minute, while difficult subjects may without loss of interest be broadcast as slowly as 84 words per minute (p. 196). For news broadcasts the best rate is approximately 120 to 140 words per minute. This speed is considerably slower than that generally used in actual news broadcasts. In their attempts to make the news flashy or to condense many items into a short period of time, news broadcasters frequently speak too rapidly for maximum comprehension. The optimum speed for any single broadcast depends, of course, on the clarity of the speaker's diction, the difficulty of the material, and the attentiveness of his listeners. A generally safe range for commercial, political, and descriptive broadcasts is from 120 to 160 words per minute.

If the material is comparatively abstract and difficult, the speaker may use repetition, although unless employed with subtlety it tends to reduce the listener's interest (pp. 196ff.). By varying his style, his metaphors, and his choice of words the skillful speaker handling difficult material may use the old pedagogical trick of telling his listeners what he is going to say, saying it, and then summarizing what he has said.

The speaker should be careful to vary the lengths of his sentences

[2] F. H. Lumley, "An Evaluation of Fifteen Radio Talks in Psychology by Means of Listeners' Reports," *Psychol. Bull.*, 1932, 29, 753-764.

to avoid monotony in the structure of his talk. The more difficult the material, the shorter the average sentence should be, and yet the crisp staccato sentence used effectively in broadcasting news and sports is not good for ordinary exposition (p. 189). Talks are most interesting and most comprehensible when the general ideas they contain are followed in the exposition by specific illustrations. If the speaker uses nothing but general terms, the listener loses interest and does not always understand the point under discussion. But a speech that uses only illustrations and does not "set" the listeners for its general implications appears scattered and meaningless. Only a few points can be introduced into a single radio talk and these must be plainly expressed. People listening to the radio are in many respects less critical and less analytical than they are under other circumstances (pp. 174ff.). The speaker must realize that listeners cannot easily discriminate separate points in his discourse; if he wishes them to do so, his script must be unusually explicit and orderly in its structure.

Before the Microphone. In the formidable atmosphere of the studio the novice may be seized with microphone fright, and wonder how in heaven's name he can speak naturally and intimately to the black thing in front of him. It does not relieve his embarrassment to be warned against such extraneous noises as nervous coughing, rattling his manuscript, and clearing his throat.

There is no sure preventive for microphone fright, although many of the larger companies have provided small, homelike studios where the speaker, if he chooses, may actually address a group of friends who have been imported for the occasion to sit before a fireplace containing an imitation blaze, and speak into a microphone dressed up to resemble a globe or a parlor ornament. Most of these devices for self-deception are unsound. The frightened speaker easily recognizes them for what they are—a form of artificial respiration. Experience alone will convince him that broadcasting is essentially a painless process and that self-assurance grows with practice. Rehearsing is a help, especially in a studio where he can familiarize himself with his surroundings, and where the microphone and controls can be adjusted to his voice. In some studios "echo rooms" have been installed to build up mechanically voices that are unsuited to the microphone. When such preparations have been made, the speaker has the comforting knowledge that he can rely upon expert technicians to see him through the ordeal.

It may help to visualize a small group of friends sitting at home in front of the receiving set, or else to have such a group present in the studio. Attention should not wander from this model group to the fearsome thought of "unseen multitudes." The voice will reflect interest and sincerity only so long as the speaker is absorbed in his message and directs it consistently to one small, typical group of listeners. He must articulate carefully and if possible pronounce sibilants softly; luscious s's and z's are annoying. His diction, however, must under no circumstances seem overelegant and affected. He should remember that intelligent variation in pitch and intonation is required to reflect humor, sentiment, and earnestness, and to compensate for the loss of his normal facial expression and gesture. While obeying all these rules, he must not forget the all-important hand of the clock.

The winner of the 1932 gold medal awarded by the American Academy of Arts and Letters for good diction on the air, Mr. David Ross, has summarized what he considers to be the essential principles of good announcing.[3]

(1) A clear speaking voice.

(2) An ability to enlist the voice in the service of good speech.

(3) A knowledge of the tonal quality of words and their psychological effects beyond their dictionary meaning.

(4) An announcer must first understand his continuity thoroughly before he can speak it intelligently.

(5) He must understand the effect of understatement as well as emphasis.

(6) He must never try to inflate by false accentuation what is essentially a simple, homey phrase to the proportions of grandeur. The phrase will die of pomposity.

(7) He must remember that he is talking to live human beings who have loved, struggled, laughed, dreamed, despaired and hoped; therefore his work before the microphone must reflect his human experience so that his audience will recognize it as real.

(8) He must bear in mind that the cheap wisecrack is as offensive as the direct insult.

(9) An announcer must know when he knows not, and make it his business to find out.

(10) If the announcer expects to be received into the homes of his hearers he must come with credentials of grace, sincerity and warm fellowship, and these may be found in his voice.

Arranging the Program. One eastern broadcaster once stated two rather cryptic rules for preparing programs. Never forget, he said, that radio is listened to chiefly by householders who open their own front doors and that there are many listeners west of the Hudson River. He meant, of course, that his program staff should never overlook the American middle class in town and rural areas, that programs should not be smart or snobbish, but simple and "folksy," that they should always respect homely virtues and homely prejudices.

Different, but not contradictory, advice comes from Mr. Orrin Dun-

[3] "Advice from a Medal Winner," *New York Times,* November 13, 1932.

lap who has studied the reasons for the success of radio programs having record runs. He lists twelve qualities making for success, together with illustrative programs.[4]

1. Naturalness (Amos 'n' Andy, the Goldbergs)
2. Voice personality (Bing Crosby, Alexander Woollcott)
3. Friendliness (Kate Smith, Cheerio)
4. Timeliness (March of Time, Edwin C. Hill and other commentators)
5. Diversity (Vallee revue)
6. Suspense (various serial sketches)
7. Drama (Grand Hotel, First Nighter)
8. Education (Damrosch concerts, Schelling children's concerts)
9. Melody (various dance bands)
10. Individuality (Mills Brothers, Phil Baker, Joe Penner)
11. Quality (New York Philharmonic Symphony Orchestra, Metropolitan Opera)
12. Humor (Will Rogers, Ed Wynn)

Mr. Dunlap's list calls attention to the fact that a successful program invariably has—as the phrase goes—a "personality." It is something that can be talked about and thought about. Sometimes it develops on its own merit, but more often it is "built up" through newspaper publicity, through catch phrases and theme songs, through a relationship with well-identified characters in the movies or comic strips, or with some well-known institution or theater. This demand for identifiability is the bond that ties the radio to all other forms of showmanship. But in contrast to the stage, the opera, the movies, or the circus, radio is under a severe handicap. Its program may take weeks of preparation and cost thousands of dollars, but when once performed it is forever ended. It cannot be given several nights in one city and then move on to another accumulating profits wherever it goes.

Endless novelty is demanded in programs; the microphone is voracious and the listeners insatiable; originality is always at a premium. For this reason it is impossible to lay down more definite rules for the construction of programs. There must always be continuous exploration and experimentation.

---

[4] Orrin E. Dunlap, Jr., "Reasons for Record Runs," *New York Times*, March 4, 1934.

Chapter XII

ENTERTAINMENT

MUSIC

ALTHOUGH for some people the sight of an orchestra and the social setting of the concert hall are significant parts of a musical experience, it is undoubtedly a fact that music loses little of its appeal through radio transmission. In fact its lack of dependence upon visual stimulation gives it a preëminent position among the varied offerings of radio. Music now consumes approximately 60 per cent of radio time, and is by far the most favored of all the types of program (p. 93). According to the expressed desires of listeners, the proportion of time devoted to music should be still further increased (p. 93). To be sure, a small minority of people, usually musical connoisseurs, cannot abide radio music. They complain that the mechanical transmission is imperfect and distorts the tonal values or else that the quality of music played is intolerable to their cultivated ears. But these ultrarefined protests count for little in the general chorus of popular acclaim. Music is the backbone of radio.

For most people the appeal of music is not intellectual but rather, in a certain sense of the word, "instinctive." Melody and rhythm coincide with the affective undercurrents of life expressing far better than language the basic feeling-tone—the mood, emotion, or desire—that underlies all experience. For this reason music has always played an important part in human culture, but until the advent of the radio it was impossible for people, unless they had the wealth of princes, to hear music without some kind of exertion. It was necessary to play an instrument, to go to a concert, or at least to attend to the mechanical needs of the phonograph. Now for a mere turn of the wrist melodies are available all day and most of the night.

It is important for the musical broadcaster to realize that the appeal of music does not depend upon its capacity for expressing the listener's mood of the moment. If this were so, then the success of radio music would be greatly reduced; joyful music would gratify only those who were in a joyful mood, and nostalgic music would appeal only to those caught during a reflective moment. The truth seems to be that so long as musical compositions express some feelings that are *common* to mankind, even though they may be deep-lying and for the time being quite unconscious, they are intelligible and ordinarily pleasing whatever the listener's state of mind.[1] Musical performance is allowed its own premises, as it were; it may express whatever it wishes to express and the listener will under usual circumstances both understand and appreciate the effect.

If the listener is musically unsophisticated, he will prefer especially those types of music whose emotional significance is obvious to him. He cannot mistake the feeling-tone in dance music, in a lullaby, in a sentimental home and hearth song, in a hymn or military march. Such forms of light music are immediately intelligible and ordinarily enjoyable to any person whatever his mood. It is, of course, true that among the forms of light music he enjoys, the listener's *preference* may lean in the direction dictated by his temperament or his present emotional state. The love-sick adolescent would probably select a luscious melody sung by a throaty torch singer rather than the old-time tunes of grandmother's day. His great-aunt Lucy would probably prefer "The Lost Chord" or "Tenting Tonight." But radio with its variety of simultaneous offerings is able to cope easily with such variations in taste.

Classical music, on the other hand, presents a somewhat different problem.[2] It is more subtle and individualistic in its appeal. Its intricate harmonic structure and its varying themes and changes of tempo do not readily reveal its moods to the untutored listener; its function is to express the strivings, ideals, imaginative projections, disappointments, or ecstasies of complex personalities.

In spite of their intelligibility and in spite of the pleasure they give, popular tunes soon wear out their welcome. Unless the selections are constantly changed they become stale and monotonous. No demonstrations in the laboratory were necessary to prove that popular pieces are liked best after few hearings, while classical compositions provide maximum enjoyment at later performances and retain their appeal even after numerous repetitions, nor that popular music loses its appeal more rapidly for musically trained persons than for naïve listeners.[3] Nevertheless, such are the facts, and they have important implications for program makers.

The public has been bombarded with popular music ever since radio

[1] C. C. Pratt, "Objectivity of Esthetic Value," *J. of Philosophy*, 1934, 31, 44; and M. Schoen & E. L. Gatewood, "Problems Related to the Mood Effects of Music," *The Effects of Music* (edit. by M. Schoen). New York: Harcourt, Brace, 1927, 150.

[2] The term "classical" music is employed here merely to distinguish compositions that are relatively complex from those that are obviously simple and popular.

[3] M. F. Washburn, M. S. Child, & T. M. Abel, "The Effects of Immediate Repetition on the Pleasantness or Unpleasantness of Music," *The Effects of Music*, 205; A. R. Gilliland & H. T. Moore, "The Immediate and Long-Time Effects of Classical and Popular Phonograph Selections," *Ibid.*, 220.

was introduced into the home. And since popular rhythms, melodies, and harmonies cannot be indefinitely varied the listener tends to become fatigued or bored with their repetition. Gradually he learns to tune in on fresher and more varied classical music whose "rhythm, accent, changes of tempo, dynamics, subtleties of phrasing, all superimposed upon the sequence of tones themselves, make possible a well-nigh inexhaustible temporal kaleidoscope of sound."[4]

Wittingly or unwittingly, then, radio is raising the level of musical appreciation in the masses. There are many signs that the transformation is already under way, the most significant being the increased demand for better music coming to the studios from people who before the days of radio regarded classical music as "toplofty." Radio has led a multitude of such listeners to undertake the serious business of *listening* to music rather than passively *hearing* it. Their appetite whetted, a new form of aesthetic desire is appearing in their lives.

The nation, however, is not about to be transformed into a vast Handel and Haydn Society, for even while people are learning to listen appreciatively to classical music they still like, and perhaps always will like, to hear popular refrains. They like to hear them as a background for their daily duties. Two-thirds of our sample audience usually engage in other activities while music is coming over the air (p. 100). So long as this is the case, simple and obvious music will be preferred. Its appreciation puts minimum demands upon attention and the sanguine moods it conveys serve as an agreeable ground for the day's routine.

One factor contributing to the enjoyment of a musical composition is its *familiarity*. In Chapter V we found that among forty-two types of radio programs listed in order of preference by 1,075 listeners, old-time favorites received first place. Most people have sentimental attachments to certain pieces. To be sure, if "The Old Oaken Bucket" were rendered several times in an evening for several days in every week it would soon wear out its welcome, but moderate familiarity nevertheless enhances its enjoyment. Familiarity means knowledge, it means associations, tied-images, and correct anticipation of the sequence of melody and words. Familiarity is said to be more essential to the appreciation of music for the untrained than for the trained listener,[5] but even the sophisticated listener likes to hear his Bach and Beethoven repeatedly. The more he knows about a composition the better he enjoys it. Familiarity means progress toward aesthetic mastery, and so long as the progress is *under way* the sense of enjoyment

[4] Pratt, *op. cit.*, 42.
[5] M. Schoen & E. L. Gatewood, *op. cit.*, 179.

is retained. Perfect aesthetic mastery, as it were, is easily achieved in the case of popular music, at which time its appeal diminishes. Aesthetic mastery is much more difficult in the case of classical compositions which retain their intriguing character for long periods of time, in some cases permanently.

If the broadcaster cares to help the listener understand classical music he will win to his station an ever-increasing audience. But musical training must be given simply, painstakingly, and with plenty of illustration. The remarks of some current commentators are of doubtful value, too sophisticated for the masses and too trite for the initiated. To say that Bach "brushed aside the narrow ideas of his predecessors and boldly strode out on new and unbroken paths" means little to the listener who knows neither the nature of the "narrow ideas of his predecessors" nor the characteristics of the "unbroken paths." If he should know them already, then the comment is useless.[6] The naïve listener can best be aided by an elementary analysis of the composition to be played without too much effusion concerning the moods and emotions of the music. When he has partially understood the fundamental structure of the composition he will appreciate the moods for himself.

In general the psychologist feels bound to say that musical broadcasters have shown skill and discernment. They are not only giving the public what it wants, but are leading it to want better things. Even the incidence of programs at the present time seems to be essentially correct: light music during the day and heavier music in the evening or on Sunday.

Like everything else connected with radio, there is room for improvement in the planning and transmission of musical programs. Musicians in the studios as well as listeners in the homes do not like to have their offerings interrupted for a station announcement or a sales talk, nor are the musicians to blame for unmusical mechanics in the control room who often unskillfully "mix" the sounds. From the point of view of the exacting conductor, Stokowski believes that harmonics and overtones are at present inadequately transmitted and that the broadcasting of musical dynamics is limited.[7] But in spite of present imperfections in policy and technique it may be said in favor of musical directors, artists, and conductors, that their efforts more than those of any other group in the studio are responsible for the firm hold that radio has on public esteem.

[6] Cf. B. H. Haggin, "Crutches for Broadcast Music," *New Republic*, December 7, 1932.
[7] Leopold Stokowski, "New Vistas in Radio," *Atlantic Monthly*, January, 1935.

HUMOR

Although radio creates comparatively few new problems for the musician, it causes the comedian a great deal of puzzlement and distress. Unfortunately for the funny man, the limitations of broadcasting are precisely of the sort that affect humorous communications adversely. Humor requires a laugh, and a laugh requires a social echo. But radio permits no echoes; it is at best a linear, semisocial method of communication, eliminating rapport between auditor and comedian. The social basis of laughter is destroyed and thereby humor itself is imperiled.

This is by no means merely an academic view of the matter. There is abundant practical evidence that humor is in fact less enjoyable over the air. There are the judgments of students that humorous portions of a college lecture are far more enjoyable if the lecture is given in person than by radio (p. 152); there is the preference of our representative population of listeners for jokes told them in a normal social group (p. 100). There is also our observation of the laughter of the two congregations, one sitting in the presence of an evangelist and the other listening to him through the loud-speaker (p. 6). The reader, consulting his own tastes, will also find that he, too, prefers to laugh in public and to face the raconteur.

Radio humor is definitely the *loser* when it is compared with the flesh-and-blood comedy of the auditorium or the drawing room. It is, on the other hand, definitely the *gainer* when it is compared with humor in print. In our experiments, the average rating given to jokes heard on the air was 20 per cent higher than the rating given the same jokes when read (p. 174). Furthermore, 89 per cent of our listeners preferred to hear a joke over the radio than to read it (p. 99). This superiority of radio humor to written humor is to be explained in precisely the same way as its inferiority to humor in the normal group. In both instances the degree of social interaction is decisive. The enjoyableness of any witticism and the amount of laughter it provokes follow a definite law, varying with the degree of reciprocal relationship existing between the raconteur and the listeners and among the listeners themselves. Exceptions, of course, must be made for the individual appeal of some isolated witticism under special conditions but in general the law is dependable.

In the following list of situations the reader will see that the order of sociability and the order for the enjoyment of humor are identical:[8]

---

[8] Proof that the situations listed are in the correct order is derived in part from the evidence just reviewed, and in part from the additional finding of our questionnaire

1. Assembly of listeners, face-to-face with raconteur. *(Most so-cial, and humor most enjoyable.)*
2. One listener face-to-face with raconteur.
3. Congregate group listening to radio voice.
4. Solitary individual listening to radio voice.
5. Congregate group reading some humorous item.
6. Isolated individual reading humorous item. *(Least social, and humor least enjoyable.)*

The radio comedian has to work against heavy odds. Not only are listeners segregated, and therefore unable to stimulate one another with their attentive attitudes and laughter, but the humorist is deprived of the use of pantomime and of costume, and, what is worse, he is wholly unable to divine the listener's responses to his jests. To be sure, the radio comedian may follow the rhythm of the day and time his program to catch people when they are in the mood for humor. If he broadcasts at the end of the day when people want to relax, he runs less danger of a cold reception; if he can tell jokes to people just after dinner, he has contented viscera as his ally. In general, however, most of the incidental conditions making for successful comedy are denied the radio humorist. Not much more than the bare joke remains for him.

This unfavorable situation might have proved almost fatal for humor on the air were it not for the timely invention of the *studio audience* which restores to the comedian some of the advantage lost when he forsook the stage for the studio. Nowadays few radio comedians dare work without a studio audience. It helps them time their witticisms. Comedy must not drag along; when the effect of one joke has worn off another must be on the way. Nor may comedy proceed too rapidly: the audience must have time to digest each sally. Since radio comedians almost invariably have stage training, they know how to take cues from the audience whose responses they can both see and hear. Listeners of flesh and blood provide guidance as well as inspiration.

Listeners at home are no less pleased with the studio audience. Most (but not all) of them report that the laughter and applause they hear make the program more enjoyable (p. 100). To know that a normal group is somewhere listening seems to satisfy their sense of the proprieties of humor; they feel less foolish when they join in the gaiety. Even the pantomime, the grimaces, and the costumes of the comedian are usually of indirect benefit, for if they heighten the laughter of the

---

that laughter is more frequent in Situation 3 than in Situation 4 (p. 100). Only in the case of Situations 5 and 6 is the relative position unestablished in our investigations, but from observations in everyday life, it seems that these ranks cannot possibly be disputed.

studio audience the listeners at home are drawn still further into the atmosphere of merriment, although a small percentage become indignant at some of the studio laughter provoked by visual cues.

The *stooge* is another invention that greatly assists the radio comedian in overcoming his handicaps. To be sure, dialogue, in which one of the speakers serves as the good-natured butt of all the jokes, is an ancient device. But radio has cleverly adapted this venerable comedy *à deux* to its own special ends. Being a form of social activity, dialogue helps to supply some of the atmosphere of social interaction in which radio humor is so deficient. Furthermore, dialogue absorbs, as it were, the normal fluctuations in the listeners' attention preventing lapses and boredom. Likewise it aids the comedian in his characterizations. When he has a contrasting voice to play opposite him he finds it much easier to delineate his own "type." The bumptious voice of a pretentious American go-getter, for example, is more easily identified and much more amusing if it has for its stooge the voice of a "silly ass Englishman."

The success of a comedian depends upon the "personality" he can achieve. He must be well identified in the public mind. No matter how numerous his puns nor how funny his jokes, if a radio comedian cannot build up a comic character he will not survive many microphone appearances. The contrasting stooge helps in the process. Another aid is a distinctive style of humor which he must keep uniform or, at most, vary only gradually over a long period of time. By specializing in one type of humor—perhaps satire on current events, rapid-fire puns, or Dumb Dora gags—he not only becomes well identified but obtains a steady clientele which finds his specialty to its taste. Another aid is the use of a silly mannerism of speech. Recent vocal trade-marks of the kind are the "So-oo-oo" of one comedian, "Vas you der, Scharlie?" of another, "You nasty man" of a third. Other shibboleths, no less elegant, are "Wanna buy a duck?" "Don't never do that," and "Some joke, eh boss?" The reason why such audible adornments seem funnier on the air than in print must no doubt be sought in the peculiar advantage of the ear for purely recognitive mental processes. Old and familiar jests seem peculiarly welcome to the ear. They have a personal and almost friendly quality, as have the sounds of everyday life which if represented in print would bore us to extinction. The ear is far more tolerant of the banalities it hears than is the eye of the banalities it reads.

All of the standard theories of humor were originally devised to take into account visible as well as audible comedy. Yet, instances in support of virtually all of these theories can be found in humorous broadcasting. Some of the jokes (probably the majority) make us laugh because we suddenly feel our superiority to the victim of the jest;

others strike us as funny because they help us work off a grudge against a type of person whom we secretly despise; others provoke a defensive laughter that protects us from painful emotions of sympathy with the victim; still others make us glory in our own sanity, as it were, and help us dispose of intellectual absurdities that otherwise would cripple our intelligences. Almost every known type of laughter seems to have an actual or possible place in radio humor. At first sight, therefore, we should expect to find humor on the air as varied and as interesting as comedy on the stage or in literature. Yet most listeners will agree that this is not the case. Not only is radio humor less varied in type, but it is distinctly less subtle. Why should this be so?

By far the greatest number of funny items on the air are "gags." A comic gag is a short joke not dependent on the context of the program and containing an incongruity that takes the listener by surprise and makes him gasp, as it were, for a whiff of rational fresh air. Ordinarily a gag is simply a two-line joke, consisting of a question that would normally demand a rational answer but whose meaning the comedian manages to distort so that the answer given is both unexpected and absurd. The most common type of gag is the pun, and puns are the steady diet of the microphone. A count of humorous sallies in a few typical programs of comedy revealed that about 40 per cent of them were plays on words.

How is one to account for this overdosage of puns in a medium adapted to more varied forms of humor? In the first place, puns are easy to manufacture and easy to understand. Every pun deals only with a simple pair of contrasting ideas, requiring neither sustained attention nor elaborate knowledge. "Why," asks the stooge, "did that waitress call you a stag?" "Because," the comedian replies, "I am a deer with no doe." In such a witticism the listener only needs to make common mental associations with each of two one-syllable words, a task requiring little effort or intelligence. The pun is the most elementary (and therefore the lowest) form of linguistic humor. It requires no preparation other than the understanding of two common meanings of one common word. More subtle humor requires a background of experience and taste not universally shared. Since radio must appeal to all classes of listeners, it cannot rely upon the peculiar apperceptive dispositions of any single class of listeners. Lawyers, doctors, Yale men, advertising men, scientists, all have some special patterns of thought that make excellent material for humorous treatment, but a jest designed for one of those special groups would certainly fail to register with the great majority of listeners.

There are still other reasons why puns are the *pièce de résistance* of radio humor. For one thing, they are brief. They do not require the highly developed situation or intricate setting of the stage play. They can be inserted as they are in vaudeville without any relation to a plot. Since radio programs are definitely limited in time and since they can seldom deal with intricate plots, it is only natural that program makers should resort to gags.

Puns have the peculiar property of depending for their effect upon the ear rather than upon the eye. They are usually ruined when they are written down. In the example given above, the effect of the terms "deer" and "doe" clearly depends upon their homophonous character with respect to "dear" and "dough." When the words are spelled the pun disappears simply because of the restraints orthography places upon the meaning of terms. Finally, it will be recalled that the ear has an advantage in provoking recognition. An effective pun requires only that two contrasting recognitions occur in the mind of the listener, simultaneously or in quick succession. The ear is well adapted to this performance. But whenever a pun is "far-fetched," that is to say, when the double meaning it arouses requires reflection or explanation, it is more likely to provoke groans than a laugh.

Due probably to the close relation that exists between the ear and the mental process of recognition, the listener seems to require a certain familiarity in the jokes he hears on the air, even though he is quick to spot and to condemn the literal repetition of a joke heard before. A delicate balance is demanded between complete novelty and staleness. Either extreme spells failure for the comedian. Like a familiar tune, a joke that is following a well-worn channel lets the listener know the direction of the solution to expect and prepares him for the point when it arrives. Yet, also like the popular tune, too much familiarity breeds contempt. A certain preparation or mental set is required and therefore semifamiliar jokes stir suitable unconscious associations into action. But if the revival of these associations is too transparent, complete recognition of the joke occurs before the point is reached and the listener experiences the peculiar displeasure that accompanies stale humor.

Ed Wynn, whose files, it is said, contain 200,000 jokes, and who introduces approximately sixty of these during every broadcast, is well aware of the balance required between ripeness and novelty. "There are," he says, "only a limited number of themes for jokes, but there is an infinite variety of twists that may be given to each of the fundamental themes. . . . It is not the story itself so much as the way it is told that draws the laughs."[9] If the bewhiskered joke is not sufficiently disguised, the offended listener often takes pains to notify the comedian of his displeasure. "Last night," he writes in, "I was surprised

* R. B. O'Brien, "After a Year Ed Wynn Finds Being Funny on the Radio a Difficult Task," *New York Times*, April 23, 1933.

to hear you tell two old jokes." Ed Wynn complains that such criticisms are unreasonable and unkind, for the listener might as truthfully have said, "You told fifty-eight new jokes last night." Psychologically speaking, the most truthful statement of all would be, "Last night you told sixty old jokes, two of which I recognized, and fifty-eight of which, though disguised sufficiently to elude conscious recognition, nevertheless prompted me through their semifamiliarity to adopt precisely the right mental set for their enjoyment." But a listener capable of such exact introspection would probably not tune in to Ed Wynn at all.

One method of varying an old joke is to place it in the mouths of new characters. The incongruity provided by contrasting types—a Greek ambassador, a flighty female, a stupid country sheriff—all involved in an "old" situation will bring more laughs than a dozen brand-new jokes. The radio always requires contrasting voices, and in humorous broadcasting this means that gross caricature will inevitably supplant delicate characterization.

In choosing his jokes the radio comedian is definitely bound by conventions, not only the conventions of the jokebook, but by moral constraints as well. The *double entendre* of stage humor is conspicuously lacking on the air for two principal reasons. The home is still the seat of all our traditions of decency, while in the theater a release of repressions is both permitted and expected (cf. pp. 14ff.). The second reason is that innuendoes of the voice are more suggestive than innuendoes of the stage, simply because, as the phrase goes, more is left to the imagination. Nudism is an accepted topic for jesting on the stage where the legal requirements in the matter of dress are observed. But as a subject for broadcasting nudism is strictly taboo.

It would be a mistake, however, to think of radio humor as always refined and Victorian. Virtually all the popular comediennes, for example, tend to be vulgar in their characterizations: they are either stupid, "horsy," or sentimentally seductive. Nearly all have the throaty voices of "torch" singers. Nevertheless, their lines are carefully edited so they will not give offense to the moral consciousness even while their "type" may be appealing to the immoral unconscious. Since human life itself is a somewhat precarious balance between socialized and unsocialized impulses, radio humor may safely reflect this same conflict. But because of its close association with the home it must incline, if anything, to favor the conservative impulses and leave the more adulterous emotions to the theater and to novels.

The upshot of the matter seems to be that the scope of radio comedy is of necessity circumscribed. It must be more conventional, more familiar, more elementary, briefer, more exaggerated, less aristocratic, and less dependent upon complex situations than humor on the stage or humor in print. Visual humor, such as is found in cartoons, in satirical novels, and visual-auditory humor as it exists, for example, in Shavian comedy, may be far more subtle and aristocratic than that which can be effectively employed on the radio. This is true at least so long as the aim of sponsors is to reach the masses. In part the limitations of radio humor spring from the deficiencies of the ear in dealing with intricate and novel material, in part from the conventions of time and sponsorship, in part also from the endeavor of comedians to reach every listener whatever his level of intelligence or education, and finally from the obvious fact that no one at the present time seems inclined to use the radio to improve public taste in respect to the comic.

DRAMA

When the listener turns the dial to a radio drama he is unprepared for the production he is about to hear. He has not read reviews of the play, nor heard it discussed among his friends; he has not paid for a ticket, nor changed his clothes, nor made a journey to the theater, nor worked himself into a holiday mood. Sitting at home with a small group of familiar faces around him, he feels none of the subtle excitement animating the patrons of the theater; he has no sense of the occasion and is not on his good behavior. In short, he lacks the physical and the mental preparation that the playwright and the actor ordinarily take for granted. Also the strained attitudes, the chuckles, or the sobs of others in the theater now have no effect upon him. He is not influenced by the physical presence of the actors and he in turn is unable to affect them by his behavior. The rapport throughout is tenuous and unnatural, easily broken by the ringing of the telephone, the baby's crying, or the arrival of a visitor. When these or any of a hundred other interruptions occur the listener may leave the audience without embarrassment merely by turning the dial.

Nor are these the only psychological handicaps under which radio drama must be played. The author is not permitted to rely upon scenery, costumes, or lighting. He may not leave any of his characterization to physical appearance, gesture, or facial expression. He dares not introduce more than a few characters into his plays. He is limited in the use of subplots. He must exclude pantomime and tableaux. He must write his play briefly, consuming precisely 15, 30, 45, or 60 minutes; he cannot risk long pauses, however eloquent they might be on the stage or screen. The "action" must be continuous, lively, and almost constantly verbalized. The only intermissions are those afforded by musical interludes.

Ordinarily a kind of social contract exists between the creators of dramatic entertainment and the spectator, whereby the latter guarantees reasonably sustained attention and two or three hours of good behavior in return for the literary skill of the playwright and the best efforts of the actors. But in radio drama the contract is one-sided. The auditor claims all of the rights and acknowledges none of the duties, not even the elementary obligation of paying attention to the play.

In the face of all these handicaps it seems remarkable that radio drama exists at all. In its early stages it was indeed a failure, until producers learned that however successful a play may be on the stage or screen it must be radically transformed before it is adaptable to the requirements of broadcasting. But it is characteristic of producers that they learn their lessons rapidly and well. With remarkable swiftness they began to compensate for the limitations of their medium, and in so doing turned failure into success. At the present time radio drama is in fact one of the most flourishing forms of entertainment on the air, ranking sixth in the table of popularity among forty-two types of programs (p. 93). It is universally regarded as one of radio's most promising children, and has been acclaimed as the new art that will guarantee the survival of broadcasting.[10]

For the most part, successful radio drama today is written directly for the microphone and differs in many respects from the drama of stage and screen. It is fashioned for an unselected audience, not for people who wear top hats and evening cloaks. The plots are generally simple and obvious, the motivation and the conflict easy to understand; and, above all, the action is quick. Opening speeches are crisper and more compelling to the attention, for within the first minute the listener must be persuaded that the production is worth hearing. Instead of raising the curtain upon a parlormaid at her dusting, the radio dramatist is more likely to open his play with a threatening storm, a cry for help, or a declaration of love.

The number of characters in a good radio play is kept within the range of easy recognition and the rôles contrast sharply with one another so they may be distinctively represented by voice alone. As a rule the characters are diversified in respect to age, sex, occupation, and culture. Any radio play is worthless unless the characters can be identified through their voices. Physical appearance, costume, position on the

---

[10] Discussions of radio drama will be found in T. H. Pear, *Voice and Personality* (London: Chapman and Hall, 1931); C. A. Buss, *Writing and Producing a Radio Play* (Madison: Library of University of Wisconsin, 1933); M. Denison, "The Preparation of Dramatic Continuity for Radio" (*Education on the Air*, 1932, 118-128); P. Dixon, *Radio Writing* (New York: Century, 1931); K. Seymour and J. T. W. Martin, *How to Write for Radio* (New York: Longmans, Green, 1931).

stage, and mannerisms are all irrelevant and the listener holds no program which names the players "in order of their appearance."

The selection of the cast for a radio drama is an art in itself. Most of the actors have been trained for the stage, but of all the histrionic abilities they have acquired the only one for which they are chosen is their skill in using the voice. The director of dramatics cares nothing for beauty, grace, physical "type," age, facial animation, or gestures. He wants actors who can *sound* their parts. Large studios have catalogues of available voices. In one we find a section devoted to "Dumb Girls," another to "Virgins." (What personal secrets the voice reveals!) There is particular demand for actors who can "double," since versatility cuts down expense and is more convenient in the studio. For this reason the file contains cross references. We learn, for example, that Belle Blossom (who was retired from the stage several years ago on account of corpulence) is still adequate, vocally speaking, to rôles requiring a heavy, a dumbbell, a French maid, a Cockney, or a negro mammy. One actor in a "March of Time" broadcast portrayed both Upton Sinclair and an accused kidnapper. Another virtuoso can depict vocally between forty and fifty different types. The earnings of such an actor are not only impressively large, but in the present period of adversity among artists, remarkably secure.

The actor trained for the stage must learn many new tricks before he is successful at broadcasting. In the studio his histrionic gestures are a hindrance rather than a help. He must learn to restrain them, also to stand still and not vary his distance from the microphone. While he stands silently waiting for his cue his postures convey nothing to the audience. He may, therefore, relax when he is not actually speaking, a privilege denied him on the stage. But a few seconds before he steps to the microphone you will see him grow tense, glance at his lines, assume character, and while he reads his part you will notice that his face is intensely expressive and that his hands are trembling with restrained gestures. The effort involved in projecting every possible fragment of conviction into the speech is reflected by these ancillary movements. The voice by itself cannot express an emotion; it can do so only with the assistance of the entire body. A good *radio* actor must first of all be a good actor.

Since the listener has neither scenery nor program to show him the time and place of an event and no visible actors to provide the motion of the play, the players' lines must convey both the action and the setting. In order not to tire the listener, they must be brief and simple, passing rapidly from one character to another, creating the illusion of movement. For example, in his play, *Le Bourgeois Gentilhomme*, Molière wrote:

First Lackey. Monsieur, your fencing master is here.

M. Jourdain. Tell him to come here to give me my lesson. I want you to see me have it.

Scene II

Fencing Master, Music Master, Dancing Master, M. Jourdain, two Lackeys.

F. M. (after having given him the foil). Come, Monsieur, square your body straight. Lean slightly on the left thigh. The legs not so widely separated. Your feet together. Your wrist in a line with your hip. The point of your sword facing your shoulder. The arm not quite so stiff. The left hand about the height of the eye. The left shoulder more squared. The head erect. A bold look. Advance. The body firm. Engage my sword in quart and keep on. One, two. Recover. Again with firm foot. A leap back. When you make a pass, Monsieur, the sword should be thrust out and the body kept well back. One, two. Come, engage my sword in tierce, and keep on. Advance. The body firm. Advance. Start from there. One, two. Recover. Again. A leap back. Parry, Monsieur, parry.

(The Fencing Master makes two or three feints at him when he says "Parry.")

M. J. Eh?

M. M. You do it wonderfully.

F. M. I have already told you, the whole secret of fencing lies in two things only, to strike and not to be hit; and as I made plain to you the other day by demonstrative reason, it is impossible for you to be hit, if you know how to turn the sword of your enemy from the line of your body: this depends solely on a slight movement of the wrist inwards or outwards.

The radio dramatist adapting this play must make it not only modern and colloquial, but must convey every bit of the action by sound alone. This is the radio version :[11]

First Lackey. Your fencing master is here.

Jordan. Well—tell him to come in—Tell him to come in—Ah, Mr. Fencing Master . . . (DOOR CLOSES) Are you gentlemen acquainted?

Dancing Master. Music Master (VERY COLDLY) Yes. . . . Yes . . . Yes. . .

Fencing Master. Come, sir . . . take your foil . . .

Jordan. Thank you.

F. M. Your salute, sir.

Jordan. There!

[11] The examples of rewriting for radio were taken directly from the radio script of Molière's *Le Bourgeois Gentilhomme* prepared by David Howard for the Columbia Broadcasting System.

(THROUGHOUT FOLLOWING THERE IS THE SOUND OF
FOILS)

F. M. Don't straddle your legs . . . Hold up your head. Look bold . . .
Advance! . . . ADVANCE . . . One! Two! . . Recover! . . Advance!
. . ADVANCE! . . One! . . Two! . . Leap back! . . Parry, sir. . .
PARRY!

Jordan. Owwwwww!

F. M. Mr. Jordan, I keep telling you that the secret of arms consists in
giving and not receiving.

Jordan. Yes . . . yes . . . I know . . . Am I better at it?

F. M. A little . . . a little . . .

The adapter also reconstructs the speeches so they overlap with one
another. He permits no single line to bear the entire burden of an idea,
for at the crucial moment when the line is spoken the listener may be
disturbed or inattentive. For this reason he uses repetition, reiterating
important ideas in successive lines. Notice in the following passage that
"news" and the "Grand Turk" are mentioned only once by Molière in
his printed play, while the radio dramatist emphasizes the news of
the event and repeats the celebrity's name three times.

(Original version)

Covielle. . . . . I have come to tell you the best news imaginable.

M. Jourdain. What is it?

Cov. You know that the son of the Grand Turk is here?

M. J. I? No.

Cov. How is that? He has a most superb suite; everyone goes to see him,
for he has been made welcome in this country as a seigneur of importance.

M. J. Upon my word! I did not know that.

(Radio version)

Covielle. I've got some great news.

Jordan. News? For me?

Cov. Yes—The son of the Grand Turk is in Paris.

Jordan. The Grand Turk? Who's he?

Cov. Don't you know?

Jordan. No.

Cov. *What!* Why, all the world knows about the Grand Turk. He's a
very important person. Why, I can't begin to tell you how the court has
been carrying on since he arrived.

Jordan. Is that so?

Calling characters repeatedly by name helps the listener to identify
their voices. In writing for the stage such a device would be consid-

ered awkward and unnecessary. Sometimes it even irritates members of the radio audience, as the following lines show.

Do you think he will be here by Christmas, Annie?
Well, I don't know, Joe, do you?
I'll bet he will, Annie, or my name's not Joe Miller.

Sound effects are more eloquent on the air than on the stage or screen. The angry slamming of a door, a menacing screech, a threatening storm, a frightened gasp, are emotionally convincing when the attention of the listener is, as it were, condensed upon them instead of fluctuating among the visual pivots of the stage or screen. Furthermore, when witnessing a stage production our eyes sometimes betray our ears. We are often aware of incongruities between the sounds made behind the scenes and the action going on in front of them. A distinctive advantage of radio is its ability to produce "close-ups" of sound, extracting the last ounce of emotional quality from even the "sounds of silence." And when it comes to producing eerie and uncanny effects the radio has no rival. Even its moments of silence, if not too long drawn out, may be fraught with sinister or joyful implications. It exploits essentially the same imaginative mental processes that are active when people lie awake at night weaving stories about the strange sounds that come to ears sensitized by the darkness and by the emotions of solitude. In order to enhance this distinctive quality of radio drama, some listeners prefer to sit in the dark or with closed eyes, for then their imaginations are unfettered by the visual constraints of their familiar surroundings and their fantasies are free.

Given the slightest encouragement the listener can build his own imaginative scene. In many cases he prefers it to the settings provided by the stage or screen for there is never a defect nor an incongruity in one's own imaginative creations. They are not confined to a proscenium arch and the bit of space behind. They may be four dimensional almost as easily as three and may include whole cities and civilizations. The listener can jump through time and space with an alacrity that defies even the advanced techniques of the stage or screen. Years can pass and centuries can change with amazing swiftness and little sense of incongruity. A few strains of music and the listener glides back to the days of the Romans; a whistle of a train and he is across the continent. No time is wasted in changing scenery or in providing continuity. All the dramatist need do is suggest to the listener that the transformation be made, and presto, it is accomplished!

This ability of the radio listener to create his own imaginative background is probably the reason why radio drama excels the stage in its productions of certain fantastic episodes (e.g., *Alice in Wonderland*) and in its portrayal of real events and real people (e.g., *The March of Time*). A purely imaginative drama done in the theater is restricted in its visual settings.

In a sense radio drama is modeled on the plays of Shakespeare. Scenery and costumes are neglected. Language alone sustains the dramatic burden. But radio drama is more radical than Shakespearean drama in dispensing altogether with visual experience. In so doing it has placed an unaccustomed burden upon the listener's visual imagery, a relatively neglected function of the adult human mind. The visual imagination of children is both fresh and compelling, but in adults it has been impaired by long adaptation to the ready-made settings of the cinema and stage and dulled by the routine of living. The advent of television will change the situation and will destroy one of the most distinctive benefits that radio has brought to a too literal-minded mankind.

Although in the past few years radio drama has advanced immeasurably in skill of production and in popularity, it is an art requiring ceaseless experimentation. It plays almost altogether in one-night stands, for the public is quick to recognize auditory repetition and to complain of monotony on the air. There is no reason to suppose that the best in radio drama has yet been written. Therefore it is a matter of public concern that this new art should be encouraged and advanced.

Now the truth of the matter is that radio drama has made more progress in countries where profits are not the prime motive in broadcasting. In Canada and in England, especially, the most successful experiments have been made, particularly in the construction of complex and costly programs. For example, the use of multiple studios is a British invention producing a remarkable blend of auditory effects. Actors may play their parts in different places, choruses may be introduced from separate studios, and so may orchestras. All may be connected with signaling devices and talk-back microphones. In this way a program originating in one studio can be blended with parts of the program coming from other studios. Overcrowding is avoided, fade outs are better, and tension in the studio is relieved. In the British Broadcasting Station in London, for example, the programs of eleven such studios can be blended if the director so desires.

Such experimentation is encouraged only when producers are permitted to throw their skill unreservedly into their art. Commercial sponsors cannot be expected to take the risk of novel procedures whose objective is aesthetic rather than economic. Nor are the private broadcasting companies disposed to shoulder the expense and the risk involved. If they did so they might lose a considerable portion of their

clientele and of their profits. But at this point the issues become political and ethical, rather than psychological, and are therefore not our
chief concern.

CHILDREN'S PROGRAMS

Andrew is a typical American boy eight years old, the son of middle-
class parents. In their home the radio is usually tuned to programs of
little interest to Andrew, but on Saturday mornings and weekdays
from five to six-thirty in the early evening the instrument belongs to
him. He knows the dial by heart and at the appointed hour he is always
to be found in the easy chair beside the box of enchantment. His mother
has had to change bath time, supper time, and bedtime for him, but on
the whole she is satisfied. Andrew, she thinks, needs the physical relaxa-
tion that listening in the easy chair provides. Besides, he is learning
many things and his play has grown more imaginative. She hears him
talking to himself, "Time turns back one hundred thousand years,"
and finds that he is imitating the exploits of Og, Son of Fire; then
suddenly time leaps ahead to the twenty-fifth century, and he plays at
cruising with Buck Rogers in rocket ships to distant planets and moons.

The psychology of children's programs is essentially the psychology
of little Andrew and his juvenile contemporaries. In studying children's programs, therefore, we can do no better than observe Andrew
carefully while he sits fascinated before the receiving set, and then
question him about what he hears.

Does he consider the radio, as adults do, to be a pleasant source of
diversion from which issues a mixture of fantasy and fact, of falsehood
and truth? Or have radio messages for him some special significance?
Suppose we ask him indirectly about the matter and get him to compare
his favorite characters in the comic strips with his radio heroes.

"Andrew, are the Captain and the Kids real or make-believe?"

"Make-believe."

"Is Dick Tracy real or make-believe?"

"Make-believe."

"How about Skippy?"

"He is real."

"How about Little Orphan Annie?"

"Real."

"Well, why are some make-believe and some real?"

"Because you can *hear* the real ones on the air."

Apparently for Andrew hearing (not seeing) is believing. When
Andrew can hear a living person speak, he cannot doubt that person's

existence.[12] His prejudice in favor of the voice is, after all, not so different from that of adults. We have already found that when adults' responses to written and to spoken messages are compared, the spoken material is distinguished for its greater interest, persuasiveness, and enjoyment (pp. 177ff.). In the case of young children for whom the boundary between reality and fantasy is at best weak and porous, radio pronouncements are especially authoritative and realistic. Stories that children would ordinarily recognize as fiction turn in the ether to solid fact. After some familiar tale has been told, studio directors often receive letters from children thanking them for "making the story come true."

Since Andrew relies so largely on auditory demonstrations as his test of reality, it is no wonder that every night for a week after hearing the "ghost bear" wail and growl he woke in terror from nightmares. In vain did his mother try to persuade him to listen to more peaceful programs. He prefers those that are exciting. Among the several competing programs on the air from five to six-thirty o'clock he always chooses those that deal with crime, mystery, and pursuit.[13] There are significant psychological advantages to the sponsor in offering Andrew these exciting stories. In the first place, they create a vivid emotional

---

[12] Although Andrew is well satisfied with his auditory criterion of reality, he is particularly convinced in the case of Little Orphan Annie. Hasn't he written her by name, giving simply Chicago, Illinois, as an address, and hasn't he received a reply?

[13] The question may be asked whether Andrew is representative in his taste for thrillers. Evidence that he is comes from the fact that sponsors, who are excellent judges of listeners' tastes, seem to be competing with one another to introduce into their children's programs the largest possible proportion of excitement consistent with parental tolerance. Stations broadcasting children's programs which contain an undue amount of horror and suspense are besieged with criticisms from irate parents. The wise sponsor, interested in creating more permanent parental "good-will" toward his program, provides excitement of a less terrifying variety. (Cf. B. A. Grimes, "Radio's Most Critical Audience," *Printers' Ink,* June, 1934; S. M. Gruenberg, "Radio and the Child," *Annals Amer. Acad. Pol. and Soc. Sci.,* January, 1935, 123-128.)

The clash of interests between sponsors and parents has recently caused one broadcasting company to intervene on the side of the parents. Admitting "editorial responsibility to the community, in the interpretation of public wish and sentiment," the Columbia Broadcasting System ("New Policies," 1935) lists specific themes which are not to be permitted in broadcasts for children:

The exalting, as modern heroes, of gangsters, criminals and racketeers.
Disrespect for either parental or other proper authority.
Cruelty, greed, and selfishness.
Programs that arouse harmful nervous reactions.
Conceit, smugness, or an unwarranted sense of superiority over others less fortunate.
Recklessness and abandon.
Unfair exploitation of others for personal gain.
Exalting of dishonesty and deceit.

consciousness greatly favoring the impression and retention of the advertising message. Likewise, the incompleteness of the serial story, cut short at an exciting moment, leaves a state of unresolved tension that not only keeps the story and the advertised product in the child's mind but brings him back next day to hear the continuation of the adventure and of the sales talk. Furthermore, successful serials for the most part are tied-in with melodramatic comic strips whose identity is well established in the child's mind. The sponsor thus gains the advantage that every propagandist seeks: a favorable, preëstablished mental content into which the suggestion may be effectively introduced.

The mind of any child is fertile soil for the seeds of suggestion, and the radio is an ideal means of planting these seeds. The techniques used in sponsored children's programs are amazingly effective.[14] First a story is chosen that is known to interest children, usually a perennial folktale or a popular comic. Unlike sustaining programs, sponsored programs are seldom experimental. The story is presented with plenty of action, exciting situations and sounds, so the child becomes profoundly absorbed. The introduction of the trade-name upon this emotional ground makes a deep impression. The suspense created by the story is favorable to the retention of the advertisement and the suggestion tends to remain active so long as the tension aroused by the story continues. At the beginning of the program the child is made to wait for his story until he has learned by heart the message of his sponsor, and again at the end, and sometimes in the middle, he is forced to transfer his sharpened interest to the product. The two become inextricable. He is told (and therefore believes) that the only way to keep his story coming to him night after night is to persuade his mother to buy the product; he is also told (and believes) that it will be a "big favor" to his hero if he will buy the goods. He is informed that his little private dreams will come true if he drinks or eats the sponsored preparation: that he will be able to run as fast as his older brothers and sisters, that his biceps will become as large and as firm as those of his radio idol, and that his batting average will reach record heights. He is sometimes led to believe that without the food advertised the meals his mother prepares are really unpalatable. The excitement, the theme music, the incompleteness of the story, the insistence of the announcer and the authority of his voice, conspire to make the child restless until he has obeyed the semihypnotic suggestions.

Perhaps most effective of all are the artful appeals to the child's

[14] An advertiser in one year invested $70,861 in children's programs. Over 10,000,-000 five-cent package wrappers were sent in as a result of the broadcasts, increasing the annual sales by $506,250. (Cf. An unpublished report of the Columbia Broadcasting System, *Radio Advertising to Children*, 1934.)

desire for gifts and trinkets. If he buys a box of Suchandsuch Cereal, and sends the top—"or facsimile thereof" (what "facsimile" might mean few children would know)—he will receive without cost an identification tag, a bandanna handkerchief, a codebook, a catalogue containing additional advertising, or some other treasure. What child can resist such an accumulation of suggestions and what parent can resist the teasing that ensues? In manipulating the plastic minds of childhood the advertisers indirectly control the more resistant minds of adults, relying, of course, upon the attitude of affectionate indulgence that virtually every parent has toward the pleading of his child.

The range of Andrew's information has increased enormously since he has become acquainted with the radio. He has learned many interesting and useful things and a few things not quite so interesting or so useful. With equal certainty, however, he reports to his parents and playmates

> that Rhea is a satellite of Saturn,
> that many "ghosts" are only the dripping of water or the squeaking of floor boards,
> that a glacier covered much of North America many thousand years ago,
> that Suchandsuch cereal will make him as strong as the school bully,
> that gypsies are dangerous neighbors,
> that brushing his teeth twice a day is a wholesome habit,
> that unless he buys Soandso's toothpaste his favorite program will disappear from the air,
> that Eatsum bread will make him weigh just what he ought to weigh, no more and no less.

All such instructions he greedily absorbs, the eccentric creeds of the consumer along with the rest of it. At the age of eight Andrew cannot be expected to discriminate truth from falsehood when both are spoken with authority.

Andrew was asked whether he preferred stories told him by the radio or those told by his mother and father. He cast his vote for the radio, giving as his reason the fact that it came more regularly and lasted longer. He might also have added that the actors he hears are more skillful storytellers than his parents. They assume neither a condescending nor a resigned air and they do not talk down to him. The voices are friendly and they use the colloquial language of childhood. Like other children, Andrew prefers "true" stories and tales told in the first person. The radio provides him with both. Furthermore, the radio provides more clever settings and more convincing action. It is one thing to hear from one's mother *about* the three bears and quite another to hear the three bears themselves. It is impossible for such an ordinary human being as a father to compete with an ethereal hero whose courage and prowess are the stuff dreams are made of.[15]

Due probably to his ability to create visual pictures, Andrew finds a special kind of charm in hearing stories without seeing the action. He likes to set the stage from the furniture of his own mind. His princesses are more resplendent than any Hollywood can produce, and his canyons and volcanoes have a style all their own. All children seem to enjoy the provocative effects of sound, and the freedom it leaves them for their creative fantasies. Television will add little or nothing to children's enjoyment of radio. It will constrain their imagery and tend to displace their aesthetic creations with a literal-minded and relatively dull reality.

One thing Andrew has difficulty with is the identity of the characters who take part in radio drama. When more than three actors are involved in a conversation he is always bewildered. He has special difficulty, which adults do not share, in keeping the actors distinct in his mind when there are weird and exciting sound effects. Especially when listening with other children he becomes so excited over the growls, the whines, and chirrups that he almost forgets to listen to the story itself. The moral for broadcasters is to keep their programs exceedingly simple. This is particularly true of programs entering the school where children listen together and sit at some distance from the loudspeaker.

To be sure, Andrew's difficulties will become less as he grows older. But here another problem arises. The radio as it is now controlled cannot afford to take proper account of age differences. To a certain extent, sustaining programs do so. One network has arranged a series of programs for children up to nine years of age, another for those from ten to fourteen, and a third for those over fourteen. But the aim of all sponsored programs is to reach the maximum number of children and the programs cannot, therefore, be designed for any particular age group. There has been comparatively little incentive to find out what types of broadcast are best suited to various age levels in childhood. In Chapter V (pp. 94f.) we listed the preferences of children at two age levels. Eisenberg found that children from ten to thirteen years old have already outgrown "children's" programs; they make no distinction between "adult" and "juvenile" programs and heartily dislike

[15] Weare Holbrook, "Synthetic Uncles," *New York Herald Tribune Magazine,* August 26, 1934.

the offerings designed for very young children.[16] More research in the
same direction is needed, covering all age groups and all types of broadcasting, commercial as well as sustaining. Such surveys need to be
widespread in order to offset the effect of local or temporary variations in the quality of each type of program. Since the majority of
children's programs in this country are commercially sponsored, and
since sponsors find it profitable to rely on stereotyped emotional appeals
suited to all ages of childhood, experimentation in juvenile programs
has been cramped.

Whatever its present imperfections may be, Andrew loves the radio.
And although he doesn't know it, he and all the members of his generation are having an experience unique in human history. Never before
has sound conveyed to children so many novel impressions, brought
them such varied entertainment, or created such immense horizons for
them. Andrew will grow up unable to remember the days when radio
was an intruder in a world of solid and circumscribed space. In contrast to his parents and grandparents he takes radio as a matter of
course and therefore feels more familiar with the world outside his
visual range. Contemporary events, no matter how distant, are immediately accessible and the art and the politics that were strange to his
ancestors now enter his house. Andrew's outlook upon the world will
surely be less provincial than that of his forebears and he may succeed
in feeling more at home than they upon a newly shrunken earth.

[16] Azriel L. Eisenberg, *Children and Radio Programs*. New York: Teachers College Bureau of Publications, 1935.

Chapter XIII

ADVERTISING

IT PAYS to advertise by radio. Three-quarters of our sample population of listeners sometimes buy products because they hear them advertised on the air (p. 102); two-fifths sometimes write down the names of products mentioned in sponsored programs; and one-third even take the trouble on occasion to note the phone number or address of the merchant sponsoring the program. A study made for a large broadcasting company shows that the purchase of radio advertised goods is 35 per cent higher in radio homes than in nonradio homes[1]; another study shows that radio advertised goods are used 29 per cent more than corresponding nonradio advertised goods.[2] Whether or not we accept these exact figures, it is nevertheless true beyond a shadow of doubt that radio has been profitably employed by the advertiser. It is the only advertising medium that has grown rather than declined during the years of depression following 1929.[3] Of the estimated 2 billion dollars spent on advertising in the United States in 1931, approximately 5 per cent was spent on broadcasting; of the half-billion spent by national advertisers in the same year, almost 10 per cent went into radio.[4]

The radio advertiser may definitely count on certain facts. He may take for granted that a radio will be found in two-thirds of all American homes. He may also be fairly sure that the average radio is turned on about three or four hours a day. When he wants to broadcast, 90 per cent of all radio stations are available to him, having any variety of coverage he may desire in any part of the country, and including all the high-powered stations (over 5,000 watts).[5] Over two-thirds of all broadcasting units in the country are affiliated with three nation-wide networks (the Red and Blue networks of the NBC and the network of CBS).[6] Through these well-equipped networks and through advertising agencies he may secure whatever assistance and advice he needs. Finally, he may be certain that although most people dislike radio

[1] R. F. Elder, *A Second Measurement of Radio Advertising's Effectiveness*. New York: Columbia Broadcasting System, 1932.
[2] R. F. Elder, *Does Radio Sell Goods?* New York: Columbia Broadcasting System, 1931.
[3] H. S. Hettinger, *A Decade of Radio Advertising*. Chicago: University of Chicago Press, 1933, 134.
[4] *Ibid.*, 135.
[5] *Ibid.*, 66.
[6] *Commercial Radio Advertising*, Senate Document, No. 137. Washington: U. S. Government Printing Office, 1932, 66-71.

advertising, they accept it as a part of the American way of life and without overt protest buy immense quantities of radio advertised goods.

Dealers and sponsors watch radio advertisements closely. They criticize them freely. Radio is comparatively new and has the interest of novelty. Radio is handy—the corner grocer may even listen to advertisements of his products while he waits on customers. If the broadcast is timed for evening hours, the current advertisement and the program can be carefully scrutinized by both manufacturer and merchant. Advertisers naturally wonder how radio compares with the newspaper and magazine in its effectiveness as a medium for advertising. They correctly suspect that each medium has its peculiar advantages and are anxious to find out precisely what they are. The psychologist should be able to point them out more objectively than do the advertising departments of networks or agencies intent upon selling printer's ink.

Advantages of the Radio as an Advertising Medium. The first and most obvious advantage of radio lies in its capacity to disseminate an advertisement *simultaneously* to a larger number of people than can any other medium. A well-designed sponsored program on a nation-wide hookup will reach a considerable proportion of the nation's 78,-000,000 listeners. Although an advertiser using magazines, newspapers, and billboards may eventually reach a large audience, his appeal cannot possibly be of so *contemporary* a nature as by radio. The fact that listeners know others are hearing the same program at the same time helps to create a feeling of kinship, enhancing the prestige of an advertiser who can entertain so many people at once.

Besides its capacity for reaching the masses simultaneously, radio advertising has the peculiar advantage, unknown to any other medium, of capitalizing the time habits of the public. If his program is attractive and if it comes at regular intervals, the advertiser enjoys the extraordinary advantage of having people *seek* his message. Most other forms of advertising have to insinuate themselves into the consciousness of individuals who are likely to be preoccupied with other matters or to be actively resistant. But in the case of radio, the individual actually *plans* to be seated in a certain chair at a certain time in order to hear a sponsored program. To be sure, he tunes in for the entertainment; nevertheless, he knows that he must listen also to the advertisement and he deliberately seeks it out night after night or week after week. This voluntary attention and friendly disposition on the part of potential customers is of incalculable advantage to the advertiser.

Occasionally the advertiser may derive other benefits from controlling the time at which the advertisement reaches the public. For psychological reasons the advertiser may want his product to be thought of at a certain time of day. Early morning, before meals, after meals, bedtime, Monday morning, Saturday night are all periods having special psychological merit.

Periodic radio advertising creates a peculiarly vivid *identifiability* for a product. The commodity becomes associated in the listener's mind with a certain time of day, or day of the week, with a favorite comedian, opera star, or other personage, with a theme song (that runs through the head), with announcements of news, of correct time, or of weather forecasts. Such associative devices aiding in the recall and recognition of products are more numerous and in many cases more effective than the corresponding devices employed in printed advertising, although, as we shall see, printed advertising has its own particular advantages in facilitating the identification of a specific product.

The study of the relative effectiveness of visual and auditory presentation (Chap. IX) contains several implications that favor radio advertising (and some that favor printed advertising). The purchase of many commodities, especially those frequently used and low in cost, is often made without much reflection or deliberation. The purchaser simply recalls the name of a brand and asks for it or else recognizes in the counter display the brand whose name he has heard on the air. The experiments reported show that auditory presentation has predilective value for both recall and recognition in the case of just such simple and straightforward announcements as advertising employs.

From the same experiments it appears that spoken suggestions have more potency than written. Obviously a hypnotist would have little success if he had to rely upon the printed word. Advertisers, to be sure, do not exactly hypnotize their clients into making a purchase, but they do employ suggestion. No one who has observed their skill in the use of repetition, positive statement, fixation and contraction of the field of attention, their avoidance of argument and of negative suggestion, can question the resemblance.

All propaganda—and, psychologically considered, advertising is one form of propaganda—relies chiefly upon the use of suggestion (pp. 6off.). The average consumer has neither time nor inclination to make a comparative and critical study of the merits of products, especially in the case of common commodities that are inexpensive. He finds it easier and on the whole far more agreeable to purchase these without consulting chemical analysts or economists as to their relative worth. The more indistinguishable the products are (cigarettes, for example), the more congenial it is to the buyer to have his mind made up for him.

Freed from the necessity of critical thought on an issue that doesn't seem to matter anyway, he good-naturedly accepts the suggestion of the strongest advertiser and adopts a brand in tribute to the advertiser's skill. Printed advertisements, of course, are also extremely potent in their suggestions but for immediate, simple, direct effects (uncomplicated by considerations soon to be mentioned) the spoken word seems to be still more effective.

ᐟAlthough the psychologist may not share the commercial attitude of the advertiser towards trading on the credulity of children, he is bound to report the efficacy of a direct aural appeal to the young folks, provided the advertiser's product is adapted to their interests. Children are notoriously suggestible; in respect to merchandise they are totally unable to make a critical judgment. Furthermore, for them the spoken word is Law; they believe it more devoutly than they believe what is written (pp. 234f.) ; and ultimately the demands of children control an immense amount of purchasing power. For advertisers, the moral is obvious—or perhaps it is not so obvious.

Advantages of Printed Advertising. Radio suffers certain limitations that magazines and newspapers escape. In printed media advertisements may be seen on more than one occasion; they may be read and reread; they lie around the house, and from time to time catch the eye. They have the peculiar advantage of pictorial quality and color, which radio can approximate only through the use of dramatic skits and musical accompaniment. Many products are much more significantly presented to the reader through photographs or artistic delineation than by spoken words. No verbal portrait alone can do justice to stream-lined automobiles, to a pearl necklace, to styles from Paris, or to new fashions in shoes. The pictorial reproduction of a product provides a valuable kind of identifiability that radio cannot achieve, a visual help to the customer in selecting that particular product from the merchant's shelves. Radio advertisers of commodities that depend upon the pleasure they give the eye can, however, use broadcasting to suggest that the listener go *see* a particular display.

New products require a considerable amount of description and rather complex promotion. Air conditioning in homes is an example. Radio advertising cannot contain long and involved discourse; if it does so its effectiveness is certainly lost. New products demand analysis and argument; they must provoke reflection and judgment, and such mental processes thrive best under visual stimulation (Chap. IX). Likewise products that have a high unit price, that are bought but once in a lifetime, or that for some other reason have an exclusive appeal, arouse hesitation and many doubts in the prospective purchaser. For this reason the case can best be presented in writing. Such goods provoke the purchaser to take his time and "shop around." He is, to be sure, still suggestible and he may indeed fall for the persuasion of some salesman, but he is certainly not likely to act in simple obedience to the voice of a radio announcer, although an announcer's suggestions may kindle his curiosity to learn more about the product. It is chiefly in respect to "convenience goods" that the purchaser is willing to have his mind made up for him and in such cases he is more likely to be obedient to the spoken than to the written word.

In deciding between the radio and the printed word, any advertiser will have to consider questions of relative cost, available talent in designing the appeal, the number of repetitions he can afford, and many other problems that are of little concern to the psychologist. The most the psychologist can say is that, *assuming all other conditions to be constant,* printed advertising is probably more effective than radio advertising for products that are new, that have endurance value and high unit price, or whose aesthetic appearance is important to the purchaser. On the other hand, radio would seem better suited to products for which the individual has repeated need, for products that are well established in public favor, for those that have low unit sales price, for those that can be bought at the corner store and require no extensive shopping, for those that are ordinarily used at a certain time each day, and for those that can make an appeal to children. It is important to remember that these generalizations are based upon a somewhat abstract analysis of the psychological factors entering into advertising appeals. In concrete instances, the influence of other variables enters, and the application of these general principles would have to be appropriately modified. In many instances the advertiser wisely concludes that his product is of such a nature that he can use *both* types of advertising advantageously.

Effective Advertising by Radio. The long list of successfully sponsored programs (e.g., *Show Boat, Rudy Vallee's Variety Hour, Amos 'n' Andy*) shows that advertisers have already learned how to bring satisfactory financial returns on their investments. The psychologist can do little more than review some of the techniques used and point out why they are effective.

In *choosing a station* the advertiser takes into account its coverage, its clientele, and its reputation. Almost 90 per cent of the listeners prefer programs coming over networks (p. 99). This fact is important for the advertiser, for even if he is a local merchant and wants only limited coverage, he will do well to choose a station affiliated with some popular network in order to benefit from the listener's habit of tuning to that station for his programs.

The *time chosen for the broadcast* is selected with reference to the popularity of different days of the week and hours of the day. Generally speaking, Saturday seems to be the worst day, for it is then that the listener's time and place habits are least dependable. The other days of the week (Sunday excepted) seem to have uniform appeal, although one day may gain temporary superiority because it contains some one or two programs of extraordinary popularity. This fact is especially advantageous to the advertiser who buys time preceding or following the favorite. The effectiveness of Saturday and Sunday advertising undoubtedly varies with the seasons for fine weather reduces greatly the size of the week-end audience. Sunday morning advertising is inadvisable for it offends those who listen to church services.

The evening is, of course, the most effective time of day to broadcast. The hours 7-10 P.M. provide the largest listening audience, 6-7 next, and 10-11 third. The noon hour, late afternoon, and late evening are more effective broadcasting times than midmorning or midafternoon. However, if a product has a special appeal to housewives, these hours should not be neglected, for housewives, it is estimated, influence 85 per cent of all money expended in retail trade.

In *arranging his program* the advertiser tries to provide people with a type of entertainment they like. He would do well to observe the listener's preferences given in Tables XII, XIII, and XIV (Ch. V.). Men's tastes differ from women's, and programs that young people enjoy often bore their elders. If a sponsor wants all types of people to hear his program he may use variety, though he should not let it become unpleasantly disjunctive. In the mornings the listening audience will be composed primarily of women, three-quarters of whom are preoccupied with household tasks (p. 100). Morning programs therefore consist generally of light entertainment which may be enjoyed with the minimum of attention: music rather than speech. Afternoon programs are also heard chiefly by women, although at this time of day they give more of their attention to the programs and enjoy a somewhat heavier diet (e.g., chamber music, dramatic sketches, narrative). Evening programs can afford to be more elaborate and more complex for then the listeners are more often willing to give their undivided attention. News events, symphonies, humorists, drama, and opera find their readiest reception in the evening hours.

With so many programs on the air it is difficult to prevent them from becoming stereotyped and repetitious. Listeners like showmanship and novelty, and most of them would prefer an improvement in quality to the great variety of programs now offered (p. 99). In striving for novelty, however, the advertiser may safely keep within certain general classes of entertainment. Popular music, drama, and news are always liked; classical and semiclassical music are increasing in favor while hearth and home songs are perhaps safest of all. The clever advertiser studies the concentration of programs and avoids during his period of time a duplication of other sponsors' offerings.

Fifteen-minute programs have rapidly increased in favor and are now greatly in the majority.[7] They are less expensive to maintain and are no doubt superior for daily or serial skits; they do not tire the listener, and reach nearly as many auditors as do the longer broadcasts. On the other hand, unless a fifteen-minute program is unusually good it has little prestige and is indistinguishable from all the other short programs surrounding it. It is difficult to build up a "program with personality" in such a short allotment of time. A half-hour program gives the advertiser more opportunity in this direction and more isolation in the radio day. His program becomes more of a figure against the background of other shorter programs. An hour's program, if done well, brings maximum prestige and isolation; but it is, of course, expensive and requires far more skill in preparation. "Spot advertisements" occupying only a few seconds or a minute of time are often effective if they are broadcast over popular stations at popular times. For the small advertiser who cannot afford expensive talent electrical transcriptions are available. Despite the tendency of listeners and networks to disparage "canned" music, these transcriptions are undoubtedly preferable to inferior artists and are cheaper and often more versatile than live talent.

The sponsor knows that the task of *inserting the commercial credit* into the program requires great skill. The advertiser must face two facts frankly. First, his message in sober truth does not have any logical connection with the entertainment he offers. Second, radio advertising is unpopular with the listeners. Of the forty-two types of subject matter judged for popularity by our population of representative listeners, advertising stood at the bottom of the list; listeners of all ages and of both sexes want less of it (p. 93). Eighty-two per cent of them are annoyed by it; and this irritation leads them greatly to overestimate the amount of time actually consumed by commercial announcements (p. 73). Remembering these facts may save the advertiser ill-will and consequently many dollars. He must restrain his natural desire to state and restate the virtues of his product; he must tell his story in a way that is newsy, graceful, informative, or helpful. Otherwise he runs the risk of giving his listeners mental nausea.

High-pressure salesmanship, like old-fashioned oratory, sounds fool-

[7] For the distribution of 15-, 30-, and 60-minute programs, see p. 84.

ish over the air. The advertiser must realize that radio is a medium demanding simplicity and apparent sincerity—the listener tunes in for entertainment and merely tolerates advertising. A dignified program especially requires a dignified commercial credit, and a brief formal announcement of sponsorship and of a product's merits is most suitable. On other programs the advertiser takes advantage of the fact that voices create stereotypes. Often he can choose, according to his need, an announcer whose voice "sounds like" a doctor's, a lawyer's, a banker's, a mother's, a good cook's, or an epicure's. Some advertisers have their scripts written especially for the announcer selected. A suave and restrained voice will not do justice to a dynamic, staccato script; a thundering voice will not fit a conservative, dignified ad.

The announcer's voice may fit the product but it is more difficult to make the advertisement fit the program. Advertisers have thought of many ingenious ways of introducing their copy. Sometimes they weave the name of their product into a dialogue or narrative, attempting to make it an integral part of the entertainment. Usually the listener suffers a kind of unpleasant shock when this is done. At times, however, if the program is of a light order and the continuity has been clever enough, the listener may actually like the trick; but clumsy insertions are always annoying. In some cases it may be possible to make the credit itself a part of the entertainment. The skepticism and humor of Ed Wynn and Ben Bernie when inserting the commercial are genial counterparts to the attitudes of many listeners. Center announcements are effectively used since the listener is caught unawares when his attention is heightened. Introducing the advertisements during the closing strains of a musical number compels the listener to follow the melody through to completion; he must allow it to make a "closure" and he is therefore unlikely to tune out so long as the music lasts, even though he may regard such an advertisement as aesthetically repelling.

The message carried by radio is fugitive; once uttered it is gone forever. It is, therefore, essential for his own good that the advertiser prolong in other ways the interest his program arouses. He does so by announcing it in the newspapers in advance, by publishing pictures of the artists he employs, by running contests that encourage correspondence between the listeners and his place of business. There are other "tie-ins" he uses: window displays, car cards, counter advertising, circulars, follow-up stories and price lists in newspapers and magazines. The extended use of such tie-ins means, of course, that he is employing not only the advantages of transient auditory appeal but likewise all those aids coming from related visual experiences as well. And all things considered, he is undoubtedly wise in so doing.

Chapter XIV

EDUCATION

EDUCATORS are confronted with a new medium for public instruction whose magnificent possibilities daze them, but whose technical and psychological peculiarities they do not yet fully understand. They hold plenty of conferences in the interest of education on the air; they write a voluminous literature on the subject.[1] But their clashes of opinion and their diverse practices are evidence enough that they have not yet found their ethereal bearings.

The commercial broadcaster and the educator are each other's friend and foe. Broadcasting officials know that educational programs from their studios help them satisfy the "public interest" clause in their licenses; consequently they are generous in their gifts of time and facilities. It is not uncommon for broadcasters to offer educators more time than they are prepared to use, with the result that the company officials themselves frequently initiate attractive educational programs for children and for adults. The larger companies also have well-organized departments to assist the teacher inexperienced in broadcasting.

Some educators are grateful for this friendly attitude and are entirely content with the present arrangements. Others feel differently. They make various accusations against the commercial companies: that the hours offered are undesirable for educational purposes, that the total time allotted is not enough (even though educators are not always prepared to use all the time that is offered), and in general, that education has to play second fiddle to the meretricious programs of advertisers. When told to set up their own stations if they do not like their present opportunities, the militant educators reply that the channels available to them are not clear and that educators cannot be expected to pay the cost of broadcasting.

The reply of the commercial companies is consistent enough. Radio, in the American system, must be a self-supporting business. Since its revenue comes chiefly from advertisers it cannot be expected to discount advertising interests. On the other hand, they argue, it is not at all impossible to give educators all the time they can profitably use,

[1] The reports of researches in radio education and of radio educational conferences may be found in the following publications: J. H. MacLatchy (edit.), *Education on the Air* (Yearbooks), Columbus: Ohio State University Press; L. Tyson (edit.), *Radio and Education* (Yearbooks), Chicago: University of Chicago Press; C. M. Koon, *The Art of Teaching by Radio*, Washington: Department of Interior, 1933; R. Lingel, *Educational Broadcasting: A Bibliography*, Chicago: University of Chicago Press, 1932.

together with far more competent advice and help than they can obtain for themselves, even while maintaining the present close relationship between business and broadcasting. They point out furthermore that educators are poor showmen. Left to themselves they would dissipate their energies into empty ether, for without showmanship in the studio the receiving sets in the home will be as dead as doornails.[2]

THE NATURE OF RADIO EDUCATION IN THE UNITED STATES.

In Chapter IV it was pointed out that some typical commercial stations devote only 5 per cent of their time to strictly educational programs. The report of the Federal Radio Commission for 1932 shows that during a sample broadcasting week (November 8-14, 1931), 12.52 per cent of the total time of 582 stations was given to programs of an educational nature. This larger estimate is based upon returns not only from commercial but from various special types of stations including those operated by universities. The distribution of this educational time is shown in Table XLIII.

TABLE XLIII[3]
How Educational Time Is Distributed

	Hours	Per cent of total time
Total broadcasting time of 582 stations for seven days	43,034	100.00
Educational programs (total)	5,390	12.52
Free (as sustaining programs from commercial stations or from noncommercial stations)	4,314	10.02
Local	3,149	7.31
Network	1,165	2.71
Paid (to commercial companies by educational organizations, or otherwise sponsored)	1,076	2.50
Local	556	1.29
Network	519	1.21
Total local educational programs	3,705	8.61
Total network programs	1,684	3.91

A report of the educational activities of the Columbia Broadcasting

[2] In October, 1934, the Federal Communications Commission invited educators and commercial broadcasters to Washington to consider these points of dispute. The upshot of the hearing seemed to be (1) that commercial companies and some educators are well satisfied with conditions as they now exist, and are vigorously opposed to further government regulation of broadcasting policy; (2) that a number of educators, represented by the National Committee on Education by Radio, are determined that further privileges shall be extended to educational interests; (3) that the Federal Communications Commission has by no means determined upon its own final policy in the matter.

[3] *Commercial Radio Advertising*, Senate Document, No. 137. Washington: U. S. Printing Office, 1932, 14.

System for the first nine months of 1934 states that during that time 26 per cent of all programs were of educational or cultural value.[4] Table XLIV is an analysis of NBC network programs for November, 1934, showing the percentages of various types of programs that this broadcasting company considered educational.[5]

TABLE XLIV

ANALYSIS OF NBC NETWORK EDUCATIONAL PROGRAMS

	Per cent of total broadcasting time	Per cent of each program type made up of educational material
Music	62.0	9.4
Literature	15.6	15.7
Lectures	7.3	100.0
Special events	2.8	4.8
Current topics	1.4	72.9
Women's	1.1	94.4
Children's	3.4	29.1
Physical training	1.8	100.0
Religion	1.5	7.6
Reports	0.1	100.0
Novelty	3.0	0.0
Total	*100.0*	*20.8*

Disparities in these various estimates of time devoted to education (from 5 per cent to 20 per cent) are undoubtedly due to differing conceptions of what constitutes an "educational" program. Charters proposes the following criterion: "An educational program is one whose purpose is to raise standards of taste, to increase range of valuable information, or to stimulate audiences to undertake worth while activities."[6] But even if this standard were adopted there would still be wide room for disagreement.

Of the 607 stations licensed in 1932, 95 were operated by educational institutions either public or private. However, of the 90 clear channels available none has been assigned entirely to an educational station.[7]

An educational broadcast may be arranged in any one of five ways: (1) It may come from some private educational station which arranges the program and pays the cost of broadcasting. (2) It may be arranged by an educational association or a state department of education and

[4] W. S. Paley, *Statement to the Federal Communications Commission.* New York: Columbia Broadcasting System, 1934.

[5] National Broadcasting Company, *Analysis of NBC Red and Blue Networks for November, 1934.* New York: National Broadcasting Company, 1934.

[6] W. W. Charters, in *Commercial Radio Advertising*, 88.

[7] *Ibid.*, 64.

be broadcast gratis by either an educational or a commercial station. Since 1932 eight state associations have supplied such programs regularly and eleven others occasionally. In addition, twenty-three state departments of education use radio in public schools. Three of these (Iowa, Oregon, Pennsylvania) have their own stations; others have free use of commercial stations.[8] (3) A commercial station or network may either arrange an educational program itself or may seek the services of educators in such an undertaking. Both of the large broadcasting systems maintain educational departments. The *Damrosch Music Appreciation Hour* (NBC) and the *American School of the Air* (CBS) are examples of elaborate and expensive programs arranged entirely by commercial companies. The National Advisory Council on Radio in Education also arranges many programs broadcast gratis by the NBC network. (4) Occasionally, though not often, educational organizations pay, just as advertisers, political candidates, or some churches pay, for the time they use. (5) Rarely does an advertiser sponsor a program that might be listed as educational. The last two methods account for all the *paid* programs in Table XLIII; the first three methods, for the *free*.

Lumley gives a sixfold classification of educational methods employed in broadcasting:[9] (1) *Straight radio lessons* where the broadcasting teacher is temporarily substituted for the regular classroom teacher; (2) *radio talks* in which subjects of somewhat general interest are discussed for pupils in schools or for adults; (3) *recitations or readings* used chiefly in English classes or for instruction in foreign languages; (4) *dialogues, interviews, debates, and conversations* used to present contrasting points of view or to make instruction more interesting by giving greater variety to the voices and permitting the method of question and answer; (5) *dramatizations and plays* for both children and adults; (6) *musical programs* with comments and explanations. Although educators believe that each type of program has its special value, they are still somewhat uncertain as to their relative effectiveness. At the present time the dialogue is rapidly growing in favor.

In addition to the 21,455,799 homes in the United States equipped with radios, educators know that approximately 60,000 schools (about one-fourth of all schools in the country) have receiving sets reaching nearly 6,000,000 children. It is no wonder they feel their new responsibility and ask how radio can be used most effectively.

[8] T. F. Tyler, "Radio Uses of State Organizations," *Education on the Air*, 1933, 342-345.
[9] F. H. Lumley, "Suitable Radio Programs for Schools," *Thirteenth Yrbk., Bull. Dept. Elem. School Principals. Natl. Educ. Assoc.* 1934, 13, 407-417.

COMPARISON OF RADIO WITH OTHER METHODS OF INSTRUCTION

Radio provides an educational medium radically different from the traditional methods of personal discourse and the printed word. The face-to-face relationship of teacher and pupil is replaced by a less personal situation, and visual presentation is entirely displaced by auditory. Unless the radio educator understands the implications of these differences he cannot expect to use the new medium effectively.

Differences between radio and the face-to-face instruction of the classroom. In Chapter VIII it was stated that the radio presentation must be regarded psychologically as more of a "closed whole" than the ordinary method of instruction found in the classroom. The absence of the teacher's gestures and facial expressions, to say nothing of the missing blackboard, give the radio talk a peculiar rigidity. Students report that their note-taking habits are distorted in a radio lecture. It is less easy to dissect the talk into major and minor points. Listeners find that they require more repetition and more concrete illustrations (pp. 199f.). The radio talk goes on relentlessly; there are no pauses in response to puzzled looks from the class. Radio permits no wholesome "mental interruptions" during which the student can come up for air and a fresh look around.

Over the air the teacher is unable to establish the peculiar rapport that emerges from circular social response. He cannot gauge the effects of his remarks, he cannot tell how long to pause after a jest until the laughter has subsided; he cannot repeat or amplify his remarks when the students seem bewildered, and above all, he cannot answer those unpredictable questions that make life in a classroom interesting. The modern practices of using a studio audience, rehearsing for smoothness, and employing dialogue with prearranged questions and answers only partially compensate for these disadvantages.

Unless the radio is installed in a classroom, the speaker cannot count on the social facilitation which in assemblies augments laughter and interest, and speeds the students' responses. When the listener is solitary, all of the phenomena that characterize congregate groups and crowds are absent. This condition is, of course, favorable to critical listening and tends to offset the prestige suggestion of the radio. The educator, unless he is also a propagandist, wishes to stimulate analytical and critical thought, and is accordingly pleased to address a scattered audience. On the other hand, he is bound to lose some of the striking advantages in enhanced interest and responsiveness that he would have in congregate assemblies.

Summarizing in a rough way the advantages of radio instruction as

compared with classroom instruction, the following points emerge—
each, of course, being relative to the precise conditions obtaining in any
particular classroom and in any particular broadcast:

radio can reach incomparably larger audiences;

figuring per capita cost its services are probably cheaper than any
other medium of instruction;

the varied content possible in its programs promotes interest and
attention;

its varied methods do the same;

dramatization and showmanship make education pleasurable;

in many regions it can supplement poor local teachers with good
radio teachers;

it probably has a favorable effect upon the exercise of visual imagination;

it can make important events and personages more real to the
pupil;

it can bring good music into every locality;

the pupil becomes less provincial in his outlook; the excellence of
talks and music heard may fire his ambition and arouse talents
that might otherwise lie dormant.

As compared with classroom instructions, radio has certain serious
disadvantages:

it cannot count upon the habits of disciplined and attentive listening that the classroom calls forth since it is usually regarded as
a medium of entertainment rather than instruction;

all visual aids in education are absent, save only the aid of visual
imagery;

spontaneous questions are impossible;

humor is less appreciated;

circular phenomena are absent, and the invention of new ideas
from class discussion becomes impossible;

there is less opportunity for the students to analyze and dissect
the presentation;

suggestibility is enhanced (though perhaps no more so than in a
congregate face-to-face assembly);

lectures are impersonal with a consequent loss in friendliness and
human interest;

students do not, as inquiry shows, favor radio education as an
exclusive substitute for classwork.

Differences between radio and reading. In Chapter IX it was shown
that the listener's capacity to benefit from auditory presentation varies

inversely with the difficulty of the material presented. For this reason the radio educator must confine himself to material that is not intrinsically difficult. He must learn, just as public lecturers have learned, that complex factual or abstract material cannot profitably be presented to the ear; it should be read rather than heard, so the student may go over it repeatedly and at his own rate of speed. For easy material, however, the radio is superior to reading on almost all counts, probably because speech is more compelling to the attention and to the interest of the student. What is heard, provided it is not too complex and involved, is normally better understood and retained, more readily recognized and recalled.

A somewhat surprising, but fairly secure, result of our experimental work is that adults of the lower cultural levels profit more by reading than they do by hearing. A good educational background quite naturally gives people an advantage in mastering both printed and spoken words, but oddly enough it gives them relatively greater advantage with the spoken word. Untrained minds are frequently quite unable to listen intelligently to material which they could, perhaps with difficulty, understand and reproduce if they read it. In listening, their attention wanders and they cannot return to pick up lost threads as they can on the printed page.

To be sure, the radio is gradually training the masses to listen. In time it may produce a nation of attentive listeners and offset to some extent the advantage that higher education gives. But in the meantime it is wise for the educator to assume that radio instruction will benefit the better educated portion of his audience more than the less educated.

Radio education is not well adapted to the needs of the individual student. In this regard it is inferior to both classroom instruction and assigned reading. The radio at present is forced to fit its programs to the *average* listener and thus run the risk of displeasing those who are either brighter or more stupid than the rank and file. The time may come, of course, when educational programs can be arranged for selected groups. As matters now stand, however, radio is best adapted to elementary, popular instruction, and to the average level of intelligence.

Another limitation of radio at the present time is the shortness of periods available for educational broadcasts. Most students devote an hour to a classroom exercise and even longer to their textbooks, but seldom does an educational broadcast extend over half an hour. Even if there should be a change in the American way of handling education on the air, subjective limits in respect to attention and interest on the part of the listener would certainly limit the length of radio lectures. In Chapter X it was pointed out that most people regard a fifteen-

minute period as the proper time to devote to serious subjects on the
air.

Students who attend classes and read textbooks sooner or later come
to the realization that true education is always a slow and arduous
process. They cease clamoring for quick solutions. Education on the
air, however, reaches multitudes who have never been initiated into the
rigors of intellectual discipline. They are likely to be impatient with
what they consider to be temporizing or indecisiveness on the part of
their radio teachers. Slow and tortuous exposition and cautious phrases
simply do not take. Snap and vividness are demanded. This is the
reason why serious-minded educators are seldom successful in their
radio teaching, and why commercial broadcasters are quite right in
maintaining that educators must first learn showmanship. Having made
a successful initial appeal to his audience, the teacher may, if he is
clever, gradually lead his listeners to read more deeply into the subject,
and finally to develop desirable habits of patience and critical thinking.

It is not quite fair to compare radio education with education in
schools and colleges whose unique advantages radio can never hope to
secure. Education by radio is much more comparable to the home study
courses conducted by university extensions, private institutes, and
Chautauquas whose instruction is planned not for selected younger
students but for the unselected adult population. Their methods, consisting of predigested readings, outlines, questions, and an invisible
corps of teachers and clerks, can still be used in radio education, but
these methods are now vitalized by the living voice that brings interest,
encouragement, and a sense of membership to all the listeners assembled in their homes at the same hour to receive instruction. Many educational institutions, especially in the West, report that the combination
of the radio with the older methods of correspondence courses has
greatly improved their success in educational work with parents, farmers, and with the adult public at large.

All in all, it is distinctly unlikely that radio will displace the established methods of personal and textbook instruction. Radio is essentially a supplementary technique of education, suitable above all else
for widening the intellectual horizons of the masses. Its powers of stimulation are immense, and its messages, if presented vividly and simply,
can provoke saner and sounder habits of thought. On the other hand,
if the messages are too involved, too protracted, or badly delivered,
they are worthless.

One evening not long ago, within a single half-hour, a prominent
network broadcast two educational programs. The first was arranged
by its own program director, and might not even be listed by the critics
of commercial broadcasting as a strictly educational offering. It was,

in fact, excellent entertainment, but it was also instructive. It dealt with *Sounds of Silence*—a clever title—and acquainted the listener with a device for amplifying such minute sounds as are made by dripping water in the kitchen sink, or by the contraction of wire in window screens under changes of temperature. Not only was the magnification of such sounds successfully broadcast, but their similarity to sounds made by "ghosts" was pointed out: clanking chains, or thuds of footsteps heard by the householder frightened by his own imagination in the dead of night. Immediately following this engaging and instructive program was a lecture by one of the world's foremost authorities on jurisprudence, arranged by an educational society and quite typical of what ambitious educators offer when they transfer their habits of the classroom to the studio. The involved, juridical language was both repellent and unintelligible to the layman. The listeners had neither preparation nor ability to follow the discourse. Everyone's time was wasted. Radio is a *new* medium of public instruction. It cannot be adapted to the grooves and ruts of present educational methods; but it can be used with incalculable profit by educators who are flexible enough to learn and obey its peculiar demands.

RADIO IN THE SERVICE OF THE CLASSROOM

In the first place, radio should always be regarded as a supplement to, and not as a substitute for, regular schoolwork. By training the children to regard it as a treat, and especially by preparing them in advance for what they will hear, it can speed their rate of learning and favorably affect the remainder of their work in school. An example of advance preparation is the "Teachers Manual and Classroom Guide" compiled by Helen Johnson for the 1934-35 programs of *The American School of the Air*. Besides giving the daily schedule, this manual provides (1) information which will help the teacher orient herself and her pupils to the program for the day, (2) references telling where the teacher may obtain pictures or lantern slides apropos of the broadcast, and (3) references to books explaining the type of music to be heard during each program.

The sharp break that a radio program makes in the day's routine, coming preferably in the middle of the morning or afternoon session, creates an altogether desirable condition not only for the reception of the radio program, but for a fresh interest in the day's work after the program is finished. But to be regarded as a treat for long, the broadcasts must have variety and quality.

Perhaps it is unnecessary to point out again that the periods of radio instruction should be somewhat shorter and more condensed than those used in the classroom, that they should not deal with subject matter that is too complex or abstract, that they should dramatize their messages or use the form of the dialogue wherever possible. Voices used must contrast sharply so the child may follow the argument and be able to distinguish the points of view represented by each character. The growing popularity of the "interview" is reminiscent of the Socratic method of teaching, although the modern pupil has the disadvantage of *eavesdropping* rather than *participating*.

The mere fact that a program is popular does not justify its existence. It must likewise contain instruction that is accurate and dependable, must be adapted to the level of the student, must dovetail into his growing store of information, and be provocative of further thought and reading. To assure these advantages, the teacher should be prepared with discussion, visual aids, and assignments to support the enthusiasm each program generates. If music lessons are broadcast, for instance, the radio instruction should be followed by capable comment and supervised practice.[10] Above all, the teacher should encourage the student to consider critically what he hears, in order to counteract radio's powerful prestige suggestion.

RADIO IN THE SERVICE OF ADULT EDUCATION

According to one investigator, adults prefer radio instruction to any other form of education.[11] They find it convenient and agreeable; more than any other agency it brings them aspects of culture and thought foreign to their rutted lives. But radio instruction cannot be haphazard. It must first of all be adapted to the medium. It must be of the informative variety, elementary, uncomplicated, with a suitable blend of repetition and concrete illustration. It should not attempt to cover as much ground as might be covered in an equivalent time devoted to personal instruction, nor should it deal with material as abstract as might be understood by reading.

Because of their brevity, radio talks should be constructed with unusual care. In their delivery, intonation, emphasis, and sentence structure must take the place of visual aids and supply the personality of the teacher. Always remembering the tendency of listeners to accept uncritically what is heard on the radio, the instructor must strive to shake them from their slumbers and provoke them to independent

[10] Franklin Dunham, "Music in a Radio-Minded World," *Musical Review*, September, 1934.

[11] H. L. Ewbank, "University of Wisconsin Studies in Education by Radio," *Education on the Air*, 1934, 334.

thought. In general the good radio teacher must have all the qualities of any good teacher—magnified.

For all its limitations radio is without doubt the most outstanding innovation in the educational world since the creation of free public schools. Yet everyone seems to admit that its effectiveness is not nearly as great as it should be. All over the country experts are experimenting in studios, schools, and universities to improve methods and to reach larger audiences. Their most serious handicap is the lack of adequate financial support. As soon as greater private subsidies are available or as soon as the federal government takes an interest in radio education commensurate with its importance, progress will be swifter.

Chapter XV

EXTENDING THE SOCIAL ENVIRONMENT

UNTIL the advent of radio the social environment of the vast majority of the earth's inhabitants was limited and cramped. Only kings, millionaires, and lucky adventurers were able to include within their mental horizons experiences that the average man has long desired but never obtained. Now at last the average man may also participate. He may attend the best operas and concerts, may assist at important hearings and trials, at inaugurations, coronations, royal weddings and jubilees. A turn of the wrist immeasurably expands his personal world. The poor man escapes the confines of his poverty; the country dweller finds refuge from local gossip; the villager acquires cosmopolitan interests; the invalid forgets his loneliness and his pain; the city dweller enlarges his personal world through contact with strange lands and peoples. It is the middle classes and the underprivileged whose desires to share in the world's events have been most persistently thwarted, and it is these classes, therefore, that are the most loyal supporters of radio. For them radio is a gigantic and invisible net which each listener may cast thousands of miles into the sea of human affairs and draw in teeming with palpable delights from which he may select according to his fancy.

There are other means for broadening the social environment; for example, books, moving pictures, and newspapers. But each lacks the quality of contemporaneity. What is heard on the air is transitory, as fleeting as time itself, and it therefore seems *real*. That this sense of the living present is important to the listener is shown by his resentment of broadcasts from electrical transcriptions. Even though such transcriptions cannot be distinguished by the majority of people from real performances, listeners feel dissatisfied. The thought of a whirling disk cannot create the sense of participation in actual events that is radio's chief psychological characteristic. It is not merely words and melodies that the listener craves. These he can obtain from a variety of mechanical contraptions. When he turns his dial he wants to enter the stream of life as it is actually lived.

The immediacy and reality of the radio voice make it a quasi-personal stimulus. It is responded to in much the same way as are voices in natural life. It is judged as congenial or uncongenial. Often, too, the traits of the speaker are pictured, sometimes with surprising accuracy. If the voice seems affected, the listener feels offended and insulted. If it is authoritative, he is, as in real life, inclined to obey its commands. If the voice sounds friendly and informal, he feels almost as if he were receiving a neighborly visit. Rarely is he indifferent to the radio voice.

The popularity of radio, then, is due above all else to its capacity for providing the listener an opportunity to extend his environment easily and inexpensively, and to participate with a feeling of personal involvement in the events of the outside world from which he would otherwise be excluded. It has brought into his home the entertainment, the mental stimulation, and the companionship of which he, as a social being, seldom tires.

A COMPARISON BETWEEN RADIO AND OTHER FORMS OF SOCIAL PARTICIPATION

In spite of the precedence and availability of other means of social contact—such as the newspaper, the moving picture, the telegraph and telephone, the concert and lecture hall, personal correspondence and conversation—radio has made a distinctive place for itself. Its success in competing with other media shows that it has unique psychological characteristics that guarantee it a secure position.

Radio and the written word. Without doubt radio is a more sociable means of communication than the written word. What is spoken is fluid, alive, contemporary; it belongs in a personal context. Time and again our experimental findings establish this point: the human voice is more interesting, more persuasive, more friendly, and more compelling than is the written word. Perhaps the only exceptions to this general rule are the telegram and personal correspondence.

Listening is likewise a sociable activity because the radio auditor knows that others are hearing the same program at the same time. Sometimes this "consciousness of kind" is dim, but often it has a salient character as in listening to the broadcast of a football game or to an address by the President of the United States. Reading, on the other hand, is an individual matter. One selects one's own reading and does it when one chooses. The awareness that others are doing the same thing may at times be vaguely present among subscribers to a periodical or newspaper. Yet in general the broadcast can induce a far more intense feeling of membership than can any printed medium.

In listening to the radio there may be a certain degree of social facilitation. The studio audience provides some of the audible cues that enhance the listener's responses, and the assembled family provides more. Such social facilitation is impossible in reading unless someone is reading aloud—a rare event nowadays. Furthermore, listening is easier than reading. Most listeners, at least during musical programs, are doing something else at the same time. They manage curiously enough to gain access to the outside world without seriously interfering with the demands of their immediate environment. Reading, on the contrary, demands undivided attention and sustained effort, only in a vague sense is it social activity at all.

Radio and the talking picture. In several respects radio offers less opportunity for social participation than does the cinema. The social conventions of the theater are more numerous than those of the radio. Entering the theater we subscribe to an unwritten code obligating us to conform to certain rules of behavior. Since we desire to give our complete attention to the film, we accept the obligation cheerfully, not expecting to sing, read, or play bridge before the silver screen as we do before the loud-speaker. As members of an audience, we are conscious of other individuals sitting around us. Their strained attention and expressions of emotion enhance our own and cause us to conform to the spirit of the occasion. This social facilitation makes our own reactions seem less artificial, less banal, less unsocial than they would appear to us if we were alone.

The combination of sight and sound undoubtedly provides a realistic presentation with which radio—until the perfection of television—cannot compete. At the present time radio drama is still of shadowy structure. It has, however, the great advantage of being felt by the listener as *contemporary*, whereas films are always, in a sense, out of date. The offerings of radio are direct and fresh; those of the films have been preserved in celluloid.

The outstanding psychological characteristic of the talking picture is its power of providing hundreds of spectators at a single time with a standardized daydream. Vaguely aware that his neighbors are likewise losing themselves in the adventurous and amorous exploits of the actors, each member of the audience feels protected and justified in his own autistic absorption. It has often been pointed out how extraordinarily antisocial are some of the attractive exploits on the screen. Paradoxically enough, conventional sanctions have grown up to protect the spectator from feeling guilt in such antisocial fantasies. With multitudes of his fellow citizens to keep him company he can indulge in outrageous daydreams whose theme is not ordinarily admitted into his socialized consciousness. The radio seldom invites such an extreme degree of emotional identification of the auditor with the actor, and its programs, furthermore, are limited by the conventions of the home. In short, it might be said that the type of social participation encouraged by radio is the type that is well integrated with conscious standards of morality, whereas the talking picture permits expression of the deeper, less socialized portions of the spectator's unconscious mental life.

Radio and television. How the psychology of television will differ from the psychology of radio can only in part be foretold. In many respects television will share the advantages of the talking picture. It will add physical substance to auditory shadow, and in so doing will enhance the constraints of the stimulus upon perceptual processes. Reality will be almost completely reproduced. As a result, there will be a standardization of the spectators' responses.

With television auditory illusions will be less effective. The listener will be critical of inconsistencies between sight and sound. Corpulent heroines and bald-headed heroes will have to go, and a storm at sea or the roar of an airplane will not be so conveniently manufactured. It will be easier than now to identify the actors in a radio drama when they speak, but shifts of scene and transitions in time and space will be far more cumbersome processes. Like the talking picture, television will demand constant and complete attention; it will not furnish a pleasant background for other tasks. The housewife who does other things while listening to radio will not benefit by television, nor will the child whose imagination is fully adequate to supply visual settings for the broadcasts he hears. Little or nothing will be added to the enjoyment of music, except perhaps in operatic productions. Indeed, it is difficult to see just what television can provide that the talking picture and newsreel do not already supply, except the one signal quality of contemporaneity.

After the era of radio, and its purely auditory art, television with its objective constraints on perception will seem literal-minded. It will bear much the same relation to radio that photography bears to etching.

Radio and the telephone. One would not ordinarily think of comparing the radio with the telephone because their functions are so different, and yet both are mechanical means of auditory communication, entering the home and extending the social horizon of the inhabitants. Although both rely entirely upon sound, the one affords only a linear, one-way communication, whereas the other is admirably adapted to circular social response. It is chiefly this element of circularity in the telephone that gives it distinctive psychological advantages over the radio. A second advantage is that it lends itself to personal uses, for in transmitting his voice, the speaker can be reasonably sure that no one other than the chosen interlocutor will hear his words. There is, however, always a certain danger of eavesdropping and partly for this reason the telephone is never as intimate a means of communication as face-to-face conversation. None the less the telephone permits a far greater variety of personal responses than does the radio, and for this reason must be ranked higher as an agency of social participation.

Radio and the formal congregate assembly. Radio does not afford as complete a means of social participation as does membership in a face-to-face group. The gregarious instinct—if such there be—is inadequately satisfied by radio. Most people, we have found, prefer to attend concerts or lectures than to hear them on the air. Membership in a formal assembly, to be sure, requires everyone present to accept the unwritten contract, binding himself to behave in the accepted manner and to submerge his individuality in deference to the convenience of others. The more formal the occasion, the more conventional must he be. And yet he likes these constraints. Church attendance, for example, we found to be little affected by the broadcasting of services, no doubt because the presence of other worshipers contributes so largely to the religious atmosphere sought by the churchgoer.

The physical presence of a speaker or artist establishes a more normal and satisfying social relationship than does the mere sound of his voice. When we can see the performer, his personality is to a larger extent a matter of observation and less a matter of inference. Although our relationship with him may at first appear to be almost entirely linear (from speaker to listener), still, even in conservative gatherings, we find ourselves responding overtly in a variety of ways—by clapping, laughing, or facial expression. The speaker in turn reacts to these signs, and a rudimentary circular relationship is established.

There is also evidence at hand to show that a listener in the presence of a speaker is more alert, more critical, and more analytical than he is in facing a loud-speaker. He finds the congregate situation more interesting and more pleasing. The bond that unites the auditor and the speaker on the air is demonstrably weaker, and the radio listener's mental alertness, on the whole, is appreciably below his customary standard.

In broadcasting, the appeal is to only one sensory channel, and seems therefore to be monotonous, whereas in the normal group the stimulus is fluid, complex, and changing. The mannerisms of the speaker in facing his audience, for example, provide breaks and divide the total stimulus into a series of perceptual patterns experienced as discrete configurations. The presence of a human face serves to give focus within the perceptual field. Radio, on the other hand, is all of a piece. It is difficult to arrange figures upon grounds or to secure variety in attention and interest. As a result the radio message has a close-knit character, and provokes more uniform and less individualistic responses in the listeners.

Radio and the informal congregate assembly. Membership in an informal assembly provides still more opportunities for social participation than does membership in a formal gathering, and consequently exceeds by an even wider margin the resources of the radio. The awareness of other auditors and of the leader is acute, and each individual has at his command a variety of means for expressing himself. He may ask questions, heckle, laugh, or comment to his neighbor. All degrees of informality are possible. Perhaps the type of assembly permitting the greatest amount of social participation is the discussion group or active committee. When contrasted with such groups the radio situation seems impersonal and even unsocial.

Radio and personal conversation. In the course of a personal conversation the sense of social participation probably reaches its peak. Here the individual is usually obliged, and is generally willing, to contribute as well as to respond. The relationship is circular, visible, variable, and personal. All of these attributes are missing from the type of participation permitted by radio. Over the air there can be no shaking of hands, no arguing, complimenting, scolding, or offering of cigarettes. Fan mail, complaints or praises by telephone or telegraph are poor substitutes. In Russia there have been experiments with talk-back

TABLE XLV

COMPARISON OF THE DEGREE OF SOCIAL PARTICIPATION AFFORDED BY RADIO AND
BY OTHER FORMS OF SOCIAL INTERCOURSE

Forms of social intercourse	"Social contract"	Feeling of kinship	Personal nature of stimulus
Books	None	None	Entirely impersonal except in rare instances
Magazines	None	Slight—in readers of periodicals	Usually lacking
Newspapers	None	Slight	Lacking except in personal items
Form letters	Slight	Slight—awareness that letter has been circulated	Lacking
Billboards and signs	None	Slight—know others will see same sign	Lacking
Personal correspondence	Moderate—answer expected	Moderate	High—depending on intimacy of relationship with correspondent
Telegrams	Moderate—response expected	Moderate	High—depending on intimacy of relationship with person telegraphing
RADIO	None	Variable—know others listening	Moderate—voice expresses personality
Television	None	Variable	Moderate or high depending on nature of program
Talking picture	Moderate—certain behavior expected in theater	High as member of an audience	Quite high—personality both seen and heard
Telephone	High—immediate response expected	High	High—familiarity of voice or curiosity about strange voice
Formal congregate assembly	High—must conform to conventional restraints	High	High—personal presence of speaker or artist
Informal congregate assembly	Moderate—conventional restraints not rigid	High	High
Discussion group	High—participation expected	High	High
Personal conversation	High	High	Maximum

TABLE XLV (concluded)

Forms of social intercourse	Contemporaneous nature of stimulus	Social facilitation	Circular relationship
Books	Entirely absent	None, unless read aloud with others present	None
Magazines	Moderate for recent periodicals	None, unless read aloud	None
Newspapers	Considerable, especially in "extras"	None, unless read aloud	None
Form letters	Slight	None, unless read aloud	None
Billboards and signs	Slight—billboards kept up to date	Some if other people looking on	None
Personal correspondence	Slight	None, unless read aloud	None
Telegrams	Moderate	None, unless read aloud	None
RADIO	Maximum	Slight—depending on studio audience and number listening in same room	Slight vicarious participation through studio audience or stooge
Television	Maximum	Slight	Slight—vicarious
Talking picture	Slight—except for latest newsreels	Moderate	None
Telephone	Maximum	None	High
Formal congregate assembly	Maximum	Moderate	Moderate—e.g., applause and laughter influence speaker
Informal congregate assembly	Maximum	High	High—e.g., asking questions
Discussion group	Maximum	High	High—give and take in discussion
Personal conversation	Maximum	None if only one other person participating; high if more than one participating	Maximum

microphones where the common man in Siberia on special occasions can have a conversation with some high official in Moscow, an impressive experience both for him and for all the listeners. In this country also there have been radio conversations with the antarctic and with aircraft. But the listeners must be satisfied with the rôle of passive listening. Radio is not conceivably a substitute for personal conversation.

These comparisons have served to establish six different factors contributing to what we have called "social participation." They are: (1) the "social contract" or obligation assumed by an individual to behave according to the particular conventional constraints imposed by custom; (2) an awareness that others are participating in the same activity, a feeling of kinship; (3) a stimulus that is perceived to be personal in nature, and (4) one that is perceived as contemporaneous; (5) contributory stimuli arising from other persons participating in the same activity (social facilitation); and (6) the circular relationship where the auditor or spectator influences the person or persons to whom he is attending. Different agencies of communication possess these factors in varying degrees and the extent to which any given form of communication provides opportunities for participant behavior varies directly with all six factors.

Table XLV presents an analysis of the various media we have considered, and compares them in respect to the opportunities they afford for social participation. The table does not, of course, present every possible comparison, nor does it allow for the numerous exceptions which special conditions create. Listening to a friend's voice over the radio would enhance the sense of social participation, whereas sitting through a boring lecture would not. The attitude of the individual may radically alter the participant relationship suggested. Only average tendencies are reported in the table.

The degrees of social participation ordinarily permitted by the vari-

FIGURE III

DEGREES OF PARTICIPATION PERMITTED BY VARIOUS
FORMS OF SOCIAL INTERCOURSE

(*Most participation*) | —Personal conversation

—Discussion group

—Informal congregate assembly
—Telephone
—Formal congregate assembly

—Talking picture

—Television
—RADIO
—Telegraph
—Personal correspondence

—Form letter

—Newspaper
—Billboards

—Magazines

(*Least participation*) | —Books

ous forms of social intercourse may be arranged roughly on a continuum (Figure III). Only average tendencies can be recorded and no permanent place can be assigned any one form because of the subjective circumstances that intervene in particular cases. The points on the continuum are determined by combining with equal weights the six factors listed in Table XLV. By this method it appears that radio, roughly speaking, occupies an intermediate position. Its virtues in respect to the contemporaneous and personal nature of its stimuli are offset to some degree by the relative absence of circularity and influence of one auditor upon another.

It will be noted in Figure III that the forms of social relationship permitting greatest participant behavior are the congregate groups. In the intermediate position fall certain long-distance media, variously distinguished for the speed, fidelity, or intimacy of their transmission. In the lowest group are the impersonal agencies of communication relying exclusively upon print. Radio's secure place among these media does not depend upon its central position in the continuum. The fact that it is both more and less participant than other forms of communication has no bearing upon its survival. What guarantees the permanence of radio is the twofold fact that it is an additional highway by which men may widen their experience of the outer world, in directions not served by other avenues of communication, and that this enrichment is secured with a minimum expenditure of energy. Radio demands little of the listener in money, effort, responsibility, or social conformity. It is one of the least exacting and yet most effective means of extending the social environment.

THE VERSATILITY OF RADIO

Every listener brings to the radio program his own peculiar attitudes, prejudices, emotions, repressions, moods, and abilities. It is these characteristics of each listener that determine the particular type of psychic experience he seeks from the program. The fact that radio has so well satisfied so many people is ample proof of its versatility in meeting the diverse demands of human nature.

The previous chapters have dealt almost entirely with the "average" listener. In reality, of course, there is no "average" listener. Although mental processes, interests, and abilities are roughly similar in the majority of people, they vary to such an extent that strictly uniform reactions are the exception rather than the rule. Radio, like any other social stimulus, must ultimately be interpreted from a personalistic point of view if it is to be thoroughly understood.

To one man radio is a technical phenomenon and in his life plays a part similar to that of his other mechanical hobbies; to another it is an economic interest engaging his attention in much the same way as do business news and advertisements in the newspaper. Another man wants nothing more from radio than a few laughs in the late evening. A housewife finds it companionable; an invalid finds it a comfort; the student of social phenomena finds it instructive. Almost everyone finds in it what he wants to find. The diversity of its offerings is so great that almost no one is left out. To write a complete psychology of radio it would be necessary to write a biography of every individual listener.

Since the "average" listener does not exist, and since it is impracticable to pursue further the idiosyncrasies of the individual listener, both the broadcaster and the psychologist find themselves centering their attention upon *types* or *groups* of listeners. There is, for example, the problem of sex differences. Men, by and large, like radio when it caters to their preëstablished interest in sports, business, financing, engineering, mystery stories, and politics. Women prefer poetry, literature, recipes, and fashion reports. Women think more highly than do men of children's programs, and they are more interested in the personalities of the speakers whom they hear.

Listeners of different ages likewise have characteristic preferences. Older people are more likely to tune in on operas, church services, news events, politics, and language instruction. Jazz singers, dance orchestras, tennis and hockey broadcasts are preferred by the young. These youthful listeners are less selective and less attentive than older people, and tend to use radio as a background for their games and their studying.

Sex and age differences are cut across by the variables of occupation and cultural background. Professional people, for example, rate news reports, classical music, and political talks higher than do nonprofessional people; students rate popular music high, news broadcasts low; laborers prefer drama to sports. A talk that is understood by some listeners will be almost wholly incomprehensible to others. Those who are well educated have an immeasurable advantage over those who are not.

Since the tastes and capacities of different groups vary so widely, the broadcaster has endeavored through the bulk and diversity of his offerings to satisfy everyone. The wisdom of his policy seems somewhat called into question by the report of most listeners that they would willingly sacrifice some of the present variety for an improvement in quality. Apparently they prefer a well-executed program that touches the periphery of their desires to an inferior program aimed more directly at their interests.

Confusing though the diversity of the listeners' tastes and abilities may be, the broadcaster can depend upon certain fairly uniform conditions. Nearly all listeners, for example, prefer as a general rule music to spoken material, male announcers to female, network to local broadcasts, and nearly all are at times annoyed by advertising. They agree, furthermore, that vulgarity and obscenity should be kept off the air, and that the religious and racial attitudes of majority and minority groups should be respected.

Every prominent program put on the air is first tested, directly or indirectly, by the foregoing criteria of public taste. The prevailing habits and attitudes of the majority of listeners are always considered; usually, too, the program is tested for its appeal to special groups. While this selection is in process there is always in the background the pressure exerted by the political and economic system within which radio has developed. Ultimately, of course, the political and economic system itself is only a derivative of the habits and attitudes of the majority of citizens. Economic and political habits are deeply ingrained, seldom questioned, and virtually unconscious in their operation. In the United States these habits have traditionally favored laissez-faire individualism. When radio appeared as a new medium of communication, it was only natural that the individualistic policies already current should be applied to it. Like the newspaper, the railroad, the telephone, or electric power, radio was allowed to develop as best it might in the hands of interested entrepreneurs competing with each other for financial profit. Competition, rather than cooperation and social planning, has been so long accepted as the American creed that the competitive attitude, deeply ingrained in every listener, has led him to submit to the sponsored program.

Because the American listener has a keen sense of *quid pro quo* in economic matters, he acknowledges the "right" of sponsors to dictate ultimately the composition, length, and character of programs. If the sponsor is clever in shaping his program to his own advantage, he is applauded for his skill. A curious psychological conflict exists in the typical American listener. He dislikes the intrusion of commercial propaganda into his hours of leisure and into his home, and yet he not only accepts the inconvenience but often admires the cleverness of the intruder. Nor does he want to pay a small tax to the government to have his programs without their sales accompaniments. Most listeners probably feel that at present they are getting something for nothing, forgetting that ultimately they pay all advertising costs. Many no doubt occasionally enjoy the skillful and novel types of advertising that creep into programs at the most unexpected spots. All in all, American broadcasting follows with considerable fidelity the psychological interests and habits of the listener, not the least among these is the listener's comfortable disposition to let competitive business alone. It is not only the immediate tastes and interests of the auditor that are respected, but likewise his ingrained and virtually unconscious socio-economic attitudes that from the psychological point of view constitute the *American Way*. Radio is not only a faithful interpreter of these attitudes, but likewise it subtly intensifies those attitudes that support the status quo in broadcasting. It is an altogether elementary psychological fact that dissenting opinions and germinal attitudes favoring radical change in the American way will not readily be encouraged by an instrument controlled by vested interests.

EPILOGUE: THE FUTURE OF RADIO

As the social psychologist, who is also a listener and a citizen, surveys the assets of the radio, the immense audience it serves, the masterful skill of its artists and its program directors, and the frequent excellence of its offerings, he cannot avoid the conclusion that the psychological and social significance of radio is out of all proportion to the meager intelligence used in planning for its expansion. Except in a few countries, it has been allowed to grow up as a device to increase the profits of a few competing entrepreneurs or as an instrument to secure the status of dictatorial governments. Both solutions are unintelligent.

Intrinsically, radio is nothing more than a highly versatile instrument of one-way communication. In itself it is neither a business nor a political accessory. But it is now forced to play these rôles by those who have gained control over it. Radio above all else is a consumer's good, yet it serves the consumer only incidentally. What the listener really wants is entertainment and instruction, unmixed with the propaganda of special interests. The expert technicians of radio, including the program managers and artists, are by the nature of their profession devoted to the adaptation of broadcasting to the needs and desires of the listener. This function requires consummate skill, and has already created a capable army of experts. But their work is now dictated by extraneous considerations—in many European countries by coercion from politicians; in America, by the prescriptions of sponsors. The length, the content, the selection, the wording, the coordination of broadcasts are not now determined primarily, as they should be, by the capacities and desires of the listener and by the intrinsic qualities of the medium, but by special autocratic interests. Neither the professional experts who work at broadcasting nor the vast population of listeners find the situation wholly satisfactory. The people who do find it so are the successful advertisers and shareholders, and those are clearly a minority group.

No human enterprise, certainly not one as young as radio, can be expected to be perfect. *The present technical excellence of broadcasting, of program construction, the prevailing decency, the integrity and skill of individual members of the new profession, all deserve high praise.* But serious dislocations none the less exist. No one who looks into the matter can deny, for example, that millions of children in the nation—radio's most loyal listeners—are being exploited (no other word will serve) by a handful of profit-makers. Nor can anyone who has perspective on the matter deny that the great majority of adults, disliking as they do advertising on the air, are badly served when they have to listen to a dozen sales talks an hour. Nor is there any doubt that the ether is overcrowded with interfering broadcasts, a direct result of competition and inadequate planning. Neither is there any question that the best hours of the day for broadcasting are devoted primarily to the interest of advertisers. In spite of its genius, its high professional codes, and its increasingly excellent programs, radio in America has room for improvement, and the improvement required is radical rather than meliorative. It has to do with the underlying profit motive which in broadcasting is, in the last analysis, not conducive to the *highest* standards of art, entertainment, education, child welfare, or even to basic freedom of speech.

In order best to serve the American public, radio should be removed from the dictatorship of private profits, and at the same time be kept free from narrow political domination. Perhaps the wisest contribution radio could make to the determination of its own destiny would be to encourage a discussion of this very topic on the air. The worst thing it could do would be to reply that "subversive propaganda" must not be permitted, for then the unpleasant retort would properly be made that propaganda is already permitted, much of it decidedly subversive to the best interests of consumers, both adult and child.

It is not the business of the social psychologist to tell in detail how radio should be owned, controlled, and administered. But it is his duty to contribute what he can to an intelligent solution of the problem so that radio may be made to serve its proper function in society. Its proper function is determined by its potential capacities : it is a marvelous social and mechanical invention, capable of giving the listener entertainment and information adapted to his tastes and to his needs. Of itself it is as democratic, as universal, and as free as the ether. Under a competitive system of operation for profit only a part of its potential benefits can be realized. But its development is not yet at an end. The radio of the future will perform still greater service if its course is guided by a more enlightened public policy, based in part upon psychological investigations and in part upon a sound philosophy of social progress.

The facts contained in this volume remain facts regardless of the interpretation placed upon them. Those who see them as possible aids in enhancing the financial profits of sponsors and privately owned stations may of course employ them to that end according to their own convictions. At the close of our factual report we are merely suggesting, according to *our* convictions, that scientific research although in itself impartial reaches the fullest justification when it is employed not in the advancement of private profit but in the promotion of the social and intellectual growth of mankind.

INDEX

HISTORY OF BROADCASTING:
Radio To Television
An Arno Press/New York Times Collection

Archer, Gleason L.
Big Business and Radio. 1939.

Archer, Gleason L.
History of Radio to 1926. 1938.

Arnheim, Rudolf.
Radio. 1936.

Blacklisting: Two Key Documents. 1952–1956.

Cantril, Hadley and Gordon W. Allport.
The Psychology of Radio. 1935.

Codel, Martin, editor.
Radio and Its Future. 1930.

Cooper, Isabella M.
Bibliography on Educational Broadcasting. 1942.

Dinsdale, Alfred.
First Principles of Television. 1932.

Dunlap, Orrin E., Jr.
Marconi: The Man and His Wireless. 1938.

Dunlap, Orrin E., Jr.
The Outlook for Television. 1932.

Fahie, J. J.
A History of Wireless Telegraphy. 1901.

Federal Communications Commission.
Annual Reports of the Federal Communications Commission.
1934/1935–1955.

Federal Radio Commission.
Annual Reports of the Federal Radio Commission. 1927–1933.

Frost, S. E., Jr.
Education's Own Stations. 1937.

Grandin, Thomas.
The Political Use of the Radio. 1939.

Harlow, Alvin.
Old Wires and New Waves. 1936.

Hettinger, Herman S.
A Decade of Radio Advertising. 1933.

Huth, Arno.
Radio Today: The Present State of Broadcasting. 1942.

Jome, Hiram L.
Economics of the Radio Industry. 1925.

Lazarsfeld, Paul F.
Radio and the Printed Page. 1940.

Lumley, Frederick H.
Measurement in Radio. 1934.

Maclaurin, W. Rupert.
Invention and Innovation in the Radio Industry. 1949.

Radio: Selected A.A.P.S.S. Surveys. 1929–1941.

Rose, Cornelia B., Jr.
National Policy for Radio Broadcasting. 1940.

Rothafel, Samuel L. and Raymond Francis Yates.
Broadcasting: Its New Day. 1925.

Schubert, Paul.
The Electric Word: The Rise of Radio. 1928.

Studies in the Control of Radio: Nos. 1–6. 1940–1948.

Summers, Harrison B., editor.
Radio Censorship. 1939.

Summers, Harrison B., editor.
A Thirty-Year History of Programs Carried on National Radio Networks in the United States, 1926–1956. 1958.

Waldrop, Frank C. and Joseph Borkin.
Television: A Struggle for Power. 1938.

White, Llewellyn.
The American Radio. 1947.

World Broadcast Advertising: Four Reports. 1930–1932.